Pivoting

Ann L. Clancy • Jacqueline Binkert

Pivoting

A Coach's Guide to Igniting Substantial Change

Ann L. Clancy
Appreciative Coaching Collaborative, LLC
Billings, MT, USA

Jacqueline Binkert
Appreciative Coaching Collaborative, LLC
Milford, MI, USA

ISBN 978-1-349-95639-5   ISBN 978-1-137-60263-3 (eBook)
DOI 10.1057/978-1-137-60263-3

© The Editor(s) (if applicable) and The Author(s) 2017
Softcover reprint of the hardcover 1st edition 2016
This work is subject to copyright. All rights are solely and exclusively licensed by the Publisher, whether the whole or part of the material is concerned, specifically the rights of translation, reprinting, reuse of illustrations, recitation, broadcasting, reproduction on microfilms or in any other physical way, and transmission or information storage and retrieval, electronic adaptation, computer software, or by similar or dissimilar methodology now known or hereafter developed.

The use of general descriptive names, registered names, trademarks, service marks, etc. in this publication does not imply, even in the absence of a specific statement, that such names are exempt from the relevant protective laws and regulations and therefore free for general use.

The publisher, the authors and the editors are safe to assume that the advice and information in this book are believed to be true and accurate at the date of publication. Neither the publisher nor the authors or the editors give a warranty, express or implied, with respect to the material contained herein or for any errors or omissions that may have been made.

Cover illustration: Jacket design by Philip Pascuzzo

Printed on acid-free paper

This Palgrave Macmillan imprint is published by Springer Nature
The registered company is Nature America Inc.
The registered company address is: 1 New York Plaza, New York, NY 10004, U.S.A.

Foreword

Coaching is fundamentally about change. The role of a coach is to facilitate new insights, deeper understanding and support the development of coherent goals. However, none of this matters if clients lack the motivation to actually go out and make the change. In such situations, coaching conversations just become full of ideas, possibilities and warm words.

A while ago I was invited to observe a coach-training session by a well-known coach-training company. During the morning, the trainer talked about the core coaching skills: active listening, open questions, reflections and summarizing. All of this was sensible and reasonable content. By the afternoon, delegates were curious about how these elements could all be brought together. One asked the trainer if she would demonstrate a coaching conversation using the core skills. The trainer asked the group of 12 delegates for a volunteer coachee. One of the group reluctantly agreed.

Sitting in a circle we observed the trainer use the GROW (Goal, Reality, Obstacles/Options, Way Forward) model to explore the delegate's objectives, his reality and a range of different options. As the conversation progressed it struck me that there was reluctance on behalf of the delegate, but this "issue" was left unexplored. Why had the delegate not resolved this issue before, when the answers seemed so obvious to us and them? Instead, moving towards a close, the trainer asked the delegate to make a commitment for action after the coaching session. The delegate voiced his reluctance: "I'm not really sure what's next." For most of us watching, this called for an exploration of this response and highlighted the ambivalence that lay behind it. Instead, the coach pushed on with a further challenge to make a commitment. The delegate replied, "I suppose I could think about doing X," at which point the trainer sat back and said to the group, "There we go, a clear plan of action." Of course we all knew that the language used by the delegate was far from a commitment to the action discussed; everything, including his body language, told us that he was unlikely to do what he had said.

Clearly, attempting to demonstrate coaching skills in front of others is difficult at the best of times and is made even more challenging when delegates have real issues that are likely to take several hours to unpick rather than several minutes. However, this experience demonstrated that the task of the coach is not simply to support a review of the past and the development of a plan for the future.

We all understand how frustrating it is when we need to simply comply with other peoples' demands—sometimes our boss or a senior work colleague. We comply but are not likely to make that commitment to going the full nine yards. As a result, we may do the minimum or look for shortcuts to achieve the goal. In contrast, when the desire comes from within, from what we believe is right, just or important to us, we will not just comply but commit. In short, when goals fit our values and beliefs, we will do everything in our power to achieve them.

Our real job as the coach is not to simply provide a framework for a coaching conversation or use core skills to facilitate a conversation, although these are important. Our real task is to help clients explore their values, beliefs, deeper emotions (often experienced through bodily sensations) and personal histories. Then we can use these as a frame with which to review the different choices for action, including inaction. Great coaches need to help clients to confront their difficult dilemmas, bringing them face to face with the consequences of their choices, to hold their coachee's feet over the fire and by so doing help them ignite the motivation within them which will act as the catalyst for change.

In this book, Ann and Jacqueline, experienced coaches, writers, trainers and researchers, offer us insights into how we can achieve this. With a highly engaging writing style, they draw the reader in, using a mixture of genuine stories and fresh insights from a range of philosophical and scientific studies in history, psychology, social psychology, biology, neuroscience and physics. They describe a new science of change that provides an explanation for the phenomenon of pivotal moments in coaching and the role that coaches play in igniting substantial change.

The result is a highly readable resource for both experienced and novice coaches alike, which coaches can use to help them ignite the motivation for change within their coachees.

University of Evora
Portugal

Jonathan Passmore

Acknowledgements

The inspiration for this book first arose in our early years of travelling and presenting on Appreciative Coaching® after our book was published in 2007. Since that time we've participated in numerous presentations, workshops and training to bring our emerging research findings to audiences of fellow coaches, consultants, scholars, colleagues and supporters. We are indebted to these individuals for their willingness to provide feedback and suggestions as we presented and tested our theory and model.

The venues involved include the UK Association for Coaching, London; Assumption University of Thailand, Bangkok; OD World Summit in Budapest, Hungary; Academy of Management conference, San Antonio, USA; International Coach Federation chapters in Chicago and Seattle, USA; Academy of Management conference in Boston, USA; International Organization Development Association in Kyoto, Japan; Society for Chaos Theory in Psychology and Life Sciences in Portland, USA; Columbia University Coaching Program 1st International Conference, New York, USA; Carolina Coaching Conference in Charlotte, USA; Institut de Coaching in Geneva, Switzerland; and a dedicated group of New York City coaches.

We would like to acknowledge the master coaches who were so generous with their coaching stories and experiences that have enriched our book. They are John Heidke, Betsy Hemming, Susan Meyer, Vince Racioppo, Bobette Reeder and Deborah Roth. We also thank our clients, both those who participated in our formal research and those we have worked with in our practices, for letting us weave their inspiring stories and experiences into our narrative. We are greatly appreciative of the interest that our publisher, Palgrave Macmillan, showed in our work when it was still in the concept stage. Also, we salute Jonathan Passmore for contributing the Foreword as well as for his support. Finally, we thank our families, friends and colleagues who encouraged us in our belief that exploring moments of substantial change was a worthy endeavour. As always, family members provided us love and support through the lengthy research and writing periods.

Contents

1	A Pivotal Journey	1
2	What Is a Pivot?	19
3	Pivoting: The Extraordinary Power of Self-Organization	47
4	Accessing the Inner Self: Beliefs	73
5	Accessing the Inner Self: Knowing	89
6	Accessing the Inner Self: Memory	109
7	Turn of the Kaleidoscope	135
8	Finding Coherence	169
References		185
Index		201

List of Figures

Fig. 2.1	Emergence of pivotal moments	42
Fig. 2.2	Variant manifestations of pivotal moments	43
Fig. 2.3	Slow awakening	44
Fig. 2.4	The coaching "chain" of events	45
Fig. 3.1	Pivoting: The power of self-organization	48
Fig. 3.2	Can you find the hidden star?	55
Fig. 3.3	What do you see? A young girl? An old woman?	56
Fig. 3.4	Answer to finding the hidden star	72
Fig. 4.1	Role of beliefs in self-organizing	74
Fig. 4.2	Comparison of two belief systems	78
Fig. 5.1	Role of inner knowing in self-organizing	90
Fig. 5.2	Blatz Beer advertisement	94
Fig. 5.3	Iver Johnson Revolvers advertisement	95
Fig. 5.4	Seven types of inner knowing	106
Fig. 6.1	Role of memory in self-organizing	110
Fig. 7.1	Model of self-organizing pivotal moments	137
Fig. 7.2	Control-Influence-Concern Model	140
Fig. 7.3	Growing vs. closing the gap	141
Fig. 7.4	Cone in the box visual metaphor	148
Fig. 7.5	Coaching cycle: The embodiment of mind, body and environment	152

List of Tables

Table 1.1	Mechanistic and generative approaches to change	7
Table 1.2	Two scientific positions	15
Table 2.1	Research results on characteristics of *aha* moments	37
Table 2.2	Research results on triggers of *aha* moments	37
Table 4.1	Major distinctions between beliefs and knowledge	76
Table 5.1	Distinctions between empiricism and rationalism	93
Table 7.1	Priming strategies observed in initial research	138
Table 8.1	Emerging Holistic Model	172

1

A Pivotal Journey

The greatest discovery of my generation is that human beings can alter their lives by altering their attitudes of mind.

—William James

Introduction

There is a moment of quiet; you can almost see the wheels turning as the realization hits, and then looking at me with a shocked expression. I think it was probably the expression of awe or surprise. It has this physical presence to it. You can watch the shift in the body—or feel it in you.

The feeling to me is that I was let in, he opened up and we could work together. It was a feeling of relief and euphoria that we were moving forward with openness and mutual listening. The resistance went away.

What usually happens to me when my client shifts, I feel it. We are both much happier, much lighter. In this case her whole tone lightened up, her attitude changed and I could feel it over the phone.

My role changed before and after the pivot. Before I was in the position of encouraging and cheerleading, but was actually on the other side of the fence from him as he was on the negative side. Once the shift occurred, we were both on the same side and the coaching was very productive.

What I had to share seemed insignificant, so my client's response astounded me. Somehow my comment triggered a cascade of awareness that changed my client in profound ways. It seemed that what we had been talking about for some time in our coaching finally gelled.

These are real stories of pivotal moments when coaches experienced the reality of their clients shifting in some way. The experience seems to be one of mutuality—their euphoria becomes ours. We chose the title of our book, *Pivoting: A Coach's Guide to Igniting Substantial Change*, to describe a topic that thoroughly captured our curiosity as researchers and riveted our attention as executive coaches. How *do* our clients make substantial change? What role do we play? What, if anything, do we contribute when clients *alter their attitudes of mind*?

We define "pivoting" as a key moment in coaching when a client comes to a new realization that changes them in some way. This shift brings with it the potential to create a fresh way of being for the client. Thus it is a moment of significance to the individual and of inspiration to the coach. Who has not felt joy and satisfaction in seeing clients undergo an inner shift that makes their life or circumstances better?

While we cannot take direct credit for a client's achievements, we know intuitively that we are somehow influential. There are times when we actually "ignite" substantial change within our clients. The question for us in writing this book was how can we repeat this *igniting* experience for our clients in a more deliberate way? Hence our desire to create a *Coach's Guide*.

While it is gratifying to see clients make a major breakthrough, not all changes are transformational. Whatever the scope of change, however, our hope is to be a source of support and encouragement—believing in clients' greatness as individuals, believing in them even during times when they cannot believe in themselves. As coaches, our purpose is to support them in making meaningful change, substantial change, in their circumstances. As researchers and authors, the purpose of our book is to share our findings and experiences about this mysterious yet engaging topic with like-minded professionals.

Living from the Inside Out

En route to giving a presentation on the topic of pivotal moments in coaching at a conference in Japan, Ann received a note from a former client. He was contacting her from Australia where he was collaborating as co-author with one of his clients. He wanted to thank Ann for being instrumental in helping him find his current life work and for being partly responsible for his incredible work project in Australia. When he started the coaching process he was an executive at a publishing company but was struggling with the management and leadership demands and feeling diminished in his position. While his career accomplishments were impressive (e.g., a Ph.D., published author, successful editing positions, recipient of editing awards, Ironman finisher, Pikes Peak Ascent finisher, marathoner), he had lost sight of his strengths, achievements and dreams. He had hoped that coaching would provide some positive way forward. He was surprised when it revealed that he wanted to find himself again, reclaim his dreams and embrace the belief that he could become his best self. He had a true quantum shift—a positive reorganization of his self-identity—as a result of the coaching, choosing to create the life he really wanted and build on all that he had accomplished. He went on to found his own business and begin living his dream: having artistic/creative control of his own writing, and autonomy and freedom to collaborate with other inspirational writers.

Receiving this note on the way to delivering a coaching workshop in Japan seemed such a synchronous event and an affirmation. The focus of Ann's presentation was on the coach as catalyst in encouraging pivotal moments. The message reminded her of her role in "igniting substantial change" within this particular individual a number of years before. For this client, executive coaching had provided a way to reconnect powerfully with his inner process and wisdom. He had become so distracted by the external pressures and demands of his career that he had temporarily lost his way. We all live the "hero's journey" to some degree in our own lives, as described by Joseph Campbell.[1] We are on a path through life that involves travails to overcome, times of crisis, moments of victory and then returning to our path hopefully transformed in some way. While some individuals do not feel victorious on their life path, others persevere and triumph. Yet we all are subject to some form or part of the hero's journey. In fact, this compelling story underlies our most cherished literature, cinema, plays and even video games.[2] Our clients have their own hero stories and singular pathways. How can they not? We are all aspirational beings and as such hunger for a successful journey in our own lives.

If our topic is about providing a guide for igniting substantial change, the passionate theme of our book is helping clients reconnect with their own inner process. Appreciative Coaching® is about living from the inside out—it's a focus on inner guidance to become one's best self, and even true self, which evolves over a lifetime. We are at a unique point in human history where the

---

[1] *The Hero with a Thousand Faces* (1949) is a seminal work of comparative mythology by Joseph Campbell in which he discusses his theory of the archetypal hero found in world mythologies.
[2] Wilcock (2013).

opportunity and expectation regarding the generative capacity of humans to change is broadly recognized in cultures around the world. We *can* change as the findings of neuroplasticity and the new scientific paradigm assure us.[3] The idea that tapping into one's inner process is key to building a fulfilling life has emerged across numerous fields of study and exploded in popular literature.[4] Knowledge about self-change is now available to anyone from any walk of life at a scale never seen before, a social movement in which the coaching profession plays a leading role. This book chronicles how to help people believe in their capacity to change by paying attention to their inner guidance.

Understanding Our Inner States of Mind

William James was a leading American psychologist and philosopher in the late nineteenth and early twentieth centuries. He was also a physician. He combined a unique blend of native intelligence, passion for understanding the human mind, insight and acquired knowledge in multiple fields, which enabled him to take a holistic view of how people change. It put him light years ahead of many of his contemporaries, who were still focused on reducing human capacity to discrete bits and pieces—thinking separated from feeling separated from behaviour separated from the physical body.

In his seminal work *The Principles of Psychology*, James examined the history of human psychology, including an introspective account and study of his own states of mind.[5] He understood that "consciousness does not appear to itself chopped up in bits … it flows."[6] He used the metaphor of a flowing river to describe what he called "the stream of thought, of consciousness or of subjective life" that is innate to being human.[7]

James felt strongly that humans had an inner process that directed them—that they had choices in how they created their lives. This was a revolutionary concept in his world, a time when scientific thought was firmly entrenched in

---

[3] Neuroplasticity is the brain's ability to reorganize itself by forming new neural connections throughout life. The new scientific paradigm is commonly referred to as a new view of the world based on findings in quantum physics, chaos theory, self-organization and complexity theory.

[4] As an example, research interest in the concept of intuition "has exploded across analytic philosophy in recent decades" and "is apparent across a broad swathe of academia (and perhaps beyond)" (Andow, 2015, p. 189). Astronaut Edgar Mitchell, founder of the Institute of Noetic Sciences, calls intuition an experience of inner knowing (Myers, 2002).

[5] James (1890).

[6] James (1890), p. 239.

[7] James (1890), p. 239.

viewing humans as machine-like and only capable of being changed through external efforts (parents, teachers, psychologists, etc.).

James developed a philosophical and psychological view of human change that was pragmatic and functional. To him, humans adapted internally and subjectively to their environment. He saw the mind and its experiences, and nature, as inseparable. Like the findings of quantum physics, which was to come years after his writings, James cultivated the worldview that the value of any truth was dependent on its use to the person who held it. In addition, he considered human response to the diverse experiences in life as never able to be objectively analysed because the mind of the observer and the simple act of observation affected the outcome of any empirical approach to truth. He described a mind–world connection that significantly impacted the modernist literature and art at the time, as seen in the "stream of consciousness" narrative device that authors such as James Joyce employed.[8]

His brilliance was to reconceive the human mind as inherently purposive and selective—*from within*.

People Are Mysteries to Be Appreciated

> *If it were not for the silence between the notes, no song could have ever touched your heart.*
>
> —The Way of Mastery

In seeking to make the most of our own lives and as Appreciative coaches striving to help others get the most out of theirs, we have, over time, broadened our view of what is possible in life. Personally and professionally, we've journeyed from a limited perspective of life (satisfied with surviving and recovering from hardships and thwarted dreams) to a belief that humans have the capacity not only to be resilient but also to thrive and flourish. American sociologist and psychologist Corey Keyes described flourishing as being filled with positive emotion and to be functioning well both psychologically and socially.[9] We are happy to report that for the most part we now live in this state, as do many of our clients.

We attribute the sense of flourishing that we feel in our current personal and professional lives to past choices we made to embrace beliefs and experi-

---

[8] James' stream of thought influenced the works of well-known authors such as James Joyce's *Ulysses*, Virginia Woolf's *Mrs. Dalloway*, William Faulkner's *The Sound and the Fury* and Samuel Beckett's *Molloy*.
[9] Keyes and Haidt (2003).

ences that focused on the generative capacity of human beings to change and evolve. These choices were heavily influenced by the philosophy and practice of Appreciative Coaching and Appreciative Inquiry, which are rooted philosophically in social constructionism. Social psychologist Kenneth Gergen's work on generative theory and social constructionism had a profound impact on David Cooperrider, developer of Appreciative Inquiry.[10]

In *Toward Generative Theory*, Gergen challenged the traditional positivist assumptions of the reigning science of social theory of the late 1970s. According to him, this science was committed to putting great weight on accumulating objective facts, demanding verification of theoretical ideas, disregarding the temporality of many social patterns and encouraging researchers to be dispassionate bystanders rather than participant theorists.[11] He advocated a generative approach to restructuring the character of social life; he wanted to raise controversy and doubt about embedded scientific biases and to offer a flexibility that would enhance the adaptive capacity of society.[12]

Gergen continued his critique of traditional scientific metatheory in the 1990s with *Toward Transformation of Social Knowledge*.[13] Cooperrider embraced this new way of thinking and described it as anticipatory theory—having the capacity to challenge the predominant cultural assumptions, to raise fundamental questions about modern life, to reconsider what has been taken for granted and to provide new alternatives for social action.[14] He placed it in a positive change context. It was a revolutionary change approach that arose in opposition to the problem-solving methodologies that were predominant at the time in social and organizational theory. The term "generative change" is more easily explained when compared with mechanistic approaches to change. Bill Veltrop, a self-described architect of generative change in the fields of organization design and learning community approaches, outlined what he saw as the differences between mechanistic and generative organizational approaches (Table 1.1).[15]

As organization development consultants, we were trained initially in the problem-solving approach to change. In fact, the prevailing metaphor for organizations was that they were problems to be solved, including the indi-

---

[10] Watkins and Mohr (2001).
[11] Gergen (1978).
[12] Gergen (1978).
[13] Gergen (1994).
[14] Watkins and Mohr (2001).
[15] Veltrop (2002).

Table 1.1 Mechanistic and generative approaches to change

Mechanistic approach	Generative approach
Treat human systems as machines, people as replaceable parts; tend to be demeaning and de-energizing	Enhance, enable and ennoble the human spirit; grow a capacity for growing
Focus on overcoming limitations, finding and fixing what's wrong—problem-solving mindset	Focus on exploring and realizing full potential, an appreciative mindset
Tend to be episodic with tightly focused outcomes	Tend to be recursive and designed to achieve multiple and even multiplying benefits
Head-oriented, focused on performance, results and metrics	Give priority to the heart, to compassion and caring
Tend to be imposed from the top down, pyramid structure	Tap into the genius of all players in the organization; naturally transform the pyramid into many circles
Implementation tends to be disruptive to "real work"	Implementation seen as real work and as woven into fabric of daily processes and practices
Learning tends to emphasize formal training of individuals	Learning tends to nurture "communities of practice" and other forms of natural knowledge-sharing

viduals who served them. Our job as organization development practitioners was to give them the tools, practices and methodologies to solve their own problems because it was in the nature of organizations to *be* a problem. When exposed to the radical perspective of Appreciative Inquiry that organizations were no longer problems to be solved but rather solutions to be embraced, we found it most compelling.

Appreciative Coaching was developed on this generative approach to change, which views individuals as mysteries to be appreciated rather than problems to be solved or fixed. Therefore as coaches we do not take a mechanistic, external perspective but instead focus on the inner process of an individual as the path to greater fulfilment and satisfaction. As we've pointed out, the inner process seems impervious to external control but may be influenced, supported and, at times, ignited to substantial change. One of the master coaches we interviewed described a pivotal moment she experienced with a client:[16]

My client was a woman in her 40s, divorced, one child and working for a major retail organization. She had been bullied at work and had to bring her supervisor

---

[16] Six master coaches were involved in our research project. They are mentioned by name in the acknowledgements.

up on charges. As a result, the organization created another job for her, one that was significantly different and in which she was working with much younger people for a much younger audience. When she came to me she was completely demoralized. She felt uncomfortable in the new role at work, her foreign accent was getting in the way, she couldn't do what was expected of her—a laundry list that left her practically paralysed. About mid-way in the coaching, she was asked at work to do a presentation to a group of senior executives. She was panicked. Her chief concern was that she would not do a good job and that she would be fired. We had been going in circles in previous sessions because she hadn't yet been ready to see herself as she was right now. I wanted to try to understand where this insecurity came from and I decided to ask about the dissolution of her marriage, and she began describing some truly heroic actions she had taken during that time period. Her husband had bullied her throughout the marriage. Finally, she had stood up to him and obtained a satisfactory custody arrangement after a long drawn-out battle. I pointed out how only a strong woman could do something like that and quickly asked who her favourite superhero was. She came up with the image of Wonder Woman. So we listed all the successful actions she had taken in handling her divorce as well as achievements from earlier jobs. The moment she started seeing herself as a kind of superhero in her own life, everything shifted for her. She went into the presentation with her executive team and delivered a strong performance. She was able to talk to her boss about her concerns with the job. She did well on her performance review. It was such a simple yet powerful experience when she allowed herself to remember and acknowledge who she really was. Wonder Woman was just a tool; the real pivot was the process of moving from seeing herself as a victim to experiencing herself as a strong woman.

If people are mysteries to be appreciated, how do we scientifically explain and replicate with other clients the success that this master coach experienced with this particular client? Would a question about superheroes addressed to another client result in the same significant outcome or, for that matter, questions about her former relationship with her spouse? On reflection and in retrospect, the inquiry process of the coach makes sense. But in the moment, the coach could have chosen any number of pathways to stimulate the client towards some type of inner discovery. Something guided her to that particular line of inquiry and support that seems to us more easily captured by a generative approach than a mechanistic one.

Understanding What Makes Us Mysterious

If we were to apply traditional scientific methodology, we would view coaching conversations and the occurrence of pivotal moments as "objects" of study, as fixed entities with innate permanent characteristics. The goal of this type of inquiry assumes that things are a certain way in the world and therefore exist independently of human experience, opinion or description.[17] This perspective understands reality as a "container of fixed entities and principles" for objective study, as opposed to a constructivist approach, which studies reality as "an ever-changing interactive process"[18] which acknowledges the fundamental role that humans play in creating knowledge.

The objectivist approach ensures that we are dealing with reality as an orderly arrangement and that there is an underlying truth to aspire to. This implies that we might not "bear full responsibility for our knowledge"[19] as researchers and practitioners. While compelling, we found the study of pivotal moments from an objectivist or mechanistic perspective to be limiting in terms of addressing the practical implications for our clients' satisfaction and well-being. We realized that our view of how the world works and of how knowledge develops has significant implications for how we best support substantial change in our clients.

Spencer McWilliams, Professor Emeritus of Psychology at California State University, is an advocate of constructivism for reasons that resonated with our own experiences and beliefs as coaches:

> From a psychotherapeutic perspective, we can help clients by facilitating awareness of the personally and socially constructed nature of beliefs and interpretations, helping them to construct more useful alternative narratives and ways of giving their lives meaning. From an individual standpoint, we can see the limitations in our own experience and the suffering and dysfunctions that arise due to attachment to the correctness of beliefs.[20]

We therefore chose to study pivotal moments from three interrelated perspectives: constructivism, pragmatism and hermeneutic phenomenology. According to McWilliams, constructivism views science as an intrinsically human activity in which we develop knowledge, interpret experience and are impacted by historical contexts. As a result, knowledge is temporal, practi-

---

[17] McWilliams (2016), p. 4.
[18] McWilliams (2016), p. 2.
[19] McWilliams (2016), p. 3.
[20] McWilliams (2016), p. 3.

cal, revisable and—most important for the field of coaching—supportive of choices for clients on their individual journeys of making meaning of their lives. Constructivism also helps coaches in understanding a range of viable viewpoints to offer clients rather than one "expert" position. At the tacit level, says McWilliams, a constructivist approach provides individuals with support in finding a better way of looking at life, and it relieves them of feeling trapped in only one way of seeing their situation.[21] From this perspective, we recognize that we live in a chaotic and dynamic world in which *processes* have priority over *objects* in terms of understanding and navigating human situations and change.

Our second perspective, pragmatism,[22] is characterized by a sceptical approach to dogma and a view that theories are "provisional, changeable, and grounded in practical results."[23] We were drawn to the pragmatist description of the world and human activity in terms of what proves useful, such as predicting events and actions, creating a better future, and increasing human equality and access to happiness.[24] Pragmatists also emphasize a view of life that places human processes, as a product of biological evolution, at the very centre of the development of both empirical and conceptual knowledge.[25]

Finally, we applied hermeneutic phenomenology as our research approach because we wanted to understand what constitutes a pivotal moment which erupts from our non consciousness, a place of continued mystery for researchers. Phenomenology is interested in the everyday, individual experiences of people and there are two perspectives of analysis of that lived experience: from the people living through the phenomenon and from the researchers who are interested in better understanding the phenomenon. The goal is to study experience as it occurs or "appears" in consciousness.

Hermeneutic phenomenology is more than a research method; it's a stance, a way of being in the world and a willingness to undergo a process so that "what is" may emerge and show itself.[26] The origin of the word "hermeneutics" is from the Greek for "to interpret." While originally it referred to the study and interpretation of biblical texts, philosophers such as Martin Heidegger and Hans-Georg Gadamer have evolved its meaning into "the theory and

---

[21] McWilliams (2016), p. 8.

[22] American pragmatists include classists John Dewey, William James, George Herbert Mead and Charles Peirce, as well as neopragmatists such as Richard Rorty and third-wave pragmatists such as Joseph Margolis.

[23] McWilliams (2016), p. 16.

[24] Rorty (1999).

[25] Margolis (2010).

[26] Gadamer (1960/1997).

practice of interpretation and understanding (Verstehen) in different kinds of human contexts."[27] Heidegger, a student of Edmund Husserl, who founded phenomenology as a research methodology, introduced hermeneutics into the study of phenomena in order to discover meanings that were not immediately apparent. Heidegger viewed existence as being-in-the-world in which many of the elements that shape us are hidden and require interpretation for existence to be understood.[28] His concern was to uncover these hidden phenomena of our lives and their meanings. Hermeneutic phenomenology goes beyond the level of description to discover meanings that are not immediately apparent[29] based on the premise that every individual's experience is unique and influenced by one's preconceptions.

How Our Story Unfolded

After our book *Appreciative Coaching* was published in 2007, we were invited to lead presentations and workshops in the USA and around the world for audiences of coaches (from beginners to master level), organization development practitioners, managers and human resources professionals. We also offered eight-week online courses based on our book, and, of course, we each had our own executive coaching practice. The more we presented on the approach and the more experience we gained as coaching professionals, the more intrigued we became about what was causing our clients to make substantial shifts in learning, perspective and even identity.

We began to acknowledge that something very interesting was happening from an inside perspective that seemed to bring coach and client together in a type of dance or interplay that often resulted in significant change. We noticed how our own internal processes, including different ways of knowing or "reading" our clients' feelings, thought patterns and energy, would inform us first and then communicate with our conscious awareness. We detected mutual interaction and processing occurring at different levels of awareness between us and our clients, for which we didn't yet have language. Something was "knocking" on our inner awareness to be heard. In truly synchronous ways, we were both experiencing the same phenomenon in our respective practices, and, because we truly enjoy research, we found ourselves veering in a new direction.

---

[27] Odman (1988), p. 63.
[28] Heidegger (1962).
[29] Merleau-Ponty (1962/1996).

Pivotal Moments: Our Interest

Executive coaching at its best allows for a creative space and time in which clients have the opportunity for alchemical moments to emerge. These are moments when clients can make significant shifts from self-limiting patterns to positive growth and development. Otto Scharmer, American economist, senior lecturer at MIT and author of *Theory U*,[30] pointed out that when we shift our habitual way of seeing and acting and redirect our attention, a different world comes forth. Coaches are often privileged to witness such events. Yet there has been little research on what actually causes or inspires these pivotal moments or learning shifts in coaching.

So we began a coaching research project, building on the power of the Poetic Principle in Appreciative Coaching and on the tool we use called "pivoting." The Poetic Principle is based on the belief that we can reinterpret our life story by constructing new ways of thinking, feeling and acting. This principle also says that our lives are choiceful. Transformative learning similarly describes this as transforming a habit of mind ("habitual ways of thinking, feeling and acting influenced by assumptions") by using critical reflection on one's frames of reference and points of view as a way to develop autonomous thinking.[31]

In addition to the Poetic Principle, Appreciative Coaching is based on four other principles, all of which are drawn from Appreciative Inquiry and which together form the theoretical base of this coaching approach.[32] They have become the filters through which we discern which methods and tools align with our coaching, and they have guided and influenced us on this journey. The five principles are summarized as follows:

1. *Constructionist Principle*: Humans construct their reality through their thoughts, language and how they communicate, interact, create symbols and construct metaphors with one another. They generate meaning and reality in their lives from their inner process in interaction with their environment.
2. *Poetic Principle*: Humans are meant to change over a lifetime and they are agents of their own change. Any number of new realities can flow from a reinterpretation of one's life story, just as there are any number of potential

---

[30] Scharmer (2009).
[31] Mezirow (1997), pp. 5–6.
[32] Orem, Binkert and Clancy (2007).

interpretations of a poem. A person's life story can be reframed, reimagined and refocused towards more hopeful and joyful action.
3. *Simultaneity Principle*: Inquiry and change happen in the same moment. By the very first questions asked, coaches begin to sow seeds of change and lead clients in a certain direction. Only from the present can the past be revisited and the future anticipated. There are no gaps between past, present and future.
4. *Anticipatory Principle*: Humans are wired to anticipate the future. Therefore visions or dreams of the future guide current behaviour in the direction of that future and lead to action to manifest that future.
5. *Positive Principle*: Change happens more readily with large amounts of positive affect. Positive attitudes, actions and connections support and build resources for change.

We have come to recognize that the very stance we took as Appreciative coaches, which included presenting, training and coaching with the five principles in mind, influenced us and led us to a deeper level of awareness that coaching was about a lot more than just goals and action plans. In a way, it seems we primed ourselves to be more and more sensitive to the nuances of the coaching interaction, especially the capacity for clients to pivot.

We could see from our experience that these pivotal moments seemed to be lived experiences that could not be quantified, predicted or planned by either coach or client. Therefore viewing pivots as an object of study from the traditional scientific approach had its limitations. We decided, however, that a pivotal moment could be explored as a process phenomenon that occurred as "humans create knowledge in ever-changing contexts."[33] From the constructivist perspective, we focused on the *process of igniting substantial change* by reflecting retrospectively on the "phenomenon" (the pivotal moment) that emerged from the non consciousness of our clients. As coaches, we either witnessed this phenomenon with our client in the present moment or were informed in subsequent coaching sessions of a shift that had occurred "offline."

Pivotal Moments: Our Path

In his collection of essays entitled, *Resistance, Rebellion and Death*, Albert Camus reminds us that "freedom is nothing else but a chance to be better." [34]

---

[33] McWilliams (2016), p. 1.
[34] Camus (1961).

In our own lives and in our coaching, we have been "driven" to better understand how humans change and how as practitioners we can aid that process. How can we improve our own lives and those of our clients? We found freedom in the Appreciative Coaching approach—freedom from the constraints of viewing our coaching clients in limited or problem-oriented ways. We have now found another level of freedom in following the constructivist approach to research, which promotes process and pragmatism rather than an objectivist position.[35] Thus we view the phenomenon of pivotal moments in terms of interrelated, changing relationships and processes that humans create as they seek knowledge about themselves and their reality.

We hope with this book to offer some partial truth that may provide further clues to understanding what causes substantial change, and we invite others to follow these clues by building on and elaborating them with fresh ideas. We acknowledge the words of caution shared by John Shotter, Emeritus Professor of Communication, University of New Hampshire, that the social constructionist perspective on understanding human process also has its limitations. He warns that "we will never be able to gain complete mastery over all that is around us—it will always be able to surprise us, no matter how familiar to us it has become."[36] This has been our experience in studying pivotal moments; we are, after all, seeking to more deeply understand the mystery of who we really are.

As part of our coach training, we usually asked workshop participants to reflect on their beliefs about human development and change; we had found these beliefs to be more and more integral to a coach's stance. We would begin our workshops by asking participants to identify where they thought they were in terms of two different positions on various principles of human change. The purpose was to help them become more conscious about what kind of influence they were bringing into coaching. We invite you to think about these perspectives as well. In Table 1.2 we have listed two different positions based on the prevailing scientific paradigms. This is intended as an awareness-building activity to help determine your own coaching stance. Take a moment to reflect on which position seems the more appropriate to you. We encountered these two positions often on our research path, depending on what construct or concept we were striving to clarify. Sometimes we were confused.

---

[35] McWilliams (2016).
[36] Shotter (2010), p. 82.

Table 1.2 Two scientific positions

Traditional scientific paradigm	Emerging holistic paradigm
Nature exists as a permanent essence, so there is an objective reality independent of human experience, opinion or description.	The world cannot be understood independent of our subjective point of view. Knowledge is constructed in communities through interpretation of experience.
Meaning is found in fixed, external truth, which humans seek to understand and which they use to evaluate and guide their lives.	Meaning is derived from relationships that are in ever-changing processes. Humans have the opportunity to create more fulfilling lives through the reinterpretation of their experience.
Science asks questions of consequence to determine the accurate account of a situation or to discover the right solution.	How questions are asked can change the very nature of a situation or solution; therefore inquiry is a tool for practical discovery.
With planning, future possibilities can be predicted and results created in a finite span of time. Planning provides security and safety.	Anticipation is a fundamental human activity which can be used to create desired futures through intention and openness to possibilities as they arise.
There is comfort in striving to achieve a life congruent with an ultimate truth and aiming to understand its essence.	Reality is constructed and therefore lacks a permanent essence. As a result, humans build positive, emotional bonds to feel comfort and hope.

What to Expect from This Book

We continue our journey in Chapter 2, "What Is a Pivot?" This was the question we asked ourselves when we did an initial literature review to better understand what we experienced with our clients when they made substantial shifts. The chapter presents a summary drawn from a range of different studies in which we were able to capture some common characteristics and trigger points of "aha" moments. We then compared that information with the learnings from our coaching research and our own experiences, and we found a discrepancy that we could not easily explain. We found three major distinctions in the types of shift that clients experienced, as well as differences in magnitude, manifestation and timing of pivotal moments. Our research and experiences showed an expanded perspective of what characterizes and triggers such pivotal experiences. These findings led us to a fork in the road and we chose to take the less travelled path.

Chapter 3, "Pivoting: The Extraordinary Power of Self-Organization," proposes a coach's theory of igniting substantial change based on self-organization.

The interplay of the aspects of belief, inner knowing and memory, which remains largely covert to clients and coaches, describes an inner process that is interwoven, multicausal and cooperative—all reflecting the dynamic patterns of self-organization. We explore the present moment as *the* access point for coaches to exploit. Only in the present moment can clients both retrieve their past and anticipate their future, literally engaging in a form of time travel to help make sense of their current situation. Through focusing their attention, coaches can help clients increase their level of self-awareness and harness the energy of their emotions for action. There is much new research on the role of positive emotions in increasing personal growth, development and capacity. The chapter concludes with the notion of embodied cognition as a key coaching strategy, broadening our notion of where bodily awareness originates and extending it beyond the purely mental.

Chapter 4, "Accessing the Inner Self: Beliefs," highlights the first of three key aspects of inner process: beliefs, inner knowing and memory. It focuses on the power of beliefs in influencing the direction of our lives. We show how igniting substantial change involves self-organization at a non-conscious level. Such a process creates an interplay of one's beliefs, implicit memory and inner knowing, and it uses the magic of the present moment to bring an insight into consciousness. We explain belief from the perspective of the tension between the traditional scientific paradigm and the current emerging holistic paradigm, and we illuminate how humans are socially wired for beliefs. At the non-conscious level we hold beliefs that we are not aware of, yet they affect how we live our lives, sometimes directly but more often indirectly. We demonstrate how beliefs can be high-level attractors for change and explain how they are constructed as part of an ever-changing interactive internal process. Beliefs play a major role in the capacity of both coaches and clients to anticipate and encourage change.

Chapter 5, "Accessing the Inner Self: Knowing," takes on the second aspect of inner process—how knowing contributes to the ease and challenge of following our own path. We distinguish the act of knowing from the idea of knowledge, and we describe how both modern and postmodern theories of knowledge have influenced our coaching philosophies and methodologies. Modes of knowing, in contrast, are active processes which coaches are constantly making use of when working with clients. We argue that there is a bandwidth of knowing in play whether we consciously acknowledge it or not. We highlight these different ways of knowing that can be better accessed for the benefit of both coaches and clients, and we suggest that all pivotal moments necessarily include this component.

In Chapter 6, "Accessing the Inner Self: Memory," we complete the presentation of the three aspects of inner process. In terms of consciousness, humans don't exist without memory because it is the holder of who we are in the present. We trace the history of the predominant view of memory and our unique human capacity to time travel. We describe some of the recent amazing discoveries from neuroscience, especially in terms of non-conscious associative memory networks and the role of priming in influencing human thought, feeling and behaviour. We consider coach priming strategies to play a key role in helping clients ignite substantial change.

In Chapter 7, "Turn of the Kaleidoscope," we connect the theory and concepts we've presented around igniting substantial change with concrete coaching stories, strategies and actions. These tools are drawn from the experiences of the master coaches we interviewed, and our own research and experiences as executive coaches, coach researchers and coach trainers. We present the power of priming and of knowing what stance we take as coaches. The priming tools we introduce include attention, feedback, discernment and making the most of the present moment. We offer ways to incorporate the concept of embodied or distributed cognition into our awareness as coaches, highlighting the key role that metaphors play. We also take an in-depth look at the importance of the coaching context as it relates to the client's internal landscape (the interplay of beliefs, inner knowing and memory).

Chapter 8, "Finding Coherence," concludes by describing a new science of change that has emerged from our hermeneutic journey. It is based on the experiences, discoveries and studies from our research project and incorporates perspectives from a range of fields. We feel that this new science helps to illuminate our path forward as coaches. We present six foundational conditions that we suggest are necessary for substantial change to occur. We share our key learnings from participating in the hermeneutic circle of research: the importance of social context and influence in coaching; learning how to integrate embodied knowing in our coaching practice; focusing on reliable measures to bring clients to higher levels of coherence; and absorbing core concepts and actions regarding the nature of insight.

In each chapter of the book, we weave together learnings from our research and our coaching, the experiences of the master coaches we interviewed, and client stories.

2

What Is a Pivot?

What sort of God would it be, who only pushed from without?
—Johann Wolfgang von Goethe

What is a pivot? This was the question we asked ourselves when we did an initial literature review to better understand what happened when our clients made substantial shifts. In our initial exploration we focused on studies of *aha* moments but we quickly discovered that the phenomenon has been variously described as cognitive insight, creative cognition, eureka moment, intuition or insight, quantum change, and epiphany or transformation—all depending on the intensity of the experience and field of inquiry. We also wondered in what ways insight differed from learning processes, and we included our own life experiences in being coached through significant insights. In our research we had observed clients making many learning shifts, frequent shifts in perspective and even some quantum changes. Were they all pivots? What specifically characterized a pivot or insight that would then distinguish it from other forms of learning?

We soon determined that the path to better understanding the nature of a pivot would not be a straightforward or uniform one. The effort seemed worthy, however, because insight is considered to be at the core of human intelligence and provides one of the most powerful ways to not only advance human understanding but also produce influential scientific breakthroughs.[1]

---

[1] Schilling (2005).

It seemed to us, as coaches, that this is what we are about as well—furthering understanding and supporting breakthroughs for our clients.

Aha Moments: A Common Perspective

Eureka! I have found it.
   —Archimedes

Our initial literature review spanned neuroscience and cognitive psychology, Gestalt psychology, social networking theory, belief systems theory, body/mind research, studies on emotion, psychotherapy, family and systems health research, transformational and spiritual literature, executive and life-coaching studies and phenomenological coaching studies. Not surprisingly, we found no definitive consensus about or understanding of what causes an experience of insight or exactly where it comes from. There was some general agreement on the characteristics of an *aha* moment, but explanations ranged from it being a strictly cognitive phenomenon to it being a phenomenological experience holistic in its nature. However, we discovered some interesting highlights that propelled us further down our initial path to decipher this mysterious experience, an experience that we can all attest to having had. We found that we could group the findings into two broad categories along a continuum: those staying within the bounds of a more traditional scientific paradigm at one end and those seeking a more holistic perspective at the other end.

Initial Literature Review: Scientific Paradigm to Holistic Paradigm

Most scientific studies on *aha* moments come from experiments in cognitive insight problem-solving in laboratory settings. This literature attempts to define and explain the underlying mechanism of insights in a quantitative, measurable manner and includes recent learnings from cognitive neuroscience in the form of neuroimaging, such as electroencephalography (EEG) and functional magnetic resonance imaging (*f*MRI).[2] It also seeks to explain the "eureka" moments of the discoveries of great minds such as Albert Einstein and Archimedes (ancient Greek mathematician and inventor to whom the term is attributed), and other highly creative individuals.[3]

---

[2] Kounios and Beeman (2009).
[3] Csikszentmihalyi and Sawyer (1995).

This field has a long and interwoven history of research involving problem-solving, creative insight, innovative science, cognitive psychology and neuroscience, all working to identify the elusive underlying mechanism of insight. Cognitive psychologist Janet Metcalfe voiced the concern of researchers in this area when she noted, "The persistent lack of a mechanism for insight, linked with the charge that the notion of insight is somehow supernatural, has shackled researchers … We do not yet understand insight."[4]

Problem-solving Literature

The term "insight" has been used in different ways in the problem-solving literature and a range of definitions can be found, a sample of which is below:[5]

- an experience during or subsequent to problem-solving attempts, in which problem-related content comes to mind with sudden ease and provides a feeling of pleasure, the belief that the solution is true and confidence in this belief;[6]
- a particular type of problem-solving sequence that happens when a problem cannot be solved using conventional stepwise methods and the problem-solver suddenly realizes (the aha experience) that the solution involves unconventional methods (the problem solver sees that the problem needs restructuring);[7]
- a type of problem situation where within the typically derived initial problem representation the goal cannot be reached and a restructured goal representation is required for the solution;[8]
- the reorientation of one's thinking, including breaking of the unwarranted "fixation" and forming of novel, task-related associations among the old nodes of concepts or cognitive skills.[9]

There are common themes underlying the concept of insight (suddenness, restructuring or reorientation, difficulty or fixation) but it is used in different

---

[4] Metcalfe (1995), p. x.
[5] Ash, Jee and Wiley (2011).
[6] Topolinski and Reber (2010), pp. 401–402.
[7] Ollinger, Jones and Knoblich (2008), p. 208.
[8] Gilhooly and Fioratou (2009), p. 356.
[9] Luo and Niki (2003), p. 316.

ways in the definitions above.[10] According to cognitive psychologist Ivan Ash and colleagues, these definitions begin with a psychological experience, move to a particular problem-solving sequence, then describe a type of problem situation and finally cast insight as a problem-solving process.[11] It is this bewildering array of how the concept of insight is applied that makes it more difficult to describe accurately.

Most cognitive researchers agree that, however insight occurs, it is different from more typical learning processes and is often accompanied by an emotional or affective response. It is usually defined as a process in which a person moves suddenly from a state of not knowing how to solve a problem to a state of knowing,[12] and it is this process that distinguishes insight problem-solving from routine problem-solving (i.e., incremental). Researchers differ in their explanations of how cognitive insight occurs.[13] For example, there are theorists who hypothesize that automatic, unconscious processes are at work in finding solutions.[14] There is experimental evidence that supports this perspective, and neuroimaging studies using EEG and fMRI indicate that insight may be the culmination of a series of brain states and processes operating on different timescales.[15]

Other theorists propose that conscious active processes, such as planning, monitoring and evaluating, are at work to find a solution.[16] Such theorists argue that insight and non-insight problems are still tackled and solved using equivalent cognitive mechanisms.[17] It has also been suggested that these two approaches may be complementary in that together they might explain the different phases of the insight process,[18] or that they both have a role to play in explaining insight, and that there are multiple ways in which insight can be produced.[19]

Insight problem-solving experiments are primarily based on giving subjects tasks (usually solving a puzzle of some kind) in a laboratory setting. The subject gets stuck on a task and is unable to make headway until they suddenly

---

[10] Ash et al. (2011).
[11] Ash et al. (2011).
[12] Schilling (2005).
[13] Ball and Stevens (2009).
[14] Chu and MacGregor (2011).
[15] Kounios and Beeman (2009).
[16] Chu and MacGregor (2011).
[17] Weisberg (2006).
[18] Jones (2003).
[19] Ball and Stevens (2009).

break free of their unhelpful thoughts and are able to find a solution.[20] Such insight problem-solving appears to have three key features: (1) individuals, after reflecting on the problem, reach a point of impasse; (2) insight into the solution seems to emerge suddenly, giving rise to an *aha* experience; and (3) problem-solvers find it difficult to describe the processes that help them overcome the impasse, or the solution processes are simply non-reportable in nature.[21]

From this literature we identified a specific definition of insight which did not precisely match our client experiences in coaching but which did contribute some pieces of the puzzle, namely that three features seem to underscore most cognitive descriptions of insight or *aha* moments: reflection and impasse, sudden awareness, and inability to explain cognitively where the *aha* or solution came from.

Network Model of Cognitive Insight

Melissa Schilling, Professor of Management and Organizations at New York University Stern School of Business, is recognized as a worldwide expert on innovation and strategy in high-tech industries. Her textbook, *Strategic Management of Technological Innovation*, is the number one innovation strategy text in the world. She has devoted some of her academic study to better explain the process of cognitive insight or sudden *aha* experiences.[22] We thought her perspective in bringing together the field of cognitive problem-solving with adaptive systems theory might offer an alternative way to think of insight.

Schilling pointed out how cognitive psychologists continue to struggle with identifying any single underlying mechanism and she proposed a network model of cognitive insight that integrates competing explanations into a single, unified view.[23] Like Metcalfe, she would like to reduce the likelihood of viewing insight as a supernatural event because of the suddenness and disconnectedness with which solutions arise.[24] She instead suggested that insights or quantum leaps of inspiration may arrive through known

---

[20] Kaplan and Simon (1990).
[21] Ball and Stevens (2009).
[22] Schilling (2005).
[23] Schilling (2005).
[24] Schilling (2005).

information-processing phases which are still amenable to scientific study and explanation.[25]

Integrating research on social networks, graph theory, complex adaptive systems, connectionism and cognition, Schilling proposed that the moment of insight may be the formation of new "small-world" network properties in the mind. This is based on the premise that systems are represented as groups of nodes that are interconnected in some way in some kind of relationship. Examples of such system relationships range from physical wiring, relationships between buyers and sellers, familial relationships and relationships between ideas. The role of deep knowledge clusters in the mind brings both benefits and costs to the insight process in terms of system impacts, according to Schilling. Some theorists have argued that insightful people have built up large reservoirs of discipline-relevant information (e.g., chess grand masters), which provide a richly connected information network for them to draw on, such as more accurate patterns of association.[26] Other theorists have suggested that such prior experience in a knowledge domain can inhibit creative problem-solving and result in "functional fixedness" where an individual can think of using an object only for its most common use.[27]

Schilling pointed to at least five prominent hypotheses on the process of insight that incorporate unexpected connections as one of the underlying mechanisms and all of which she finds congruent when viewed from a network perspective.[28] She built on the three features of the cognitive insight process described above by emphasizing the role of unexpected connections: (1) there is some type of problem-solving gap that needs to be resolved to achieve coherence; (2) information needs to be reorganized in order to search for a solution; (3) a mental block or impasse must be overcome in viewing the problem; (4) a transference or abstraction of structural elements from one problem to another problem may occur (includes priming or external suggestions); and (5) some type of subconscious random recombination of ideas or free association results in a solution.

Small-world analysis in social networks is rooted in work by mathematical graph theorists. Research began in this area with studies estimating both the average number of acquaintances that people possess and the probability of two randomly selected members of a society being linked by a chain of no

---

[25] Schilling (2005).
[26] Schilling (2005).
[27] Schilling (2005).
[28] Schilling (2005).

more than two acquaintances.[29] This type of research was popularized by psychologist Stanley Milgram with his studies on links in social networks.[30] His work was featured in a play by John Guare in 1990, *Six Degrees of Separation* which was later made into a movie. The premise was that everyone in the world is connected to everyone else in the world by a chain of no more than six acquaintances, hence "six degrees of separation."

Schilling applied this small-worlds concept to cognitive networks to create her unified theory of cognitive insight.[31] Briefly, she posited that each case of insight from a network perspective represents the addition or change of nodes (elements or sets of information) and links (connections or relationships between nodes) or both. While this process is not unlike typical learning processes, the key difference is that insightful learning forges nodes or links that result in a more substantive shift.[32]

In summary, Schilling proposed that cognitive insight occurs when an atypical association results in a "shortcut" in an individual's network of representations. This causes a reorienting of the individual's understanding of the relationships within and among the affected representations and may prompt a cascade of other connections. This atypical path could be forged through a random recombination process or through subconscious or conscious directed search.[33] Schilling seeks to stay within the scientific paradigm in her explanation of insight as a cognitive process and offers a theory that incorporates the diverse findings found in insight problem-solving studies. We found that her explanation was still unable to fully account for moments of self-described epiphany that a few of our research clients experienced.

Gestalt Concept of Insight

Gestalt psychology was a major contributor to developing a concept of insight that went beyond a strictly cognitive definition and which revolutionized the field of learning at the time. Ash and his colleagues provide us with a brief history of the development of the Gestalt concept of insight.[34] In the early twenti-

---

[29] Schilling (2005); researchers de Sola Pool and Kochen (1978).
[30] Milgram (1967).
[31] For a full account of her model, we refer to her article, "A 'Small-World' Network Model of Cognitive Insight" (2005).
[32] Schilling (2005).
[33] Schilling (2005).
[34] Ash et al. (2011).

eth century, psychology was becoming an empirically based and experimental science, and theorists such as Alexander Bain proposed that all learning and knowledge were based on passive association, linking mental processes with physical sensations. This did not address spontaneous thoughts and ideas. He was an early behaviourist relying on reinforcement and association to explain creativity. This approach to psychology—assuming that all learning was based on the building of incremental associations—was what the Gestalt movement in psychology reacted against.

Gestalt psychologists proposed that in order to truly explain learning and behaviour, theories must address internally generated relationships between memories or ideas that are formed. This means that "any psychological process or behavior that is based on an organism's subjective internal mental representation of a situation, and is not simply the objective co-occurrence of environmental stimuli, would be an insight phenomenon."[35]

The difference between the two learning approaches (behaviourist and Gestalt) is interestingly demonstrated by Ash and colleagues by contrasting the investigation of problem-solving behaviours of animals. Edward Thorndike was an early proponent of behaviourist learning theory, and B. F. Skinner's theory of operant conditioning was based on Thorndike's ideas. Thorndike put cats in a "puzzle box" containing different levers and switches, one of which would release the cats from the box (desirable outcome). The cats' problem-solving behaviours started with random movements until they happened to interact with the release device. Only over multiple trials did the cats' behaviour become less random and more focused on the release device. The takeaway from this type of problem-solving behaviour was that solutions were discovered slowly through trial and error and new information was only acquired incrementally over time as the cats associated the release device with the desirable outcome.

In contrast, Wolfgang Köhler, German psychologist, phenomenologist and co-founder of Gestalt psychology, described a very different problem-solving pattern in apes. He conducted experiments which significantly contributed to the understanding of insight learning.[36] He observed how chimpanzees solved problems, such as reaching for bananas that were placed out of reach. He watched how they stacked wooden crates to make ladders or used sticks as limb extensions in order to grasp the food. Köhler concluded that the chimpanzees were not succeeding through trial-and-error methods but rather were insightful in how they purposefully found solutions. He proposed that

---

[35] Ash et al. (2011), p. 4.
[36] Köhler (1956).

when the initial attempts to solve the problem failed, the apes abandoned behavioural trial-and-error strategies and began cognitive trial-and-error strategies where they mentally searched for new functional relationships between prior experiences, and it was this reasoning that led to the discovery of new relationships.

Thus Gestalt psychologists described learning that involved internal cognitive processes as "insight learning", in contrast to gradual learning by association.[37] In addition, what is singular about Gestalt insight versus classic problem-solving is that impasse or initial failure plays a central role in insight learning.[38] As Ash and colleagues pointed out, the original Gestalt conception of insight was more encompassing than just a problem-solving mechanism or generator of *aha* moments: it was a general principle that learning based on reasoning or thinking (i.e., Gestalt) is qualitatively different from learning based on association (behaviourism).[39] According to Ash et al., classic insight problems were laboratory stimuli designed to be highly likely to lead to fixation or impasse but with no guarantee that solvers actually experienced impasse.

Gestalt psychology was considered by its proponents as a way of escaping from the "prison" of behaviourist psychology with its focus on associations and which Köhler famously described as "the implication that human life, apparently so colorful and so intensely dynamic, is actually a frightful bore."[40] As a school of thought, Gestalt psychology focused on the nature of perception as a process by which humans interpret and organize sensations to produce meaningful experiences of the world. Gestalt (German for "whole") founded a new holistic attitude towards psychology and Köhler is well known for his quote: "The whole is different from the sum of its parts." One of the basic tenets of Gestalt theory is that humans do not perceive the world discretely but rather they grasp the whole before the individual parts enter consciousness using continuous whole processes in the brain.[41] For example, we do not think of a car as an amalgam of its parts (fenders, engine, seats, windshields) but rather as a whole idea greater than its parts—an automobile.

We found that Gestalt research more closely reflected what we observed with our clients and experienced in our own moments of substantive change,

---

[37] Ash et al. (2011).
[38] Ash et al. (2011).
[39] Ash et al. (2011), p. 24.
[40] Köhler (1959).
[41] Wagemans (2015).

moving us towards the holistic end of the continuum. The Gestalt stance did indeed seem to bring more "colour" into our attempt to describe these different kinds of change we witnessed or heard about from clients. Gestalt theory is also well known for its visual figure-ground perception which we found to be a significant perspective in exploring how coaches draw on different modes of knowing when working with clients.

Insight and Intuition

Another area of research we reviewed related the concepts of insight and intuition. Two examples were from psychotherapy, one exemplifying the scientific paradigm and the other reflecting a holistic paradigm. A third writer defined insight and intuition from the perspective of the arts, science, mathematics and religion.

Hans Welling, a psychologist in Lisbon, Portugal, considered intuition to be a common factor in psychotherapy and proposed a five-phase process model to explain how intuition plays a direct role in therapists' hunches, hidden insights and uncanny feelings that turn out to be important to therapy.[42] His perspective was focused on explaining the practitioner's insight rather than the client's. He proposed that intuition is a cognitive process based on pattern discovery and recognition and not the counterpart of rational thought or some type of direct knowing. He defined it as a process in which knowledge is increasingly revealed through a cognitive unfolding but which is also an integrative process that the mind uses when dealing with new and complex information. He proposed that both intuition and insight reside within a purely cognitive perspective. He acknowledged, however, that there seems to exist an inner compass that accompanies the decoding process of intuition that needs further investigation. He also could not adequately account for the "feeling of knowing"[43] that is often experienced.

Psychotherapist Clara Hill wrote *Helping Skills: Facilitating Exploration, Insight and Action*.[44] She speaks from the perspective of helping clients achieve new understandings about themselves, their thoughts, their feelings and their behaviours. Although clients can and certainly do achieve insight on their own, she noted that hearing new ideas and receiving feedback from caring helpers with a different perspective can help clients develop a deeper level of

---

[42] Welling (2005).
[43] Welling (2005), p. 43.
[44] Hill (2009).

awareness and understanding. She proposed a three-stage model incorporating exploration, insight and action.

Hill defined insight as helping clients see things from a new perspective, making connections between things and understanding why things happen. She described insight as not only a sudden *aha* but also incorporating what Carl Rogers defined as something that comes gradually as the person develops sufficient psychological strength to endure new perspectives.[45] For Hill, insight must be emotional as well as intellectual so that it can then lead to action; in other words, it must be deeply felt as well as cognitively understood. The emotional insight helps create a sense of personal involvement and responsibility which can then result in behaviour change. In Hill's insight stage, therapists focus on fostering awareness and facilitating insight, and she defined the helper's role as coaching the client to gain insight rather than being the one to provide it. She recommended numerous interventions to help clients attain insights, including interpretations, probes for insight and thoughtful questions. Hill has also participated in numerous studies on the attainment of insight using dream work.[46] A recent investigation by Baumann and Hill indicated that when therapists used probes for insight, the clients gained more versus less insight during the insight stage.[47] We found Hill's work with insight to more closely resemble what we were experiencing with our clients.

Researcher and writer Kathleen Housley explored the similarity of the concepts of insight and intuition in religion and the arts to those in science and mathematics, including their attribution of *aha* moments to supernatural causes.[48] According to Housley, ambiguity was an essential component in the definitions of both insight and intuition. She pointed out how insight can either mean a deep understanding that comes slowly, arising from prior knowledge, or be an instantaneous breakthrough that comes *ex nihilo*. Intuition, on the other hand, she defined as an inner knowing that seems to appear without use of rational thought or observation. She identified some common emotions and feelings that pertain to both insight and intuition: a sense of intensity; a sense of timing and time (as in something momentous is happening); feelings of surprise, even joy, when it occurs (think eureka!); and the frustration of explaining in words what one has just experienced.

---

[45] Rogers (1942).
[46] Hill et al. (2006), Hill et al. (2007), Knox, Hill, Hess and Crook-Lyon (2008).
[47] Baumann and Hill (2008).
[48] Housely (2009).

She noted that philosopher and mathematician Kurt Gödel experienced mathematical intuition as a kind of "knowing" that defied mathematical formulation (like a sixth sense). In contrast, Catholic theologian Bernard Lonergan, who penned a monumental work on insight,[49] saw moments of insight as an indication of the very existence of God. Housley found a biblical parallel in the Hebrew phrase "seeing the thunder" (Exodus 20:18) when the Israelites are gathered at the base of Mount Sinai while God speaks to Moses on the mountain. The people hear voices and trumpets. They see flames, clouds and lightning, but they also *see* the thunder, suggesting that insight is perceived by the total self, not just a single sense. This implies the necessity for watchfulness and preparedness, a state of full sensory alertness. One also needs to recognize the significance of an insight, once it occurs, and to integrate it. In addition, according to Housley, the role of action in creating the situation in which insight can occur was also prevalent in Jewish religious thought. She viewed this perspective as important for understanding insight because it clarified that anyone —not just gifted mathematicians and scientists—can experience insight.

Housley went on to critique psychological and biological studies of insight based on word games, visual brain teasers and math puzzles as not insight but a normal form of mental processing drawing on underlying methodologies and patterns that a good puzzle-solver figures out, either suddenly or slowly. She also saw flaws with the visual problem-solving studies. For example, people who do well in these tests tend to have strong visual skills, can move objects around in their mind's eye and can keep track of patterns, all specific intelligence skills that not all people possess.

For Housley, another major difficulty with using puzzles to study insight is that the person knows there is an answer and that the puzzle has been solved many times. The individual also knows that some kind of mental restructuring is necessary so they are already primed to try a radically different approach. On the other hand, when Isaac Newton asked about the nature of gravity, he didn't know there was an answer. In fact, scientists and mathematicians often don't know if their questions even make sense. To Housley, one more serious difference between insight problems and true insight was that test problems are "knowledge-lean," meaning that the test-taker doesn't need to possess any specific body of knowledge to solve them whereas scientists and mathematicians work within rich domains of knowledge.

Housley questioned the premise of the psychological approach that insight is preceded by a problem or impasse. She stated that many examples from

---

[49] Longergan (1957).

science and mathematics show insight coming unbidden and unburdened in a profoundly holistic manner as experienced by scientists such as Gödel and astrophysicist Roger Penrose. Housley again used the phrase "seeing the thunder" to describe a way of perceiving in which the total self, not just a single sensory apparatus, is actively involved. We appreciated Karen Housley's perspective as truly expansive and discerning.

Insight and Body–Mind Connection

This research emphasized the holistic aspect of pivotal moments and suggested the body–mind connection as a viable way to access *aha* experiences.

Researcher in kinesiology and health sciences Vietta Wilson and colleagues proposed that *aha* experiences are natural ways to help individuals become aware of their internal processes and to understand how mind and body affect each other.[50] They assert that the *aha* experience can change the person's belief system, lead to awareness and increase their sense of control, thereby enhancing their confidence and competence. They began with bodily movement and activities (somatics) to trigger an *aha* experience that they consider is felt rather than explained. They provided some examples of somatic techniques that experience has shown evoke the *aha* effect:

- *Aeroplane* movement with the arms to increase body rotation results in the *aha* experience that any tension in the body affects the whole;
- *Threading the Needle* movement demonstrates how precise work causes body tensing and immobility leading to an *aha*;
- *Arm Lift by Partner* generates an *aha* awareness about the effect of negative emotions in the body.

They noted that practitioners should be prepared for individuals to become stuck before they are able to understand, reintegrate or perform. They began with the body as the entry point to insight as opposed to the cognitive researchers who use mind puzzles to trigger *aha* moments.

In her *Quantum Skills for Coaches: A Handbook for Working with Energy and Body-Mind in Coaching*, Annette Simmons used quantum physics to define an intuitive process which focuses on the interconnection between the body and mind through energetic (vibratory) resonance.[51] She proposed that thoughts

---

[50] Wilson, Peper and Gibney (2004).
[51] Simmons (2009).

and language have energetic vibration and that individuals actually become the essence of the thoughts they think and the words they speak. Thus they develop "energetic footprints" from their life experiences that are lodged in the energy form of their bodies. She suggested that coaches should go beyond cognitive limitations when working with clients and connect directly to the client's body-mind. This can impact clients who then feel an energy shift from within and experience an *aha* moment. In her model the body understands the *aha* experience first and then informs the brain, primarily using the energy of emotions in the present moment. Her model incorporated such approaches as neurolinguistic programming (NLP), psychodrama, cognitive-based therapy, kinesiology and emotional intelligence.

Quantum Change, Epiphany and Transformation

Another category of research literature included studies and writings on profound experiences of insight. These were variously described as quantum shifts, epiphanies, transformational experiences and defining moments. As we found some of our coaching clients self-describing their pivotal moments as "epiphanies," we considered it necessary to briefly review this type of literature as well.

> *When an electron is hit by a photon of light, it absorbs the energy of the photon and jumps to a higher energy state. In fact, it can suddenly and spectacularly jump up to a higher and expanded orbit, an instantaneous transition that can be applied as a metaphor for sudden psychological or mystical transformations.*[52]

William Miller, a psychologist at the University of New Mexico, used the term "quantum change" to refer to sudden, dramatic and enduring transformations that affect a range of personal emotion, cognition and behaviour, and which occur both within and (mostly) outside psychotherapy.[53] In his clinical field of addictions, Miller revealed that it is common to encounter reports of sudden and permanent transformations, often spiritually profound. In his research he was surprised to find that transformational change had rarely been addressed in modern psychology and that there was not even a psychological term for the phenomenon. While there have been discussions within humanistic psychology of profound subjective experiences, such as mystical and peak experiences, they have typically been ones that could not account for abrupt, enduring change.[54]

---

[52] Wood (2006).
[53] Miller (2004).
[54] Maslow (1971).

In a book they co-authored, Miller and fellow psychologist Janet C'de Baca shared the results of a study in which they interviewed 55 people from all walks of life who had experienced discontinuous transformational changes, and from these accounts they were able to identify some characteristics of quantum change.[55] They found the following commonalities: distinctiveness (people knew that something extraordinary was happening to them); surprise (their experience was unbidden and uninvited); benevolence (the experiences were often joyful and freeing, and the individuals felt safe, loved and accepted); and permanence (they felt changed permanently and often at the level of personality). Miller observed that part of the permanence seemed to be that quantum changes occurred at the level of identity—people experienced more than just a change in behaviour; they felt truly transformed.

Miller also identified two types of quantum change. First, the *mystical (epiphany)* type is considered to be more dramatic (think Joan of Arc), lasts a few minutes and the experience is distinctly different from normal consciousness. It often leaves the person altered in benevolent and permanent ways. Second, the *insightful* type of quantum change occurs more within the conceptual world of psychotherapy but still incorporates sudden realization or knowing that is different from *aha* insights of ordinary experience. The effect seems to be a reorganization of one's perceptions of self and reality, accompanied by intense emotion and a cathartic sense of relief and release. Miller also identified some common areas of transformation in the narratives: sudden release from chronic negative emotion (e.g., fear, resentment, depression, anger) replaced by a pervasive sense of well-being, safety and joy; often an abrupt and enduring shift in one's central values (e.g., possessions are no longer as important); changes in relationships from superficial to deeper with greater intimacy; and sometimes feeling interconnected with all of humanity and creation.

Another perspective on personal transformation is the concept of "defining moments", as articulated by researchers CaSondra Devine, and leadership and organization development professor, William Sparks, at McColl School of Business, Queens University in Charlotte, North Carolina.[56] They viewed personal transformation as an evolutionary process or as an instantaneous event, such as a dilemma or tragedy that disrupts the order of life. They drew on the transformative learning research of Jack Mezirow with his ten steps to a new perception of the world, as well as from religious theorists W. H. Clark and James E. Loder. They found some interesting commonalities around

---

[55] Miller and C'de Baca (2001).
[56] Devine and Sparks (2014).

stages of transformation in the areas of religious experience and behaviour that are merged and summarized here: unrest and conflict or disorienting dilemma; self-examination; search for a resolution or exploration of options; conversion crisis (sudden breakthrough) or intuitive insight; release and openness for new patterns of thinking and being; sense of peace, release and inner harmony; and interpretation, verification and reintegration.[57] Mezirow's ten steps of transformative learning theory did not include sudden insight.

Coaching Studies

Finally, we reviewed some coaching studies focused on *aha* moments and insight-oriented coaching, one based on phenomenological research and two on the use of insight-oriented methodology in executive coaching engagements.

Psychologist and coach Leigh Longhurst[58] used phenomenological methodology in a study of the *aha* moment using the Co-Active Model of life coaching[59] to explore whether psychological *aha* moments were fundamental to transformational change. She reduced first-person accounts to common themes through a grounded theory analysis. Co-Active coaches collected data from client participants in the form of diaries that captured the lived experience of the *aha* moment, and they supplemented them with questionnaires and interviews. Longhurst considered life coaching as belonging to the field of "insight" psychology alongside psychotherapy, Gestalt and transpersonal psychology. She thought the phenomenon of insight should be studied in its own right and not confined to the role of cognitive problem-solving tasks.

Longhurst defined the *aha* moment as the prime device by which clients in life coaching achieve transformational change. The results of her study, presented within Ken Wilbur's Spectrum of Consciousness[60] framework, showed that *aha* moments could be experienced at varying levels of intensity and that they were felt in the body as well as, or instead of, in the mind. Respondent accounts described *aha* moments as if they were an "orchestral affair" integrating body experiences (sudden rush of energy felt in heart, chest, stomach, gut or solar plexus); mind experiences (changes in perspectives or beliefs and a releasing of negative self-talk or thinking patterns); felt experiences (relief, calm, excitement, inner knowing or intuition); soul experiences (uncovering

---

[57] White (2004).
[58] Longhurst (2006).
[59] Whitworth, Kimsey-House and Sandahl (1998).
[60] Wilbur (1989).

deeply held values, sense of connection with others/the universe); spiritual experiences (beyond the physical body, epiphany); and non-dual experiences (subject/object duality shattered, sense of interconnectedness with all things).

She proposed that *aha* moments were best understood in terms of holistic body-mind theories that see the whole organism as conscious and purposive. She articulated some observations/conclusions:

- The difference between an *aha* moment and just learning something new is that the *aha* is felt in the body.
- Changes in perspectives, beliefs, self-talk, decision-making powers and clarity of ideas are labelled as a core category of mind experiences. Mental *aha* moments have to do with a change in beliefs or perspectives, or strengthening of the ego through releasing negative thinking patterns.
- Felt experiences of *aha* moments are always associated with relief, peace, calm, sometimes excitement and an "inner knowing" or intuition.
- Unearthing of hidden values to build life purpose and meaning can be a central function of the *aha* moment.
- Reports of experiencing beyond the realms of the physical body are labelled spiritual experiences, such as inner knowing or intuition.
- *Aha* moments can occur at any level and depth on the spectrum of consciousness with insight occurring at the mental level, intuition happening at the level of the soul, and epiphany experienced at the level of the spirit.

Two further case studies[61] described successful executive coaching engagements that were based, among other methodologies, on insight-oriented coaching. Such coaching focused on psychological insights into limiting patterns and then action that resulted in successful outcomes. In one case study, executive coach Karol Wasylyshyn[62] worked with a CEO client applying four methodology factors: a holistic approach (work–family integration); deep behavioural insight; active involvement of top corporate executives; and sustained relationships. In the course of the coaching, the client experienced a psychological insight that had important implications for his personal life and for his interaction with leadership. Wasylyshyn used a technique she created called the "visual metaphor," which showed self-described representations of the client in current, transitional and future leadership states.

---

[61] Wasylyshn (2005), Wasylyshyn, Gronsky and Haas (2006).
[62] Wasylyshn (2005).

The second case study described survey results of a commissioned coaching programme to improve emotional competence in a global company.[63] An insight-oriented coaching approach called VISTA was applied. This was designed to deliver psychological insight and to influence sustained behavioural change. It was based on an empirically tested model of brief psychotherapy that integrated psychoanalytic, interpersonal, object relations, self-psychology, and cognitive-behavioural and systems approaches. Clinical psychologist Hannah Levenson's[64] cyclical maladaptive pattern was applied to help clients change any idiosyncratic vicious cycles or patterns involving self-perpetuating behaviours, self-defeating expectations and negative self-appraisals. The approach used a rapid sequence of delivering and applying insight, supporting clients' courage to change (through a pragmatic coaching agenda) and providing positive reinforcement of progress/sustained efforts.

Literature Review Summary

The exploration process we went through, which involved matching existing research and theory to our observed and personal experiences, brought up more questions than answers but also provided some useful data. For example, we were able to summarize the common characteristics of *aha* moments and their potential triggers from among the diverse studies of inquiry (Tables 2.1 and 2.2).

We also realized that insight or *aha* moments were more of an embodied experience than we had anticipated. Limiting our exploration to only the cognitive psychological sphere would not give us full comprehension of insight. Instead we needed to complement the cognitive and neuroscience studies with a descriptive, first-person phenomenological account of how insight is experienced. We found other researchers who thought similarly.

Psychologists Diego Cosmelli and David D. Preiss with the Pontificia Universidad Católico de Chile in Santiago are looking to better understand the experience of creative insight using both biological and biographical evidence.[65] They proposed that the phenomenon of creative insight has a dynamic past–future interplay that may be at the core of the experience.[66] They pointed out how the cognitive problem-solving process restricts the concept of creativ-

---

[63] Wasylyshn et al. (2006).
[64] Levenson (1995).
[65] Cosmelli and Preiss (2014).
[66] Cosmelli and Preiss (2014).

Table 2.1 Research results on characteristics of *aha* moments

Characteristics of *aha* moments
Preceded by impasse
Change in attitude
Sudden clarity
Shift in belief
Physical response
Emotional response
Sense of inner knowing
New neural connections made
Sudden awareness (holistic in nature)

Table 2.2 Research results on triggers of *aha* moments

Potential triggers of *aha* moments
Impasse
Directing attention
Shifting of thinking patterns
Shifting of emotional patterns
Using body intelligence & movement
Shifting language
Exposing belief patterns
New neural connections made

ity to a specific task and moment in time when it is clear that short-term activities and experiences are always embedded within longer periods of time.[67] They further noted how the time-restricted insight problem-solving approach has had a long history, extending back to the Gestalt movement. At that time, however, problem-solving behaviour was observed in open-ended situations as in Köhler's work with chimpanzees. They pointed out that by the end of the twentieth century, experiments were primarily conducted with closed-ended problems and characterized as only sudden and abrupt.

In building the elements for a phenomenology of creative insight, Cosmelli and Preiss proposed that the moment of insight is quite similar to a "tip-of-the-tongue" experience in which the insight is not necessarily a quick *aha* but can be protracted.[68] Insights make sense because they are a combination of recognizing the previous context in light of the new context—a past- and future-oriented interplay. Cosmelli and Preiss suggested that the spontaneous occurrence of *aha* moments makes them a natural target for phenomenological inquiry since they are part of the ongoing flow of experience. We agreed.

---

[67] Cosmelli and Preiss (2014).
[68] Cosmelli and Preiss (2014).

We compared the information from our literature review to the learnings from our coaching research and our own experiences, and we found a discrepancy that we could not easily explain. As we said earlier, these findings led us to a fork in the road and we took the less travelled way.

Aha Moments: An Expanded Perspective

When Ann began coaching her, Irene was a newly appointed high-level executive in a federal agency and was hoping to learn and develop in her new role.[69] *She was challenged in a number of ways in her new position. First, she reported to a demanding and mercurial boss. Second, she had been promoted up the ranks for her ability to get things done and for her excellent people skills. Now, however, she was expected to learn how to manage strategically, not tactically, at her new level. Third, she had an ingrained pattern of taking care of those under her supervision, often at personal cost to herself. In the coaching, Irene revealed how difficult it was to learn how to trust and delegate accountability to her direct reports while at the same time shielding them from her aggressive boss. She was convinced she should know in detail everything going on in her department. She knew that the stress of seeking to "do it all" was impacting her overall ability to lead. But it was not until more than half-way through the coaching that she began to understand how much her old pattern of taking care of others was actually fostering a "propping up" dynamic of which she took the brunt. She realized she needed to spend more time "being" a strategic leader and less time "doing" things that were the responsibility of others. She also observed how her perceived weak points or shortfalls were actually leadership opportunities for those she managed.*

Over the Christmas break, something happened to Irene that she was excited to report at the next coaching session. As she told it, she was working out on her treadmill at home when she was struck by a self-described "epiphany." She suddenly "knew" at a deep integrative level that most of her professional life she had put others before herself and had cared more for them than for her own well-being. It was a deep knowing that had an immediate and strong impact on how she wanted to view herself moving forward—to be first in her own life. The results of this deep insight enabled her to consciously shift to a sense of identity which now incorporated her own feelings of worth. The rest of the coaching engagement was devoted to setting up actions and processes that would support her reorganized sense of identity.

---

[69] We have changed the name of clients in the coaching stories to protect their anonymity.

Ann was struck by how this client's pivot, self-described as an "epiphany," represented aspects of a more expanded perspective of *aha* moments. The deep knowing aspect of this type of insight is difficult to explain within the scientific paradigm. It did not occur in aid of solving a puzzle or while being creative in resolving a situation. It resembled more what Carol Rogers identified as something that comes gradually as an individual develops enough psychological strength to embrace a new perspective or sense of self.[70] It was similar to what Kathleen Housley described as a deep understanding that comes slowly, or that William Miller categorized as a mystical or insightful type of quantum change that left the client altered in a benevolent and permanent way. It appeared to be a reorganization of her perceptions about self and reality.

The awareness moment occurred well into the coaching engagement following many conversations regarding the limitations of her current patterns and the opportunities that were available for her to find new ways of leading. What caused the awareness to occur when it did? Was there a tipping point? What, if anything, did Ann's coaching contribute? The outcome was clear: the client experienced an internal shift that enabled her to find a new, higher level of coherence about her life. As her coach, Ann could sense the difference in her client pre- and post-Christmas epiphany; it felt like interacting with a different person.

Coaching Research Project

What are the breadth and depth of the role we play in supporting our clients to positively reframe their unwanted perceptions and perspectives? We wondered what happened when our clients had *aha* moments, a deep insight or even a shift in perspective. What caused these changes to happen? What influence did we exert? What were we not yet aware of in terms of our interaction with clients? It was clear that we as coaches did not plan or predict when these shifts might happen and that our clients shared in the surprise when they occurred. It seemed that clients who experienced shifts in perception seemed able to transform their limiting belief systems or habits of mind and move towards greater self-direction. This process of "meaning-making" has been defined by psychologist Robert Kegan as a person's "ever progressive motion

---

[70] Rogers (1942).

engaged in giving itself a new form."[71] At times, this new form can be a substantial or transformational change.

As Appreciative coaches, we hold the belief and stance that new realities can flow from a reinterpretation or a reframing of a situation or aspect of life. This is based on the Poetic Principle, one of the foundational elements of Appreciative Coaching. As co-developers of the Appreciative Coaching model, we have built on this principle to identify the actual "event" of *pivoting*. We have defined it as a key moment in coaching when clients come to a new realization. We use the term "pivots" to name these key opportunities that appear in coaching.

Clearly, these are important concepts in our approach, which originate from the generative (not problem-solving) philosophy underlying Appreciative Coaching. We start with constructive and positive premises regarding change. Our major focus is helping clients to shift to the positive, to what they want, to solutions (thus pivoting them away from the negative, what they don't want, problems). It seemed a natural next step for us to explore how we could support this occurrence more often, more consistently and at deeper levels. In essence, we wondered what needs to happen to better understand the capacity and power of these pivots so we could help clients bring more of their best and true selves to light. We started our research project with the following questions in mind:

1. What does a pivotal moment look like? What are its characteristics?
2. Where and when does it happen?
3. What conditions support it?
4. What role do coaches play?
5. How do we contribute to clients experiencing pivotal moments?

Coaching Research Design

Our study used an interpretive research design based on the hermeneutic circle of study, which involves making sense of experience and putting what is learned into practice. It included:

- *Phenomenological reflection*: the study of lived experience through retrospective reflection of something that can't be "solved"—only more deeply understood;
- *Hermeneutics*: the study of interpreting and understanding something that "appears" in personal experience.

---

[71] Kegan (1982), p. 8.

We incorporated our interpretive point of view as it developed over time into our reflective practice, drawing on formal theory and research, our coaching experiences and those of other master coaches. These became our sources of information as we wrestled with sorting out the research and experiences describing the phenomenon of pivotal moments. Our research components included:

- examining our own coaching through the review of transcripts;
- undertaking an initial literature review on the topic of insight and *aha* moments;
- presenting our preliminary findings to master coach audiences to gain further understanding and perspective;
- collecting and tape recording stories of pivotal moments from master coaches;
- reviewing transcripts for evidence of pivotal moments and any coach strategies related to pivotal moments;
- incorporating the pivotal moments we witnessed in our clients from our coaching practices;
- bringing our personal learnings and sharing from our own stories of pivotal moments;
- developing our theory as we conducted our research;
- writing this book as part of the hermeneutic circle of understanding and interpretation, further developing, deepening and organizing our thoughts.

We worked with 12 executive coaching clients, each one coached by phone for nine one-hour sessions over a period of six to nine months. We audiotaped and transcribed all of the sessions then conducted a grounded theory analysis of the transcripts. While coaching, we completed structured protocols before and after each session, as well as phenomenological reflections on identifying the degree and type of pivotal moments, language used, client's affective responses and the appearance/interplay of Appreciative Coaching principles. We also recorded the coaches' feelings, sense of timing and any coach learnings resulting during the session. Clients completed pre- and post- questionnaires and final reflections.

Initial Coaching Research Learnings

Our research yielded a number of key learnings around the range of client experiences of substantial or incremental change. First, we observed three major *magnitudes* of shifts in our clients:

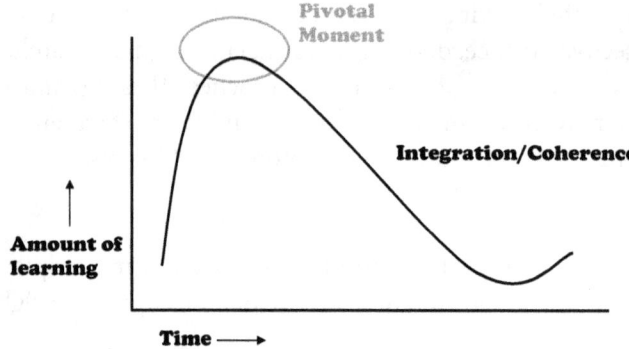

Fig. 2.1 Emergence of pivotal moments

1. *Learning shifts*: acquiring a new skill but not changing one's inner values or associated belief system; similar to routine or "puzzle"-induced cognitive problem-solving;
2. *Shifts in perspective*: changing an inner value and associated belief system but retaining the same sense of identity; shift in patterns involving experience of insight;
3. *Quantum shifts*: changing one's inner sense of self-identity often described as defining moments, epiphanies or insights; often representing a shift from a wounded identity to a healed one.

All of our research clients were subject to some type of learning shift as a result of the coaching. Most experienced some shift in perspective during the coaching but only a few underwent quantum shifts. As a result of these learnings, we identified a range of pivotal moments with only shifts in perspective and quantum shifts involving an inner change of value, beliefs or identity. These changes involved an experience of insight (mild to intense) and brought greater coherence to clients' sense of self. We based these definitions of self-organizing levels of belief and change on the work of Robert Dilts, well-known developer, author, trainer and consultant in the field of NLP.[72]

Our research also revealed that the *manifestation* of shifts differs. These experiences can be immediate *aha* or eureka (creative insight) moments or *liminal* shifts of slow awakening that include phases of letting go or breaking down to make a new whole and/or slow hunches developing over time and building through connections (Fig. 2.1).

We proposed that all pivotal moments are the result of a combination of the amount of learning, length of time and level of integration or coherence

---

[72] Dilts (1996, 1998).

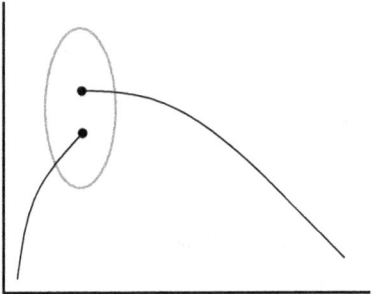
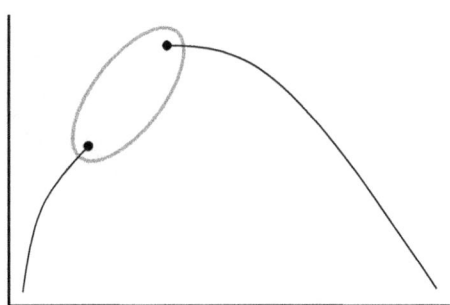

Immediate, sudden *aha* moments   **Liminal (over time), gradual awakening. "Not there ... there" phenonmenon**

Fig. 2.2 Variant manifestations of pivotal moments

experienced. We found differences in the manifestation of the shifts (immediate or liminal) and in their timing, which could be during a coaching session (in person or on a call), in between coaching sessions (offline) or after the end of a coaching engagement (Fig. 2.2).

John was a new CEO of a for-profit hospital. While not new to being in a CEO position, he was new to the healthcare field. He was struggling with bringing his leadership team together, some members of which resented having a CEO come from outside healthcare. He began to question his leadership abilities and spent numerous coaching sessions expressing his insecurity and doubts about being able to build a cohesive team. He and Ann spent time exploring the origins of his doubts, and talking about his ability to transfer and apply his leadership team skills from his former position. Ann had known him in his previous CEO role and observed him as very effective with his leadership team. She suspected that his lack of content knowledge regarding the healthcare field was interfering with the application of his known team skills. He was agitated during the coaching calls. Then there was a break between coaching sessions. When Ann next talked to him, John showed up to the meeting as a different person. Gone was the agitation, self-doubt and insecurity. In its place was his usual confidence and positive energy about leading team members. Ann could immediately sense the difference and queried him. John's response was nonchalant, acknowledging that he felt fine once he remembered he was father of a large family and was accustomed to working as a team at both home and work. It remained a non-issue for the remainder of the coaching engagement.

Ann was surprised by how John had moved from a place of "not there" (unresolved situation) to now being "there" (situation resolved). What aspects

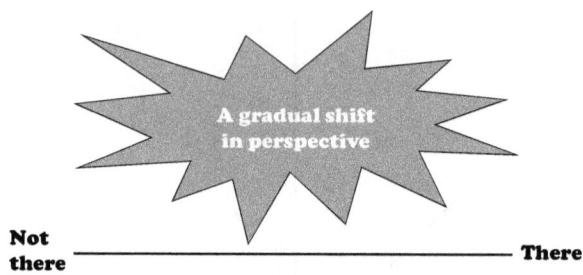

Fig. 2.3 Slow awakening

of their previous coaching, if any, had contributed to John's shift in awareness? He did not articulate what had caused the shift or if it came as an insight, unlike Irene's epiphany, which she was more than happy to share in great detail and with much emotion. Was John's a learning shift or was it a slow pivotal moment, insightful in nature? As coach, Ann experienced a sudden shift in John's sense of presence from when she had last coached him. It was a strange sense of moving from "not there" to "there" (Fig. 2.3).

Overall, more of the research clients seemed to experience substantial shifts via liminal or gradual shifts in perception. The liminal process of awareness seems to parallel the pattern of chaotic systems of self-organization in which new structures evolve out of the interplay between randomness and order.[73] Liminal shifts seem to involve a state of "creative space and time" during which clients experience a period of transition where normal limits to thought, self-understanding and behaviour are relaxed, allowing for a state which leads to new perspectives. Such states of liminality are like a threshold or "realm of pure possibility whence novel configurations of ideas and relations may arise."[74] We wondered how this learning might impact our role as facilitators and primers of change.

From analysing the transcripts, we had already gleaned an initial list of priming actions and behaviours that we had engaged in and which will be presented in Chap.7. There have been many neuroscience priming research experiments over the years which substantiate the significance of the level of influence that coaches could have with their clients. We became keenly aware that as coaches we are constantly priming and encouraging our clients to think and act differently. From these learnings, we developed a simple model incorporating what we have discovered so far about the "chain" of events in coaching sessions that impact our clients' ability to change. From the litera-

---

[73] Mills (2002).
[74] Turner (1967), p. 97.

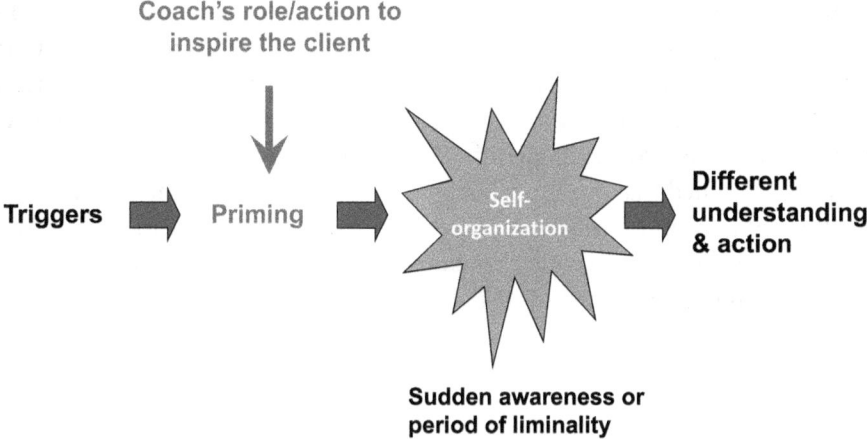

Fig. 2.4 The coaching "chain" of events

ture review, we had identified some triggers that seemed to support substantive change, and we knew that the power of pivots was an important factor in facilitating clients in different types of inner self-organization, whether sudden or over time (Fig. 2.4).

By this point we knew we had enough information and validation for us to further explore what made up a pivotal moment and what role coaches play. We identified three key factors we knew were essential to igniting substantial change:

1. Focusing the client's attention on what they want to change to and move towards (not what they *don't* want);
2. Using priming strategies as a way to act as catalysts for clients (they need help to make new connections);
3. Recognizing that shifts in perception occur initially non-consciously, then rise to consciousness as an insight or *aha* (therefore they cannot be predicted or controlled by coach or client).

Stepping Forward on the Path Less Travelled

Our literature review and analysis of coaching transcripts led us to propose that pivotal moments are subjective lived experiences of dynamic self-organization that seem holistic in their integrative impact on clients. We learned that *beliefs* were attractors for change and played a key role in how open or closed clients and coaches would be to the process of transformation. We were already aware of how we personally used different modes of *inner knowing* when coaching, from deep empathy to expert intuition. And we discovered that we were already adept at priming our clients (like any experienced/master coach), which is a key construct in associations in *memory*. Besides making connections, memory is also the holder of who we are.

We determined that our model of pivotal moments would include the areas of attention, priming, emotions, beliefs, inner knowing and memory. In terms of access, we became even clearer about how precious the *present moment* is when working with clients.

3

Pivoting: The Extraordinary Power of Self-Organization

Access and expression are both conditions of the present.

—A Course of Love

A Coach's Theory for Igniting Substantial Change

How does it happen: the miracle of change we are privileged to observe and co-experience—these pivots our clients make? As coaches, we were both fascinated and humbled by our clients' capacity and courage to overcome obstacles, to shift their limiting perspectives and, in some cases, to reorganize their sense of self-identity. Through our research we began to assemble the components we recognized and experienced as happening in real time with our clients that could feasibly contribute to a coach's theory for igniting substantial change.

We saw that access to their inner process was not only essential but also fruitful for clients to discover their true choices in life. Through the coaching process, the interplay of their beliefs, their inner knowing and the connective aspect of their memory could be stimulated to allow for reframing and new possibilities. As coaches we recognized that the present moment was an access point for us to interact and participate with our clients at this deeper level. Our coaching conversation was the potent time and place for this to occur.

Expression, we observed, is what happens as a result of making optimal use of the access we have. Coaching in its essence is helping clients to express new thoughts, feelings and actions that lead to desired results. The question then becomes, what can we employ as coaches to better support clients in

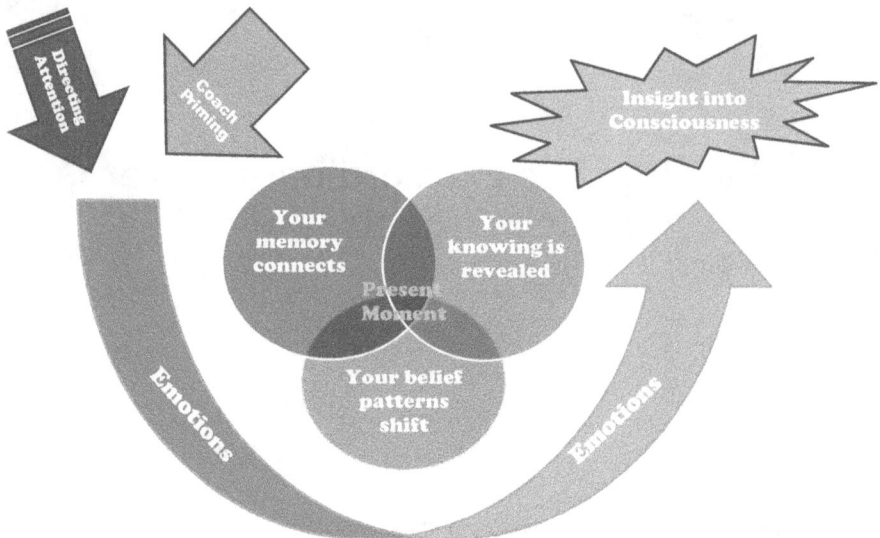

Fig. 3.1 Pivoting: The power of self-organization

accessing their inner process and expressing their desires? Clearly, directing attention can help clients access their inner process. Science tells us that whatever clients focus on will grow, and time will flow to wherever they put their attention. So how do we help them place and keep attention on what they want to add or grow in their lives? Awareness of emotions is another pathway to inner process—are they focused on limiting thoughts linked to negative emotions or have they embraced empowering thoughts leading to feelings of hope, inspiration and joy? The model described above represents what we consider to be the elements of self-organization that embody potentiality in every coaching conversation. Directing attention; priming; the interplay of the inner processes of beliefs, inner knowing and memory; and the expression of emotions are the "tools" we have at hand in real-time, present-moment coaching sessions. Any one or combination thereof could be enough to elicit a self-organizing event. Of course, neither the coach nor the client is privy to the timing of such insight (Fig. 3.1).

Theoretical Base of Our Model

The client presented himself during his coaching with Jackie as a traditional, top-down alpha leader. He took control of the initial coaching conversations, seeking to side step the agreed-upon coaching goals that might require deeper change. Jackie decided to bide her time, her experience and expert intuition advising her to "do nothing" for a while until an opportune moment presented itself for him to make some figure/ground shift in understanding about himself. This finally occurred during the sixth session when Jackie offered to help him better understand the results of a recent conflict-management assessment that highlighted his need to change certain of his actions and behaviours. She knew that putting attention on the survey results might cause some positive shift if he felt it was his choice to change. She had anticipated that he would probably resist any intimation that he had to change because of external pressure. Intentionally, Jackie presented the results in a format that appealed to his intellect. She hoped to capitalize on any positive emotions he might generate if he could logically justify the change without feeling wrong or without tapping into his sense of emotional vulnerability. It was unexpected when he suddenly experienced a pivotal moment in the coaching session. He recognized how he was perceived by others as overly directive and commanding. He had received 360° feedback prior to his coaching engagement about his dominant leadership style and it now made sense to him in a non-threatening way. He saw how others experienced him as being aggressive in his manner. By his eighth session he had a three-way mid-review with his coaching sponsors who were impressed with his insight and subsequent change in behaviour.

There are moments when clients self-organize and we are able to witness it as Jackie did with her client. These shifts may vary in intensity (from a learning shift or change in perspective to experiencing a quantum shift) and in duration (from an immediate knowing to slow realization over time). Whenever these experiences of insight occur, however, we know they emerge from the interaction of specific conditions and opportunities:

- They arise out of inner process and direction.
- They are the result of a holistic (i.e., interactive with environment) constructivist process.
- They are revealed through a non-conscious mode of knowing.
- They take place in the present, which is *influenced*, not determined, by both the past and the future.
- They are the result of a self-organizing human system in which the brain is fundamentally pattern-forming (i.e., anticipating the future as well as reacting to the present and past).
- They occur with affect (usually positive feelings of relief, wonder, hope and joy).

Our proposed theory of igniting substantial change is based on the constructivist approach, the philosophical movement of pragmatism and the tradition of hermeneutic phenomenology, all of which encompass the conditions necessary for transformation. Constructivism informs the coach's role in facilitating clients to a greater awareness of how their personally and socially constructed beliefs and interpretations can be reconstructed or reframed to give their lives more meaning and autonomy.

Pragmatism emphasizes the practical application of ideas by acting on them and testing them in human activities rather than through contemplation. Pragmatists consider thought to be an instrument or tool for prediction, problem-solving and action. The pragmatic outlook informs the coach's role of ensuring that their clients lead useful lives of their own choice, helping them create a better future and encouraging them to strive for equality and personal happiness. The emphasis is on promoting clients to be intentional in the events and actions they choose in building a meaningful life for themselves. Finally, hermeneutic phenomenology deepens understanding of how clients become open to the "revealing" of their own inner process, be it inspiration, insight or subtle guidance. Any inner awakening or shift in perspective is an "event" for clients, and their coaches involuntarily become participants in witnessing or assisting them in interpreting and sharing what they have experienced.

Self-organization: Interplay of Beliefs, Inner Knowing and Memory

In Chapters 4, 5, and 6 we explore how each of these three elements of self-organization contribute to the likelihood of substantive internal shifts occurring. Research tells us that for clients to change how they see themselves and their capabilities, they need to shift their *beliefs* about themselves. They need to bring to awareness hidden or conflicting beliefs that are often most evident in their behaviour and language. We have introduced the notion of how opening clients up to their own inner wisdom, process and ways of *knowing* can help them access useful, empirical data about their lives. *Memory* plays a key role in accessing non-conscious knowledge and generating new associative networks that can reorganize one's beliefs, perspectives or even sense of self into an insight that erupts into conscious awareness.

We infer that these three hidden components are closely interwoven, multi-causal and cooperative. They reflect the dynamic patterns of self-organization—phase transitions as old ideas break up and something new is created.[1] Think of the flow of a river in which patterns emerge and disappear as opposed to the

---

[1] Kelso (1995).

static landscape of the river.² Our clients' sense of reality is generated out of their choices (informed by beliefs and knowing), events (actions) with their environment and the potentialities of those events. As complex human systems, our clients are engaged in endless pattern formation and change.

As neuroscientist Scott Kelso tells us, emergent properties are a significant feature of all complex systems, and cooperation among the components of a system is what creates new patterns in a self-organized manner.³ He sees the brain not as a computing machine but rather as dwelling in "metastable states" where it is "poised on the brink of instability where it can switch flexibly and quickly" as it anticipates the future and reacts to the present.⁴ For Kelso, both the brain and overt behaviour follow natural laws of self-organization. In a personal anecdote, he explained how the experience of an idea he had in 1980—based on the "let your fingers do the walking" advert from *Yellow Pages*—enabled him to demonstrate phase transition in human hand movements which become the foundation of his subsequent well-known work in coordination dynamics. He described, in hindsight, how the emergence of this idea was a kind of phase transition in itself: a concept was planted in the subconscious where an association of ideas took place which abruptly emerged, quite spontaneously and unsought, into consciousness.⁵ His is an apt description of the experiences of insight that we witness with our clients and which our proposed theory seeks to illustrate.

Accessing the Authentic Self

The aha moment felt like a full alignment with self and source. It felt like being empowered, worthy, spot on—actually the best feeling of aliveness. I was connected. I was buzzing with clear confidence to a degree I've never experienced before. For a split second, I thought I was observing and then I was flooded with—this is real— you are fully present. I was living fully as my AUTHENTIC SELF—blending of the greater part of me, connected to my source and my physical self. My physical body was full of power and emotion and indicating I was righteous and wise. My physical body had all the information and I knew/felt the clarity of the situation. I was surprised by the intensity and even though I could not put words on it at the time I understood I was plugged into something great that the situation called up within me.

---

² Kelso (1995).
³ Kelso (1995).
⁴ Kelso (1995), p. 26.
⁵ Kelso (1995), p. 46.

This written account of an *aha* moment was sent to Ann by a former client. She knew Ann was researching this topic and thought she might be interested in her first-person description. She explained that the insight came in response to an inner desire to go from old behaviour to new behaviour, and knowing that the body was the link. Her recounting was similar to other such experiences with the elements of physical, emotional and spiritual levels of awareness and that instant recognition of an authentic sense of self. These are the types of substantive change that we would like to support and encourage in our coaching, when the internal timing and opportunity arise. Following are suggestions we've discovered about ways to help clients (and ourselves) enhance access to such moments of authenticity.

Potency of the Present Moment

A century ago, Einstein's special and general theories of relativity destroyed the idea of time as an absolute, universal constant. He found solace in his revolutionary sense of time and a month before his death he wrote a letter consoling the family of his lifelong friend Michele Besso who had just died: "Now he has departed from this strange world a little ahead of me. That means nothing. People like us, who believe in physics, know that the distinction between past, present and future is only a stubbornly persistent illusion."[6]

How do we define the present moment? This is a question that has been pondered by philosophers, scientists, practitioners and spiritual traditions over thousands of years and across virtually all fields of study and cultures. For our purposes we are viewing the present moment from the richness of the constructivist, pragmatic and hermeneutic phenomenological perspectives and from the scientific foundation of quantum physics. We also value it as the most important access point through which to engage our clients. We find it similar to the fourth core coaching competency of the International Coach Federation: coaching presence (being fully conscious and creating spontaneous relationships with clients, employing a style that is open, flexible and confident).

Belief in the feasibility of substantial change necessitates embracing a different perspective of time than that of Newton's external linearity. According to Newton's linear concept (still ingrained in Western culture and society), time is conceptualized as proceeding along a fixed line from past through present to future. In this view, the present is only one brief blip on this line, the future is unknowable and the past holds supremacy. It is not an empowering

---

[6] Folger (2007).

perspective that would embolden individuals to construct the life they want, create the future they desire or be open to ways of inner guidance. The locus of control is almost exclusively outside the individual, and the individual is largely considered to be the sum total of their past.

Newton's absolute time cannot account for the multitude of experiences of temporality that we routinely experience as humans: the cyclical time of our biology and the natural world, the sense of flow when the passage of time disappears, synchronicity, intuition, sudden leaps of insight or abrupt change. Fortunately, the new scientific paradigm, and the sustained beliefs of natural philosophers and theorists through the ages,[7] now support a more holistic interpretation in which the past, present and future are an integrated whole.[8] The mind and environment are understood as simultaneous parts of a greater Gestalt or life-space as well.[9] The following holistic assumptions about time underpin a transformative approach to coaching:

- Past, present and future co-occur as an integrated whole, and each part is influenced by the other parts.
- Both the present and the future can influence change in people.
- Being agents of their own actions and attitudes is necessary for people to have self-responsibility and human dignity.
- People can reconstruct the meanings of their past.
- People can change in ways that are inconsistent with their past.
- People are best understood in relation to their present contexts.
- People have access to multiple experiences of time.[10]

If we look at the meaning of the present moment from its pragmatic potential as coaches, it is a time associated with experiencing events directly, when an individual may be freed from past patterns and open to receiving information from sources other than one's conscious mind. The present moment encompasses direct sensory experiences, reconstructing memories, and anticipating ideas, images and desires for the future. The present moment in coaching is rife with interactive mental time travel as we share this lived experience with our clients. And who knows what may be revealed in the present moment for coaches and clients? That is the mystery, potential and practicality of accessing the present moment in coaching conversations.

---

[7] For example, Heidegger, Piaget, May, Husserl, Whitrow, James, McGrath and Kelly are just a few of the modern theorists.
[8] Clancy (1996).
[9] Lewin (1948).
[10] Orem, Binkert and Clancy (2007), pp. 64–65.

Directing Attention

My experience is what I agree to attend to.
—William James

As part of our research findings we identified attention as a pathway of revealing. Directing attention can allow or catalyse clients to re-form patterns of thinking, feeling and action at a deeper level. Directing attention and making use of the present moment are considered to be sound methodologies for most coaching approaches. We point out that directing attention is also a major tool for shifting clients' perceptions, which is often a precursor to substantive change. To illustrate this point, we share an activity we have used in our workshops to highlight what occurs when we shift perceptions.

Seeing the Star

In Fig. 3.2, look for a five-pointed star in the pattern. As you look for it, try to be aware of the search strategies you use to detect it. Do you squint your eyes? Do you methodically scan the pattern? Do you look away and back again? Do you get frustrated or remain calm? Obviously your mind has already quickly searched your memory for an image of a five-pointed star to begin the activity. It might even have brought up recollections of drawing or cutting out stars as a child. As you engage in solving this puzzle, your memories, strategies and feelings will be subjective and unique to your lifeworld experience.

Here are some hints if you are having difficulty finding the star: it is situated in the upper left corner of the pattern and three points of the star are white. The moment you find the star (even if you have to look at the answer), be aware of how you feel. This is an example of a small cognitive insight exercise. Its purpose is to raise your awareness about what's happening visually and cognitively as you try to pick out a particular star image from the overall pattern. This act of becoming conscious of something shifts it from being the *ground* to becoming the *figure*. Again, this is what we do with our clients when we want them to shift their attention or perception from what they don't want or what is limiting, to what they desire or wish to move towards. An interesting consequence of finding the star in the pattern is that you will now see the star if again presented with the pattern. It is now in your consciousness.

Note: The location of the star can be found at the end of the chapter.

Fig. 3.2 Can you find the hidden star?

Shifts in Perception

Each time we direct the attention of our clients, we create an "event" in our clients' process. It is a movement of focus to the conscious level. Another way of saying this is that when we direct the attention of our clients, we are shifting their awareness from what has been *ground* to what is *figure*, from what might have been non-conscious or blind to them to what is suddenly real or of importance. The figure–ground perception is a principle of Gestalt psychology, whose theorists[11] proposed that the whole is greater than the sum of its parts (e.g., seeing an orange in the whole is different from seeing its individual components of stem, rind, pith, segments, juice, etc.) (Fig. 3.3).

When we view the whole, say Gestaltists, a cognitive process takes place in which the mind leaps from comprehending the parts to realizing the whole. Thus we visually and psychologically go through our days trying to make order out of chaos from the seemingly endless disconnected bits of information that we take in. The focus at any given moment is considered to be the figure and everything that is not the figure is the ground. As our attention shifts, the ground also shifts so that an object (or idea, thought pattern, etc.) can go from figure to ground and then back.

---

[11] The prominent founders of gestalt theory are Max Wertheimer, Wolfgang Köhler and Kurt Koffka.

Fig. 3.3 What do you see? A young girl? An old woman?

Ground is also thought of as background or negative space. Camouflage, for instance, is the deliberate alteration of figure–ground so that the figure blends into the ground. In Fig. 3.3 the visual is another demonstration of how we visually and conceptually shift our perceptions based on what we perceive as the figure and the ground. What do you see? A young girl? An old woman? Both images are there but you cannot focus on both of them at the same time—one must be the figure and the other the ground in order for you to comprehend each of the images. In another example, we might ask, "What is the shape of the Atlantic Ocean?" In most cultures we learn to comprehend the continents as shapes (or figures) and the ocean as ground. We simply perceive oceans as "there" without any definitive shape. It is a habit of seeing that is so ingrained for most of us that it has slipped into our non-awareness.

These demonstrations clarify the power of conscious intent that results from directing attention. Figure–ground perception is at work in every coaching conversation. If the focus is on problems, clients cannot also be focused on solutions. As coaches we are constantly making choices about how and when to help our clients focus on what is important to them. But we don't always know if what we are directing attention towards will turn out to be minor, major or of no consequence at all. However, there are times with every client when we sense or intuit or feel or think that shifting their perception may be beneficial in some way.

In the story above, Jackie strategically engaged in shifting her client's perception by directing attention to what she deemed to be the opportune time of openness for the client to be able to see himself with different eyes. It worked, but this was not something she could have predicted or imposed by using external pressure. Directing attention can be a powerful pathway or access point for both coach and client, as well as the vehicle to reveal what may be hidden.

Mindfulness, Attention and the Present Moment

Mindfulness as a spiritual practice, philosophy, methodology and/or tool is currently a hot topic in Western education, healthcare, training, research and professional coaching. Academic programmes talk about its broad application in the fields of technology, medicine, social services, psychology, consulting, law enforcement and the justice system, athletics and clergy, to name a few.[12] Because of the intense interest in this approach and its embeddedness in the experience of attention in the present moment, we also see it as a link to our model from the perspective of inspiring coaching-based philosophy, methodology and tools.

The literature of mindfulness as a philosophy and spiritual practice is vast and beyond the scope of this book to summarize, let alone interpret. We know it has its roots in ancient Buddhist texts, some of which are now incorporated into Western Buddhist psychology.[13] In the Buddhist context, according to cognitive and Eastern psychologist Eleanor Rosch, mindfulness is a simple mental factor that can be present or absent in a moment of consciousness.[14] However, Buddhist mindfulness as a spiritual practice is not a simple technique or type of consciousness but rather an entire mode of knowing and being in the world. Rosch defines it as a relaxation and expansion of awareness, "a letting go even into deep states of not knowing, access to wisdom knowing beyond what we think of as consciousness or the mind, and an open hearted inclusive warmth toward all of experience and to the world."[15]

The Light of Buddhadharma Foundation International recently published a talk by renowned Buddhist meditation master in the Theravada tradition,

---

[12] For example, Master of Arts in Mindfulness Studies at Leslie University in Cambridge, MA, started by Nancy Waring, who studied under Jon Kabat-Zin, who is considered to be a forefather of mindfulness studies and programmes in the USA.
[13] Rosch (2007).
[14] Rosch (2007), p. 259.
[15] Rosch (2007), p. 261.

Phra Luang Por Jamnian Seelasettho. His "Dhamma Talk on Practicing the Middle Way" was given under the revered Bodhi Tree in India,[16] where he referred to Four Foundations of Mindfulness but in the context of other primary teachings of the Buddha: the Noble Eightfold Path and the Seven Factors of Enlightenment, all ultimately leading to the Middle Way. He spoke about the Four Foundations of Mindfulness as mindfulness of the body (*rūpa*), sensations/feelings (*vedanā*), mind (*citta*) and mental phenomena (*dhamma*), and he urged followers to view all four of those as impermanent, unsatisfactory and empty of self—a type of seeing that progressively leads to the direct experience of *anatta* (not-self, impersonal), *sunnata* (emptiness) and *nibbana* (extinction, liberation from all suffering), tracing the path to freedom.[17] He encouraged his followers to understand not only with their intellect but with their mind, and to understand that consciousness moves throughout the body at different centres (i.e., he referred to chakras in a unique way to denote the location/centre in the body where the mind lodges at times in certain states).[18]

We recognize the complexity and depth of the genesis of mindfulness as an Eastern philosophy, a system of teachings and spiritual practice. As a spiritual tradition, mindfulness has a dimensionality to it that Western application does not always infer. This underscores Rosch's concern about the level of interpretation and application of these profound Eastern principles to Western thought and action. In terms of our model of substantial change, we resonate with the idea of mindfulness as a mode of inner knowing if practised appropriately, but again emphasize that this is a philosophy and system of teachings and practice beyond our personal and professional level of experience. Mindfulness as practised and applied in the West, however, can be influential and supportive for coaches hoping to ignite substantial change in their clients. We heartily acknowledge the benefits of mindfulness as a therapeutic approach with sound methodology and tools of wide applicability.

In Western culture there has been no commonly accepted definition or model of mindfulness that is acknowledged across fields of study. Jon Kabat-Zinn, Professor of Medicine, is considered a forefather of the mindfulness movement in the USA. He studied meditation with Buddhist teachers and founded the Stress Reduction Clinic in the University of Massachusetts Medical School in 1979, adapting Buddhist mindfulness teachings. He later went on to develop his well-known Mindfulness-Based Stress Reduction programme, dropping the Buddhist framework and focusing on mindfulness in

---

[16] Seelasettho (2013).
[17] Seelasettho (2013), p. 5.
[18] Seelasettho (2013), p. 1.

a scientific context.[19] His programme is designed to help patients cope with stress, pain and illness using mindfulness as a process of bringing a specific quality of attention to moment-by-moment experience.[20]

In 2004, psychologist Scott Bishop and colleagues articulated a proposed operational definition in the hope of finding a professional consensus on a model of mindfulness.[21] We were impressed with the clarity that they found in their definition, which not only captured the complexity of the philosophy and approach underlying mindfulness but also provided a useful methodology for Westerners. According to Bishop, "mindfulness in contemporary psychology has been adopted as an approach for increasing awareness and responding skillfully to mental processes that contribute to emotional distress and maladaptive behaviour."[22]

His group proposed a two-component model of mindfulness: self-regulation of attention to keep it focused on immediate experience, and adopting an orientation towards one's experiences in the present moment that is curious, open and accepting (i.e., with no judgment). In this model, mindfulness involves a direct experience of events in the mind and body but is not a practice in thought suppression. Bishop and his colleagues described it as a way of regulating attention that can lead to insight into the nature of one's mind, and also adopting a detached perspective on one's thoughts and feelings. This promotes learning to experience one's thoughts and feelings as subjective rather than valid, and as transient rather than permanent, offering a way to be "decentred" about oneself.[23]

Bishop proposed that mindfulness is closer conceptually and operationally to those constructs that involve a *process* of self-observation (e.g., introspection, reflection, observing self) rather than an outcome of acquiring self-knowledge (e.g., insight, self-awareness).[24] From the perspective of a coaching theory of igniting substantial change, we find his view of mindfulness as a process to be similar to our stance of clients engaging in a constructive process of reflection and deeper understanding that is drawn from their inner guidance. Some type of mindfulness practice that encourages clients to stay in contact with their inner process supports our model. He also distinguished between "mindfulness meditation" and "concentration" forms of meditation

---

[19] Wilson (2014).
[20] Kabat-Zinn (1990).
[21] Bishop et al. (2004).
[22] Bishop et al. (2004), p. 230.
[23] Bishop et al. (2004), p. 234.
[24] Bishop et al. (2004), p. 235.

that invoke deep states of relaxation by restricting the focus of attention to a single stimulus, such as a word, sound or sensation.[25]

Mindfulness has made its way into the field of learning[26] as well as into the study of emotions, such as helping-related emotions.[27] And it is currently a significant topic in the field of coaching and leadership development. To name a few coaching-based researchers and practitioners, authors Richard Boyatzis and Annie McKee included the concept of mindfulness in their book *Resonant Leadership*, focusing on how self-awareness through mindfulness can help to calm executives in times of crisis.[28] Author and coach Jonathan Passmore, together with psychologist Oberdan Marianetti, explored the research and application of mindfulness as a tool for helping both coaches and clients to better manage stress and improve performance.[29] In an exploratory study of 45 adults randomly assigned to three health programmes, coaching researchers Gordon Spence, Michael Cavanagh and Anthony Grant investigated a health intervention that integrated mindfulness training with cognitive behavioural solution-focused coaching.[30] Douglas Riddle with the Center for Creative Leadership has presented on the three keys to mindful leadership coaching.[31]

Clearly the notion of mindfulness in today's fast-paced world is an attractive concept and its application has proved effective in a range of studies: the brain and immune system (better stress regulation),[32] enhanced relationships (loving-kindness meditation)[33] and educational settings (children's attention and social skills).[34] As mentioned earlier, we approach the philosophy of mindfulness from the perspective of offering access to a direct way of knowing with appropriate understanding and practice. Most salient for our coaching model is using mindfulness as a strategy for expressing awareness through attention. We are drawn to the idea that living authentically in the present moment is predicated on a high level of mindfulness (attention) on the part of the coach when in dialogue with clients. Methodology and tools in mindfulness for coaches and clients will be taken up again in Chapter 7.

---

[25] Bishop et al. (2004), p. 238.
[26] Langer (2000).
[27] Cameron and Fredrickson (2015).
[28] Boyatzis and McKee (2005).
[29] Passmore and Marianetti (2013).
[30] Spence, Cavanagh and Grant (2008).
[31] Riddle (2012).
[32] Tang et al. (2007).
[33] Hutcherson, Seppala and Gross (2008).
[34] Napoli, Krech and Holley (2005).

Expanding Our Awareness

Awareness is attention that occurs in the present moment and which is situated in our body with its complex interplay of thoughts, emotions, actions and environment. Expanding and sustaining our awareness levels can enable us to be fully present for our clients' growth and development. Equally, for our clients to be successful, they need to develop greater facility in their own self-awareness and in their awareness of their environment. The coaching relationship is an intersubjective experience, and an interconnected sense of awareness underlies this constructive process. How can we help our clients to construct a desired reality without giving it our mutual awareness?

Emotions as Expressions of Energy and Awareness

At the request of her husband, Ann went to a handgun shooting range in their hometown. It was something he suggested they could do together that might be interesting. Neither of them were gun owners nor particularly drawn to target practice. As they were walking into the building, Ann began to feel uncomfortable and queasy. Her hands started sweating and her breathing sped up a little. She felt lightheaded and was wondering what was going on. She had done some clay pigeon shooting years before and hadn't had any such reaction. When she looked around, there were handguns in glass cases and individuals shooting them at paper targets. She realized she was anxious and afraid, but couldn't understand why until suddenly a memory popped up. When she was in her early 20s she and a male friend had picked up two hitchhikers while driving home from a concert. Once in the back seat, one of the hitchhikers pulled out a handgun and held it to the head of Ann's friend as he was driving the car and demanded to be driven to a particular spot. Needless to say, the situation went downhill from there but fortunately neither Ann nor her friend was injured; the gun was not fired. The hitchhikers eventually took what little money Ann and her friend had and left them stranded in a field. It was a terrifying experience at the time, more than 30 years ago. After realizing the source of her emotions, Ann was able to stay in the building and actually fire a handgun and do some practice target rounds with her husband. She did so with some concern but no longer with a sense of fear and anxiety.

Ann was completely surprised by this strong emotional response and memory which showed up, involuntarily, in the present moment. It felt like intense time travel—having the past thrust into the present through the feelings expressed. It felt contextual in terms of the juxtaposition of the two events in her personal history. She surmised that it was the first time since that long-ago event that she was in the presence of handguns being used openly. She had first experienced her body reacting physiologically with the memory association (past context), and then it surfaced as awareness and conscious recollection (present context).

Such vivid autobiographical memories, research shows, tend to be of emotional events, whether negative or positive. Part of the reason for this is that positive and negative emotional experiences also register a memory in cell tissue and sometimes the body responds emotionally, manufacturing emotional chemicals, *before* the brain has registered a problem.[35] Unexpected memories or revelations can occur in a coaching conversation and bring with them emotion to be expressed, as Ann experienced when her past erupted into the present moment, unbidden and with expanded awareness.

History of Emotions: The Social Dimension

Recent years have seen an explosion of new and renewed interest in the study of emotions across the humanities, natural sciences and even in the context of cultural, social, political and economic events in history.[36] Interestingly, historians have been engaged in a new area of study in their field: the history of emotion. They have pointed to philosopher Friedrich Nietzsche as their inspiration. In the late nineteenth century, Nietzsche called for a more vivid, probing and emotional form of history-making than just describing conditions as fixed and never-changing.[37] According to historian Erin Sullivan, the last decade has seen a great rush in her field to finally address Nietzsche's observation, and writing has proliferated on describing a history of emotions that looks at the expressions of feeling across a variety of times, places, cultures and contexts.[38]

French historian Lucien Febvre was well known in his field for advocating that the study of history be dynamic and human focused. He was an important figure in promoting a history of emotions, building on Nietzsche's suggestion. In his 1941 essay entitled "Sensibility and History: How to Reconstitute the Emotional Life of the Past," he spoke of emotions as being contagious and relational, a concept which current historians have embraced as a foundation for exploring the social dimension of emotions.[39]

---

[35] Myss (1996), p. 35.
[36] Biess et al. (2010).
[37] Sullivan (2013).
[38] Sullivan (2013).
[39] Febvre (1941/1973).

3 Pivoting: The Extraordinary Power of Self-Organization 63

To historian Ute Frevert, emotions are a hot topic for a reason—because they are dynamic and mobile in cultures, what was culturally prominent at some point in the past changes over time. For example, she has studied the social emotions of honour and shame that were prominent in domestic and international politics and interpersonal relationships in European societies in the nineteenth and twentieth centuries. These social emotions are now said to be disappearing, to be replaced by different emotions, such as empathy and compassion.[40] She observes that nowadays emotions seem to be the object of constant individual and social manipulation, with "emotional intelligence" emerging as a buzzword of our times.

According to Sullivan, historians of emotion attend to "the way culture talks about particular emotions, paying attention to how feelings are valorized, marginalised, scientifically defined, or religiously encoded."[41] They acknowledge the different strands of thinking and feeling that may co-exist in a society at any given time and focus on the socially oriented nature of much emotional experience and expression.[42] This widened perspective of how emotion is simultaneously personal, social and even political (given the systems of power in control) can only sharpen our perception of how to help our clients find clarity around their own conflicting contexts of emotional expression.

Just as historians are concerned about the role of emotions in their multi-lens perspective (social, cultural, political and economic) on historic events and eras, we propose that coaches should be aware of how their clients are embedded in their own social, cultural, political, economic and organizational communities and systems that reflect specific emotional contexts. Clients and coaches are influenced and shaped by the greater social attitudes towards emotions in the contexts in which they move, whether cross-cultural, transnational, regional, local or familial.

In a forum in 2010, five international historians, who have contributed significantly to this new field, participated in a virtual round table.[43] They were asked to explain the reasons for the current historical interest in emotions. Their responses are of consequence to coaches because they describe the parallels of social and individual emotional contexts that can hopefully give us

---

[40] Sullivan (2013), p. 97.
[41] Sullivan (2013), p. 95.
[42] Sullivan (2013), p. 95.
[43] In 2010, historian Frank Bies with the University of California, San Diego, invited colleagues Alon Confino (University of Virginia), Ute Frevert (Max-Planck-Institut für Bildungsforschung), Uffa Jensen (Universitat Gottingen), Lyndol Roper (University of Oxford) and Daniela Saxer (Universitat Zurich/ETH Zurich) to be part of a virtual dialogue.

a deeper grasp of how to interpret and work with emotions in the coaching process.

Historian Frevert pointed to the prominence of neuroscience since the 1990s as a reason for the increased interest in emotion. Findings in neuroimaging have been a boost to psychological research, including new possibilities for measuring emotions and better understanding the link between cognition and emotions.[44] Historian Daniela Saxer attributed interest in emotion to the social influence of popular ideas around self-management, including catchphrases from self-help literature, advice from business management and popularized scientific concepts, all indicating that personal emotions should be groomed as an important element of self-care. According to Saxer, this seemed to suggest that whoever wants to get ahead socially and economically needs to take emotions seriously.[45] Saxer also saw an influence from the field of economics, which considers itself to be a universal science of human behaviour and has contributed to this trend by studying emotions as factors in economic transactions.[46]

Historian Uffa Jensen referred to the rise of postmodern theories that have reshaped the field with a renewed focus on cultural and political theory, especially with the new political climate after the events of 9/11 in the USA. She has observed that emotions such as hate, fear and paranoia are now dominant in the political language of emotions which international terrorism uses and mobilizes.[47] Lyndal Roper at the University of Oxford pointed out that there are now more women in the historical profession, many of whom have grown up with the legacy of feminism and are more comfortable with the emotional and the subjective.[48] In addition, she explained how emotions are not only physical and mental but can also be collective, linked to action, and yet have a physiological component.

Alono Confino at the University of Virginia associated a history of emotions with the history of memory in that emotions, like memories, are absolutely individual yet originate from the symbols, landscape, practices and language shared by a given society.[49] He viewed the making of emotions, personal and collective, as being embedded in a specific cultural, social, economic and political context. Therefore he found it of value to history to explore how people construct emotions, make sense of them and use them. For Frevert

---

[44] Biess et al. (2010).
[45] Biess et al. (2010), p. 69.
[46] Biess et al. (2010), p. 69.
[47] Biess et al. (2010), p. 69.
[48] Biess, et al. (2010), p. 70.
[49] Biess et al. (2010), p. 71.

it was clear that studying emotions is a way to discover more about human motives, about what triggers actions, about what influences decisions and about what causes people to bond or not.[50]

The Role that Positive Emotions Play in Awareness

In flipping the collective/individual coin, we see the amount of influence that our clients (and we as coaches) are subject to given our multiple contexts. Much of it is below the level of conscious attention, and much of it is derived from negative emotional influence given the current political, cultural and social contexts. Think of the myriad marketing and advertising images and language used to sell products to keep us safe or healthy from the negative influences of our environment. Think of the focus of the majority of news stories. Neuroscience tells us that our brains have a negativity bias to aid us in survival.[51] Now that we have been alerted to the negative social emotions embedded in our multiple systems, what is happening at the individual level?

Although there is no commonly accepted definition of emotion across fields of study, an accepted psychological construct states that an emotion is a complex psychological state that involves three distinct components: a subjective experience, a physiological response and a behavioural or expressive response.[52] Another definition similarly states, "Emotions are short-lived experiences that produce coordinated changes in people's thoughts, actions and physiological responses."[53]

Most early psychological research on emotions was focused on the tendency to action which seems to infuse both mind and body, simultaneously narrowing an individual's action urges (e.g., flight in fear, attack in anger) while simultaneously mobilizing the body to take those actions, such as increased blood flow to large muscles in fear.[54] This perception of emotions as leading to specific actions has been linked to human evolution and seen as a trial-and-error learning process in response to environmental events. As a result, these "action" emotions have become genetically embedded in humans and animals as the flight or fight instinct. This evolutionary perspective that negative emotions have specific action tendencies has challenged researchers

---

[50] Biess et al. (2010), p. 68.
[51] Hanson and Mendius (2009).
[52] Hockenbury and Hockenbury (2007).
[53] Fredrickson and Branigan (2005), p. 313.
[54] Fredrickson and Branigan (2005), p. 313.

to account for the purpose and nature of positive human emotions such as joy and contentment.

Although emotion theorists who support specific action tendencies have tried to extend their theories to include positive emotions,[55] social psychologist Barbara Fredrickson has argued that positive emotions do not share this hallmark feature of promoting and supporting specific action.[56] Instead she asks, if positive emotions do not share this action feature, what good are they? Do positive emotions have any evolved adaptive value? Since her seminal article, "What Good Are Positive Emotions?," appeared in 1998,[57] Fredrickson has worked diligently on researching and solidifying a theory of positive emotions that is based on a non-action premise: her broaden-and-build theory. She has been at the leading edge of this new science of positive emotions and established a Positive Emotions and Psychophysiology Laboratory, first at the University of Michigan and then at the University of North Carolina, Chapel Hill. She focuses on acknowledging and growing a repertoire of positive emotions at the individual level, and understanding the consequences that such positive expression can have in broadening and building personal resources in multiple areas (e.g., cognitive, psychological, social and physical).

Fredrickson has also targeted ten representative positive emotions for further research based on laboratory evidence that these emotions are frequently experienced in people's daily lives. She listed them in order of frequency with the exception of "love", which she identified as the most frequently experienced positive emotion: joy, gratitude, serenity, interest, hope, pride, amusement, inspiration, awe and love. She related each emotion to the resources it generates and its thought-action tendency.[58] By no means comprehensive, a brief compilation of some of her salient research projects and findings follows:

- *Undo Effect of Positive Emotions*: The seeds for Fredrickson's broaden-and-build theory came from work with Robert Levenson in which they examined the "undo effect" of positive emotions on negative emotions, specifically fear.[59] Levenson posited that the evolutionary meaning of positive emotions might be to function as efficient "undoers" of states of autonomic nervous system arousal produced by certain negative emotions.[60]

---

[55] Fridja (1986), Lazarus (1991).
[56] Fredrickson and Branigan (2005), p. 314.
[57] Fredrickson (1998).
[58] Fredrickson (2013).
[59] Fredrickson and Levenson (1998).
[60] Fredrickson (2013), p. 8.

The results of their studies suggested that positive emotions serve as useful resources for regulating negative emotional experiences in daily life.

- *Broaden-and-Build Theory*: Fredrickson has contended that the form and function of positive and negative emotions are distinct and complementary. For example, while negative emotions narrow individuals' thought-action tendencies by calling forth specific actions (attack, flee), many positive emotions broaden individuals' thought-action tendencies, prompting them to pursue a wider range of thoughts and actions, such as play, explore and integrate.[61]
- *Broaden Hypothesis*: Positive emotions widen the array of thoughts, action urges and percepts or mental concepts. The broaden effect of positive emotions extends into the social domain with individuals being more likely to expand their circle of trust and show greater perspective and compassion for others.[62]
- *Build Hypothesis*: The expansive form of positive emotions spurs the development of resources, thereby increasing resilience and capacity for inner growth and optimal functioning. Positive emotions build personal resources and abilities which can be *cognitive*, such as mindfully attending to the present moment; *psychological*, such as maintaining a sense of mastery over environmental challenges; *social*, such as giving and receiving emotional support; or *physical*, as in warding off the common cold.[63]
- *Positive Emotions and Attention*: Fredrickson's research confirmed the view that positive emotions broaden the scope of attention and awareness. While anxiety and depression are correlated with a bias to narrow one's scope of attention, positive emotion traits (e.g., well-being and optimism) correlate with a bias to broaden the scope of attention.[64] Because positive emotions arise in response to diffuse opportunities instead of narrowly focused threats, they momentarily broaden individuals' attention and thinking, enabling them to draw on higher-level connections and a wider range of ideas.[65] In another study, Fredrickson and colleagues provided evidence that positive emotions forecast broadened cognition, such as holistic processing and flexible attention.[66]
- *Positive Emotions and Mindfulness*: Fredrickson and colleagues have done numerous studies on positive emotions and mindfulness, including the impact

---

[61] Fredrickson and Branigan (2005), p. 314.
[62] Fredrickson (2013).
[63] Fredrickson, Cohn, Coffey, Pek and Finkel (2008), p. 1045.
[64] Fredrickson (2013).
[65] Fredrickson et al. (2008), p. 1045.
[66] Johnson, Waugh and Fredrickson (2010).

of loving-kindness meditation on building personal resources,[67] the role of positive emotional reactivity in promoting flourishing,[68] and the impact of positive psychology interventions as predictors and consequences of long-term positive behaviour change.[69] According to Fredrickson, these studies confirm that increased positive emotions support the build hypothesis of creating personal resources and of learning to self-generate positive emotions.

- *Broaden-and-Build Theory and Biological Resources:* Fredrickson has been further exploring research findings that people who express more frequent positive emotions can build biological resources for health. Her studies have already shown a link between positive emotions shifting cardiovascular patterns towards health. In addition, she and her research collaborators have been investigating whether a stable rise in positive emotions could produce reliable changes in gene expression, especially around the immune system's regulation of inflammatory processes.[70]
- *Upward Spiral Theory of Lifestyle Change*: A key long-term goal of Fredrickson's laboratory has been to investigate whether and how positive emotions alter people's bodily systems and non-conscious motives in ways that ultimately reinforce lifestyle change and sustain positive health behaviours. She has proposed that positive emotions can "knit" people to new positive health behaviours as well as raise their overall psychological propensity towards wellness (i.e., be motivated by non-conscious desire rather than rigid willpower).[71]

As we can see from the breadth and depth of Fredrickson's work, there is much to be gained for coaches in further exploring this relatively new area of research on positive emotions. We have focused primarily on her groundbreaking work to underscore the potential available to coaches in helping clients grow their personal inner resources. Fredrickson's research directly links positive emotions to increased growth, development and capacity. We are well aware that there are many other life-enhancing, positive approaches to understanding human emotion and resiliency that include positive psychology approaches, Gallup's StrengthsFinder and positive emotion laboratories at universities around the world. We briefly acknowledge the unique work of the Institute of HeartMath, which has explored the relationship between mental

---

[67] Fredrickson et al. (2008).
[68] Catalino and Fredrickson (2011).
[69] Cohn and Fredrickson (2010).
[70] Fredrickson (2013).
[71] Fredrickson (2013).

and emotional systems to find internal coherence, and which has looked to the heart as a source of intelligence and intuitive guidance.[72]

We leave our discussion on emotion with this reassurance about our capacity as individuals to seek the positive in our lives. One of the most consistent, prevalent and robust biases documented in psychology and behavioural economics, according to neuroscientist Tali Sharot, is the "optimism bias" phenomenon.[73] This is defined as the difference between a person's expectation and the actual outcome that follows. It appears that we humans show a remarkably consistent and strong bias to predict the future by overestimating the likelihood of positive events and underestimating the likelihood of negative events. This optimism bias has been observed across gender, race, nationality and age. Perhaps it also reflects the human spirit at play—unquantifiable and unquenchable.

Embodiment: A Coaching Awareness Strategy

As we conclude this chapter, we seek to answer a final question about the elements of self-organization: From where does awareness arise and who is in charge of it? In the seventeenth century, Rene Descartes' proposition, "I think, therefore I am,"[74] helped to form the foundation for reason and science in Western philosophy. He proposed that the mind and body were two separate and distinct entities and that the mind took supremacy as only the mind could sense the body. This has been part of an ingrained worldview in the West that has relegated knowledge, wisdom and intelligence primarily to mental cognition and the mind. The body was considered to be along for the ride.

This subordinate role of the body in terms of innate knowledge and intelligence is being challenged on numerous fronts. There is a new interdisciplinary field developing in which researchers are studying how mind, body and environment mutually interact and influence each other. *Embodied cognition* is a hot topic due to the recent rise and resurgence in the interest of embodiment from such diverse perspectives as artificial intelligence and robotics, social psychology, phenomenology, anthropology and spiritual traditions.

We borrow the concept of embodiment as a way to explain how awareness is dispersed in coaching. Embodiment is a strategy of awareness; we are interacting with our clients on multiple levels of intelligence and awareness—cognitively, emotionally, physically, environmentally and intuitively—whether we are consciously aware of this or not. The concept of embodiment

---

[72] McCraty (2015).
[73] Sharot (2011).
[74] Descartes (1637/1986), p. 65.

represents the active constructive process we are engaged in when coaching. For example, tacit and enactive knowledge are based on the physical action of interacting with the environment—it's an active way of knowing, influencing and learning. Thus "our bodies are not *merely* life support systems for a mind or self, but [they] are absolutely interdependent."[75] We believe that the essence of coaching is engaging in this active constructive process with clients, a strategy of embodying in which we are aware of one another at a deeper level.

We present some definitions of embodied cognition which we feel are relevant to a better understanding of embodiment as a key coaching strategy. We do not presume to represent or adequately explain the complexity and wonderment inherent in this concept and experimental research. We begin with a definition from *The Embodied Mind: Cognitive Science and Human Experience* by Eleanor Rosch, Evan Thompson and Francisco Varela, an early and seminal work:[76]

> By using the term *embodied* we mean to highlight two points: first that cognition depends upon the kinds of experience that come from having a body with various sensorimotor capacities, and second, that these individual sensorimotor capacities are themselves embedded in a more encompassing biological, psychological and cultural context.

This definition is helpful in understanding the necessity of extending beyond a purely cognitive stance in coaching. For us to be truly educated about our level of influence as coaches we must assume responsibility at a conscious level for what we bring to the relationship.

Scientists Rolf Pfeifer and Josh Bongard offer another definition. In their book *How the Body Shapes the Way We Think*, they challenged the classical notion of the mind controlling the body and explored embodiment, how the body affects intelligence.[77] They defined embodiment as the idea that the body is actually required for intelligence to occur and that many features of human cognition are shaped by aspects of the body beyond the brain, such as the motor system, the perceptual system, and the body's interactions with the environment. There exists a subtle interplay or balance between neural activity (brain), the morphology of the body's shape and its material properties, and interaction with the environment to achieve certain tasks.[78] The brain does not control the body; rather, the two systems interact and intelligence is distributed throughout the organism—it is a flat system, explained Pfeifer and Bongard, where components influence each other. Even the way we walk

---

[75] Harle (2007) p. 589.
[76] Rosch, Thompson and Varda (1991), pp. 172–173.
[77] Pfeifer and Bongard (2007).
[78] Pfeifer and Bongard (2007), p. 20.

3 Pivoting: The Extraordinary Power of Self-Organization

or pick up a glass of water has cognitive qualities. To illustrate, the fact that muscles are elastic and that the weight of one leg increases when the other one is lifted are as much a part of the movement of walking as are the reflexes and brain centres involved in this action, according to Pfeifer and Bongard.

In the field of artificial intelligence and robotics, researchers have discovered what has been called "Moravec's paradox." The principle was articulated by Hans Moravec, Rodney Brooks, Marvin Minsky and others in the 1980s. Moravec, researcher and futurist, wrote, "It is comparatively easy to make computers exhibit adult level performance on intelligence tests or playing checkers, and difficult or impossible to give them the skills of a one-year-old when it comes to perception and mobility."[79]

He described how in the large, highly evolved sensory and motor portions of the human brain are encoded a billion years of experience about the nature of the world and how to survive in it. He viewed reasoning as the newest aspect of human thought that could only survive because it was supported by the much older and more powerful unconscious, sensorimotor knowledge.[80]

Rodney Brooks, former director of the MIT Computer Science and Artificial Intelligence Laboratory, has been a key contributor to the field. He challenged his peers to think about how intelligence or intelligent behaviour comes about without the need for rational thought.[81] In his forward to Pfeifer's book, he pointed out how even Alan Turing, in creating his machine of computation and intelligence, approached his model from watching real people's observable behaviour in carrying out computations with pen and paper and following fixed rules. Turing modelled what a person does, not what a person thinks.[82]

So from where does our awareness arise? When humans experience an *aha* moment or an event of deep knowing, it seems to involve the body and mind holistically, without separation. It is felt physically, emotionally, mentally and often spiritually. It is a happening with multiple dimensions involving intelligence at multiple levels, and it is situated in an environment. These deep moments of change are not controlled by a thinking brain; in fact, the thinking brain appears to be "informed" along with the rest of the body as the awareness sweeps through.

In working on this passage for the book, Ann experienced one of those events of deep knowing. She was struggling to articulate the holistic nature of self-organizing when the "knowing" passed right through her body with a strong physical reaction

---

[79] Moravec (1988), p. 15.
[80] Moravec (1988), pp. 15–16.
[81] Pfeifer and Bongard (2007), p. 353.
[82] Pfeifer and Bongard (2007).

of vibration, intense feeling and mental insight—all happening at once in the presence of a colleague, while sitting on her couch. Who was in charge of that awareness? Her experience was of a single awareness permeating her being.

Implications for Coaching

Our journey thus far has invited us to extend our perspective of coaching beyond a purely cognitive stance. Embodied cognition represents the collapse of the body–mind dualism while at the same time offering much greater awareness of how our cognition occurs in different ways. For us to be truly educated about how deeply we influence our clients and/or are influenced by them, we must assume responsibility for the only vehicle we bring to coaching—ourselves—and whatever awareness, expertise, emotional maturity, mastery and tools we have embodied. For coaches it would appear that the gift of embodiment *is* awareness. When we embody anything, we use all of our senses and abilities to create full awareness, and whatever we are aware of we can change.[83] In the next three chapters we explore the role that beliefs, inner knowing and memory bring to pivotal moments of self-organization.

Fig. 3.4 Answer to finding the hidden star

---

[83] Day (2009).

4

Accessing the Inner Self: Beliefs

We prefer to believe what we prefer to be true .

—Francis Bacon

Accessing Our Inner Process

Cognitive neuroscientists tell us that around 95 % of how we act, make decisions, feel and behave occurs at the non-conscious (i.e., subconscious, unconscious) level of unobserved processes. This leaves the self-conscious mind (also known as the neocortex or executive function) responsible for less than 5 % of our cognitive activity—an astounding fact to consider for those of us in the business of coaching. It appears that our inner process encompasses a vast network of interconnected thoughts, beliefs, memories, feelings, knowledge and intuition whose existence is now being reaffirmed through the lens of neuroscience and related experimental studies.

Recent empirical evidence supports the findings of psychological theorists such as William James, Sigmund Freud and Carl Jung, who long ago suggested that unconscious phenomena included repressed feelings, automatic skills, subliminal perceptions, thoughts, habits and mindless reactions.[1] Jung, for example, captured his life story as "the self-realization of the

---

[1] Westen (1999).

unconscious."[2] He believed that everything in the unconscious sought outward manifestation, and that the personality wanted to evolve out of unconscious conditions and experience itself as whole. He poetically described it as "The longing for light is the longing for consciousness."[3] He also lamented that he could not use the language of science to trace this process of growth in himself because he couldn't experience himself as a scientific problem. He turned to the idea of personal myth instead as more accurately portraying the singularity of his life.

This notion of personal myth resonates with those of us in the coaching field because each client we work with has a life story—a mythology about themselves. Some aspects of the client's story we discern are conscious and accurate, while other elements, perhaps because of what isn't said or what is glossed over or what feels incongruent, we detect are not accurate or lack coherence. As we work with clients, we become aware at subtle levels of the beliefs they hold about themselves and the world that they may be blind to. A personal myth is, after all, what one has come to believe about oneself and, as this chapter points out, we are heavily influenced by external belief systems (Fig. 4.1).

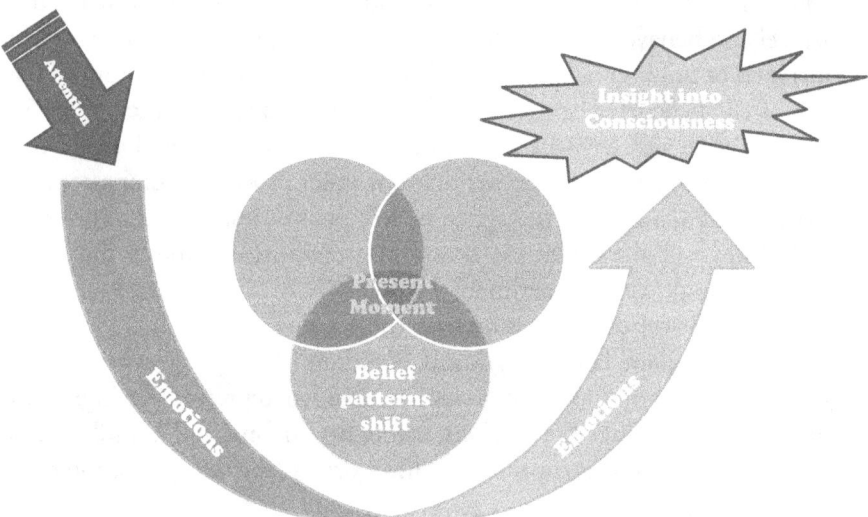

Fig. 4.1 Role of beliefs in self-organizing

---

[2] Jung (1965).
[3] Jung (1965), p. 269.

What Are Beliefs?

The *Oxford English Dictionary* traces the roots of "belief" to Middle English from Old English. The word appeared in about the late twelfth century and was used to refer to things held to be to true owing to religious doctrine. "Faith" referred to loyalty or allegiance to a person based on duty. In the fourteenth century, "faith" began to take on a religious connotation while the concept of "belief" gradually diminished to the generalized modern definition: the mental acceptance of something as true.[4]

Scholars from divergent fields have difficulty in defining "belief" because its meaning depends on the context in which it is used and how it is distinguished from terms such as "knowledge," "attitudes," "values," "judgement," "ideology," "perceptions," "internal mental processes" and "action strategies."[5] Anthropologists, social psychologists and philosophers, however, have agreed on an acknowledged definition: "Beliefs are thought of as psychologically held understandings, premises, or propositions about the world that are felt to be true."[6] Psychologist Milton Rokeach defined beliefs as "any simple proposition, conscious or unconscious, inferred from what a person says or does, capable of being preceded by the phrase 'I believe that'."[7] He also suggested that all beliefs have three components: cognitive (person's knowledge about what is true or false, desirable or not); affective (capable of arousing affect of varying intensity, taking positive or negative positions); and behavioural (leads to action when activated).[8]

Robert Dilts defined core beliefs as very general and basic beliefs that will influence anything that comes after them.[9] Core beliefs are also made up of critical relationships between people and it can be difficult to distinguish between beliefs we have modelled from others (e.g., parents, teachers and society) and our own beliefs.[10] Experience and context play a role in the formation of beliefs. Mathematicians J. L. Usó-Doménech at the University of Castellon, Spain, and J. Nescolarde-Selva at the University of Alicante, Spain, have posited that beliefs arise through experience and that experience needs previous beliefs and reason to be assimilated; therefore beliefs, reason and

---

[4] Belief (n.d.).
[5] Pajares (1992).
[6] Richardson (1996), p. 103.
[7] Rokeach (1968), p. 113.
[8] Rokeach (1968).
[9] Dilts (1990).
[10] Dilts (1990).

Table 4.1 Major distinctions between beliefs and knowledge

Beliefs	Knowledge
Refer to suppositions, commitments and ideologies	Refers to factual propositions and the understandings that inform skillful action
Do not require a truth condition	Must satisfy a truth condition
Cannot be evaluated	Can be evaluated or judged
Episodically stored material influenced by personal experiences or cultural and institutional sources	Stored in semantic networks
Static	Often changes

experience are based on each other.[11] Contexts also play a role, they explained, because they are dynamic and changing constantly as people have new experiences and change their beliefs and ways of reasoning.

The term "belief system," according to Usó-Doménech and Nescolarde-Selva, tends to be used differently depending on the context (e.g., psychology, anthropology or political science). Belief systems are structures of norms that are interrelated among several beliefs. They are the stories that individuals tell themselves to define their personal sense of reality.[12] Apparently, each of us has a belief system that we utilize to make sense of the world around us. Usó-Doménech and Nescolarde-Selva proposed that people are capable of constructing all kinds of individual beliefs by which they tell stories about how the world works and then use these belief systems to cope with events in their lives so that the world makes sense. They noted that belief systems do not need a basis in reality as long as they consistently provide adequate explanations for our lives.[13] They are also reinforced by culture, theology, and experience and training in cultural values, stereotypes, political viewpoints and so on. Perhaps one way to refer to these belief systems in coaching is to talk about the personal myths that we and our clients carry with us that we believe make our lives singular.

Scholars have also attempted to distinguish between knowledge and beliefs. Learning theorist Frank Pajares drew a distinction between knowledge (based on objective fact) and beliefs (based on evaluation and judgement) and pointed out that the difficulty is finding the border where knowledge ends and beliefs begin.[14] Table 4.1 describes the major distinctions between the two.[15]

---

[11] Usó-Doménech and Nescolarde-Selva (2015).
[12] Usó-Doménech and Nescolarde-Selva (2015).
[13] Usó-Doménech and Nescolarde-Selva (2015).
[14] Pajares (1992).
[15] Savasci-Acikalin (2009), p. 4.

It appears that beliefs play various roles in the coaching conversation. First, coach and client each bring core beliefs at a deep level of memory and conditioning that can impact behaviours and choices in unseen ways. Second, these personal beliefs create a story or personal myth that we then carry with us and use to make sense of the world. Coaches can often glean clues from clients' stories or personal myths that may help them to shift client perceptions. Third, we have belief systems based on the social, cultural, organizational and familial contexts we dwell in, yet beliefs are also intertwined and susceptible to our changing experiences and contexts.

Paradigm Shift in Belief

Research across multiple fields (e.g., biology, epistemology, neuroscience, philosophy, psychology and self-organization) yields no commonly accepted or shared definition of "belief" as either a construct or a system. Biologist Bruce Lipton proposed that this can be explained to a great extent because of the cultural and scientific belief system and historical context in which we are currently embedded.[16] According to Lipton, we are in the midst of a paradigm shift, moving away from the Newtonian mechanistic worldview in which material reality was considered to be the sole legitimate realm of science with all other aspects of reality being relegated to philosophy, religion or fiction.[17]

This paradigm of scientific materialism is shifting to what Lipton described as a holistic paradigm, a structured worldview which seeks to incorporate both the seen and unseen aspects of our human reality.[18] Lipton suggested that with this evolution we are being required to confront our internal conscious and unconscious limitations and misperceptions about the capacity of human nature and human potential that we have inherited from scientific materialism.[19] Thomas Kuhn in *Structure of Scientific Revolutions* argued that the evolution of scientific theory does not emerge from the straightforward accumulation of facts but rather from a set of changing intellectual circumstances and possibilities.[20] Thus our cultural and societal beliefs, from which our personal beliefs arise, are influenced by and constructed from the scientific context in which we live.

---

[16] Lipton (2009).
[17] Rock and Page (2009).
[18] Lipton (2009).
[19] Lipton (2009), p. 65.
[20] Kuhn (1970).

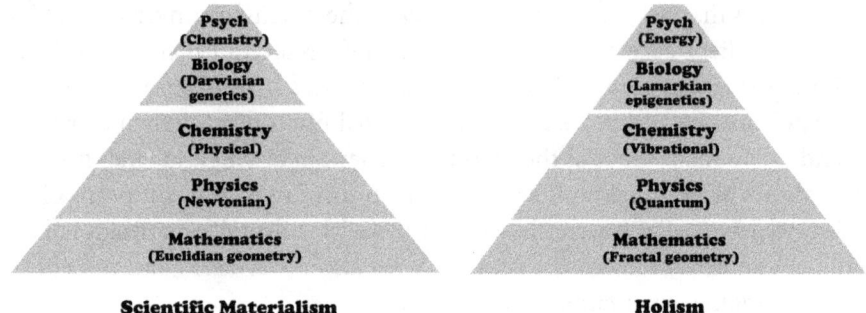

Fig. 4.2 Comparison of two belief systems

David Rock and Linda Page, in *Coaching with the Brain in Mind*, referred to the following quote from theoretical physicist Henry Stapp, describing the power of cultural and scientific beliefs on human development:

> Martyrs in every age are vivid reminders of the fact that no influence upon human conduct, even the instinct for bodily self-preservation, is stronger than beliefs about one's relationship to the rest of the universe and to the power that shapes it. Such beliefs form the foundation of a person's self-image, and hence, ultimately, of personal values.[21]

Stapp went on to point out that the values we hold depend on what we believe and that what we believe is "strongly influenced by science."[22] Lipton has noted the crucial influence of science on our human belief systems. He has proposed that studies on the structure and behaviour of the natural world are intricately linked and can be organized under the structure of one concept of "science" rather than separated by conventional fields of knowledge, such as mathematics and physics. According to him, if this accumulated knowledge were pulled together under one roof it would resemble a multitiered building, with each floor built on the scientific foundation of the supporting lower levels. Each floor would represent a basic scientific discipline, beginning with mathematics as the ground floor.

Lipton compared the belief system of the scientific materialism paradigm with that of the emerging holistic paradigm, making it clear that when the belief system within a lower level of science changes, the belief systems on the higher levels must change accordingly (Fig. 4.2).

---

[21] Stapp (2007) in Rock and Page (2009), p. 31.
[22] Stapp (2007) in Rock and Page (2009), p. 32.

Lipton's holistic paradigm has some useful applications for the field of coaching in terms of how we can better understand the "big picture" of beliefs in the process of human growth and development. He listed what he called some relevant new science facts in the holistic paradigm:

- *Mathematics*: Fractal geometry emphasizes the self-similar patterns of organization found at all levels (self-organization, chaos theory).
- *Physics*: Matter and energy (spirit) are inseparable. In the quantum universe (physical or non-physical), energy waves or thoughts are entangled and embedded within an invisible energy matrix called the "field". No structure can be separated out from the field or source. Because it is the *observer* who creates the reality, we co-create reality with our beliefs, perceptions, thoughts and feelings.
- *Biology*: Epigenetics now controls genetics meaning that certain circumstances in life can cause genes to be turned off (become dormant) or turned on (become active). Thus epigenetic molecular mechanisms represent a physical pathway along which consciousness moves. Our field of beliefs and perceptions, individually and collectively, determine our biology and our reality.
- *Psychology:* The subconscious mind controls 95 % of our behaviour through biological-cognitive programmes obtained primarily from the field of beliefs. When we seek to access and better understand our subconscious beliefs and emotions, individually and collectively, we can take more creative control of our lives.[23]

For Lipton it has been all about the story we tell ourselves regarding reality and our place in it that is the origin of human self-consciousness, that neurological mechanism that gives us the freedom of choice.[24]

Socially Wired for Beliefs

In the broadest of terms, the story that Lipton has implied that we tell ourselves is based on a social system of beliefs. In fact, it may be that we are wired to be social as the new field of social cognitive neuroscience suggests. Researchers such as Matthew Lieberman have posited that our need for social connection with others may be the most fundamental requirement for human

---

[23] Lipton (2009), pp. 342–343.
[24] Lipton (2009).

survival, and that our identities are formed by the values lent to us from the groups we belong to.[25] He suggested that while we might think that our beliefs and values are core parts of our individual identity, he has found a neural basis for personal beliefs that overlaps significantly with one of the regions of the brain primarily responsible for allowing other people's beliefs to influence our own.[26]

Lieberman identified three major neural adaptations that have led humans to evolve a socially malleable sense of self. First is the discovery of the brain's default network of social cognition. This means that during times when the brain is at rest (i.e., not occupied with a task), we think about other people, ourselves and the relation of ourselves to other people. According to Lieberman, the brain's free time is devoted to thinking about the social world and our place in it. *Connection* is a default mechanism for human survival, ensuring that infants are cared for and groups are formed. He also linked social pain and pleasure with biological pain and pleasure. For example, our sensitivity to social rejection is so key to our well-being that our brains treat it as a painful event.

The second neural adaptation is the human capacity for *mentalizing*, which allows us to imagine what other people are thinking or feeling and to react to their future events. We have mirror neurons that enable us to imitate others and to do mindreading or imagining of others' situations, and to generate answers when we want to know the why of someone's choices or behaviour. Empathy, a process in which we are able to feel another's experiences, is a key aspect of this adaptation and contributes to the principal of reciprocity, an important mechanism for growing social connection.

The third neural adaptation is what Lieberman called *harmonizing*, a term he borrowed from Eastern philosophy and culture where it is considered essential for successful group living. Suggestibility and the process of being persuaded have been researched in *f*MRI studies, and results support the premise that many of our beliefs and values are transmitted through the self that exists as a conduit to the social groups we are involved in, from family to school to country.[27] Lieberman suggested that we incorporate socially derived impulses to supplement our natural impulses. "The social world imparts a collection of beliefs about ourselves, our morality, and about what constitutes a worthwhile life," and we often "cling to these beliefs as though they are

---

[25] Lieberman (2013).
[26] Lieberman (2013).
[27] Lieberman (2013), p. 193.

unique ideas."[28] He described these beliefs and values as being "snuck in from the outside"—like a Trojan horse—which our brain then makes use of to construct and update the self.[29]

Western Philosophy and Beliefs

The perspectives above do not yet include a philosophical definition of beliefs. According to the *Stanford Encyclopaedia of Philosophy*, most contemporary analytic philosophers use the term "belief" to refer to the attitude humans have whenever we take something to be true.[30] To believe something, in this sense, does not necessarily involve actively reflecting on it. Many of the things that humans believe are quite mundane—for example, that the sun will come up, that it's the twenty-first century, that my coffee cup is resting on the table. Forming beliefs is therefore considered to be one of the most basic and important features of the mind, and the concept of belief plays a crucial role in the philosophy of mind and epistemology (the study of the nature and scope of knowledge).

The "mind-body problem," considered to be central to the philosophy of the mind, is partly the question of whether and how a purely physical organism can have beliefs. Much of epistemology is based on questions of when and how beliefs are justified or qualify as knowledge. As we've seen, distinctions are made between beliefs, opinions, truth and knowledge. For many philosophers, what humans think about the world may not match up with the way the world really is, so there is a distinction between belief and truth. But there are other philosophers, such as postmodernists and existentialists, who think that such a distinction can't be made. These philosophers take a sceptical attitude towards certainty and see truth as much more fluid. To have certainty, according to postmodernists, humans would need to be able to "stand outside" their own beliefs and look at them and the world without any type of perspective or mental lens. However, that is not possible because our cognitive structure (made up of intellectual and social backgrounds, biases, moods, genetics, beliefs, preferences and passions) influences how we perceive what is true about the world and we cannot remove all of these lenses.[31]

---

[28] Lieberman (2013), p. 192.
[29] Lieberman (2013), p. 192.
[30] www.plato.stanford.edu.
[31] Pardi (2015).

Neurophilosophers such as Paul and Patricia Churchland, Daniel Dennett and Lynne Rudder Baker[32] adopt yet another perspective by asserting that since beliefs cannot be explained in a scientifically valid way, they do not exist. Dennett in his book *Consciousness Explained* described how consciousness arises from the interaction of physical and cognitive processes in the brain.[33] These neurophilosophers expect that neuroscience will one day uncover deeper levels of understanding that render the concept of beliefs no longer useful.[34] For example, neuroscientist Kathleen Taylor[35] suggested that beliefs may be like memories from a neural standpoint; the more something is repeated or intensified, the stronger the neural pathways become. Thus repetition and the emotional draw of ideas would create the neural version of beliefs.

Beliefs from the Constructivist Perspective

Belief as a global construct does not lend itself easily to empirical investigation from an objectivist perspective. According to Pajares, "Many see it so steeped in mystery that it can never be clearly defined or made a useful subject of research."[36] As coaching scholars-practitioners, we hold a constructivist perspective of beliefs. We see the development and expression of an individual's belief system as a changing interactive internal process. In fact, we suggest that *we are our beliefs*. We borrow from one of the key principles of quantum physics: the observer creates the reality. In other words, as Henry Ford so eloquently stated: "Whether you think you can, or you think you can't—you're right."

In a coaching session with Jackie, an executive and heir apparent for the legal counsel of a major corporation spoke critically about herself regarding her fear of performing high-level legal tasks. Even though she was successful in executing those tasks, she felt uncomfortable about these fearful emotions. Jackie reminded her that despite her trepidation she faced each situation and completed it successfully—she could count on herself. They talked about what that meant when she could rely on herself to be brave and confident no matter the situation. This observation helped to pivot the client's self-concept from being fearful to being brave. The client realized that, by definition, no one is brave without feeling scared. The belief that it

---

[32] Brann (2015).
[33] Dennett (1991).
[34] Brann (2015).
[35] Brann (2015).
[36] Pajares (1992).

was wrong to be fearful was the non-conscious belief that Jackie helped bring to awareness. The client was then able to shift her negative perspective about herself to a more affirmative belief about her competency and bravery. Jackie noted that the consequences of the change in her client's belief in herself cascaded positively throughout the rest of the coaching engagement.

The client (observer) in this case created a new perspective for herself. She reinterpreted her conditioned response of believing that being fearful was a deficit to realizing she was being heroic because of her fear. It resulted in a shift in her belief about herself. Lipton has pointed out how belief is not a trait that can measured on a scale but rather resembles the state of being pregnant—either one is or is not—there being no middle ground.[37] In other words, we either believe or not, but what happens when many of our beliefs are not evident to our awareness or that of others? Research demonstrates a strong link between beliefs and the non-conscious, which is one aspect of this concept that has substantial agreement among diverse theorists.

In researching the role of beliefs in the practice of teaching (which has parallels to the role of beliefs in the practice of coaching), most learning theorists agree that all teachers hold beliefs about their work, their students, their subject matter, and their roles and responsibilities.[38] Both psychological and learning theorists generally agree that beliefs are generated through a process of enculturation and social construction with the following core aspects being relevant to coaching[39]:

- Beliefs play a key role in interpreting knowledge.
- Beliefs arise through experience.
- Beliefs vary in strength.
- The earlier a belief is incorporated, the more difficult it is to alter.
- The more central or core a belief, the more resistant to change.
- Newly acquired beliefs are most vulnerable to change.
- Beliefs provide personal meaning and assist in defining relevance.
- Beliefs strongly affect behaviour, although there is still debate as to whether beliefs influence actions or vice versa.
- Beliefs are used to selectively retrieve material from memory and to build causal explanations to create self-fulfilling prophecy.
- Individuals have a continuum of beliefs from factual to evaluative.

---

[37] Lipton (2009).
[38] Pajares (1992), p. 314.
[39] Pajares (1992), Mansour (2009), Rokeach (1960, 1968), Lai et al. (2014), Hawkes (2003).

- Highly resourceful persons are better able to control the effects of negative personal beliefs.
- Positive personal beliefs are directly related to adaptive functioning (e.g., coping effectively, managing difficulties, promoting mental health).
- Beliefs, attitudes and values organize together to form a functionally integrated cognitive system.
- Beliefs cannot be directly observed but only inferred.

In terms of igniting substantial change, beliefs offer access to the vast network of interconnected thoughts, memories, feelings and ways of knowing that exist in the non-conscious. In his transformative learning theory for adult learners, Jack Mezirow confirmed the usefulness of gaining access to these deeper levels.[40] He talked about transformative learning as a way to effect change in a person's frame of reference (worldview), which includes their "structures of assumptions"—a combination of associations, concepts, values, feelings and conditioned responses that reflect "habits of mind" and "a point of view."[41] He categorized these habits of mind as habitual ways of thinking, feeling and acting influenced by assumptions that form a set of codes (or beliefs) that may be cultural, social, educational, economic, political or psychological in origin.[42] These habits of mind become articulated into a specific point of view which then shapes a particular interpretation (of one's worldview) and which assigns causality.[43]

Mezirow believed that learners, through critical self-reflection, could examine their worldview in light of their own particular belief or value system, which included both habits of mind and meaning perspectives.[44] He found the underlying habits of mind to be more durable (harder to transform) than a person's point of view because they seemed to operate outside awareness but, through critical reflection, might be transformed.[45] He also made an interesting distinction in his levels of self-reflection between consciousness and *critical consciousness*, inferring that by becoming critically aware of how we see ourselves and our relationships we can discover the belief systems that shape the way we think.[46] This is the type of assistance that coaches can be uniquely trained to contribute.

---

[40] Mezirow (2000).
[41] Mezirow (1997).
[42] Mezirow (1997).
[43] Mezirow (2000).
[44] Kitchenham (2008).
[45] Mezirow (1997, 2000).
[46] Lundgren and Poell (2016).

Ann often uses assessments in her coaching, and one of her more practical applications is the Thomas Kilmann Conflict Mode Instrument, which presents five different modes of conflict (competing, collaborating, compromising, avoiding and accommodating). One mode is no more effective than another; it is the conflict situation that dictates which mode or combination of modes might be best used. Individuals, however, tend to have "favourite" or "default" modes, and one of the learnings is to broaden one's repertoire of skills in each of the modes and, depending on the situation, be conversant in applying the different approaches. She was coaching a CEO who scored high in collaborating and competing and very low in compromising. Because of much experience in debriefing this instrument, she was quickly aware that the client had made some unconscious judgements about the different modes. He valued the collaborative and competing modes (his top two scores) and viewed the compromising approach unfavourably (his lowest score). After discussing his different experiences in handling conflict, Ann made the distinction between one's intent going into a conflict situation and which conflict mode was actually used. The client suddenly realized that he actually used compromising extensively but didn't acknowledge it because he learned when growing up that it was a form of failure. It was better to compete or collaborate.

Beliefs and Quantum Theory

The transition phase from the scientific materialism paradigm to the unfolding holism paradigm reveals how they differ fundamentally in their beliefs about the role of consciousness and human self-determination. According to Stapp, classical physics created a material picture of human beings, promoting the idea that the physical world was composed of tiny bits of matter whose interactions controlled everything.[47] Thus a person's conscious thoughts and efforts could make no difference at all to what the body/brain did—whatever a person did was considered to be fixed by local interactions between tiny mechanical elements. This materialist conception of reality was challenged at the beginning of the twentieth century. Max Planck's discovery of the quantum of action in the mid-1920s founded a new basic physical theory developed by the physicists Heisenberg, Bohr, Pauli and Born, who brought the consciousness of the human observer into physics as an essential role.[48] The quantum theory of reality intentionally incorporated conscious human choices into the structure of physical theory.

---

[47] Stapp (2011).
[48] Stapp (2011). This became known as the Copenhagen quantum theory.

Stapp explained, "The conception of self is the basis of values and thence of behaviour, and it controls the entire fabric of one's life. It is irrational, from a scientific perspective, to cling today to false and inadequate nineteenth century concepts about your basic nature."[49] Stapp was mystified that some modern physicists want to "improve" on orthodox quantum theory by excluding "the observer"—a stance in direct opposition to what he considered to be the most "glaring failure" of classical physics: its inability to accommodate human consciousness, its very creators.[50]

Role of Self-Organization

With the breakthrough of quantum physics in the twentieth century, the core perspective of reality shifted from matter to events (actions), and the potentialities for those events to occur. The concept of self-organization emerged initially out of systems theory. It was soon adopted by physicists and researchers in the fields of complexity and chaos theory as a way to account for the spontaneous evolution of living matter from states of relative simplicity and disorder to states of relative complexity and order.[51] It was a new discovery method first applied with inanimate and physical systems but then extended to other varied contexts. Now it is considered central to the description of biological systems, with examples of self-organizing behaviour extending into natural science literature and the social sciences, such as economics and anthropology.[52]

Models of psychological systems also now incorporate the concepts of chaos, non-linear dynamics and self-organization.[53] Self-organization has been applied as a model for understanding growth, change and development in psychological systems, such as addressing why various belief systems link up with one another to create family dysfunction.[54] The dynamic nature of self-organization is what makes it attractive to practitioners and researchers in the field of human and organizational change. Self-organization, for example, can help explain sudden jumps in behaviour or chaotic behaviour (i.e., non-linear transitions in mental states). Self-organization in psychological systems

---

[49] Stapp (2011), p. 143.
[50] Stapp (2011), p. 143.
[51] Kurakin (2011).
[52] Kurakin (2011).
[53] Barton (1994).
[54] Barton (1994).

signifies a process by which a structure or pattern emerges in an open system without the direct involvement of the outside environment.[55]

Robert Dilts has combined NLP and self-organization theory to describe how people can become aware of and change their beliefs.[56] He has asserted that people naturally and spontaneously change beliefs throughout their lives.[57] In his application he described self-organization theory as a branch of systems theory that relates to the process of order formation in complex dynamic systems (e.g., humans). This process creates a new paradigm for perception and change. Self-organizing systems organize their own behaviour in relation to their environment, and beliefs can act as "attractors" which help to create and hold stable patterns within the system but which can also be "destabilized" to create a new point of balance.

Implications for Coaching

As has been pointed out, non-conscious beliefs have an effect on our actions and behaviours. Edgar Schein, former professor at MIT Sloan School of Management, noted that unconscious assumptions can distort data and the way in which individuals perceive the world, which in turn affects behaviour.[58] As an example, if we believe that people will take advantage of us, we will behave in ways that will coincide with those expectations.[59]

Chris Argyris, American business theorist and co-founder of the field of organization development, viewed humans as designers and implementers of their actions. Individuals design their diagnosis of reality and implement their actions through an internal "master programme" made up of two components: the espoused theory and the theory-in-use.[60] Individuals are able to articulate their espoused theory but rarely behave consistently with it. They are unable to articulate their theory-in-use yet consistently use it when they act. Theories-in-use have two basic components, according to Argyris.[61] First are the values that the individuals attempt to satisfy (called the "governing variables"); and second are the behavioural strategies that people use. All

---

[55] Barton (1994).
[56] Dilts (1998).
[57] Dilts (1996).
[58] Schein (1985).
[59] McGregor (1967).
[60] Argyris (1983).
[61] Argyris (1976).

behaviour is designed to satisfy as many of the governing variables as possible. These unconscious variables therefore guide behaviour.

In coaching there are always at least two internal belief systems in play—that of the coach and that of the client—both of which are heavily influenced by external systems. The internal systems are made up of conscious and nonconscious beliefs about change and reality, and they inform and influence who we are as coaches and clients. A deeper understanding of the role that beliefs play in facilitating or preventing change seems critical for transformative coaching.

While as a profession coaching is firmly based in quantum and constructivist perspectives of reality, as practitioners we might not personally embrace some of the belief systems underlying the scientific foundation of our profession. For example, what are our own theories-in-use when working with clients? How do we take into account the unseen aspects of who we are? Clearly we are strongly influenced in terms of our perception of reality and our beliefs about the capacity of humans to change and evolve.

5

Accessing the Inner Self: Knowing

A person often meets his destiny on the road he took to avoid it.
—Jean de La Fontaine

Accessing Our Inner Process

The second point of access to our vast non-conscious network is that of *knowing*, specifically *inner knowing* as it relates to supporting our clients in making substantial change. This chapter is framed from the perspective of seeing human development as adaptation, change, learning and growth, and it explores how knowledge and ways of knowing can support and/or impede this active process. We feel kinship with the somatic philosophy of Thomas Hanna, a self-proclaimed follower of pragmatism, who stated, "The goal of philosophy is not, finally, the trans human goal of eternal abstract truth, but the human goal of temporal, ongoing experiential freedom."[1]

We make a quick journey through highlights of modern and postmodern theories of knowledge and their impact on the field of coaching. Clearly the study of living organisms is a very complex area that Hanna not-so-humorously described as "a baffling tangle of theoretical, philosophical and metaphysical uncertainties—uncertainties that have haunted science since its Renaissance origins."[2] We do our best to carve a useful path through the uncertainties.

---

[1] Hanna (1986), p. 3.
[2] Hanna (1986), p. 3.

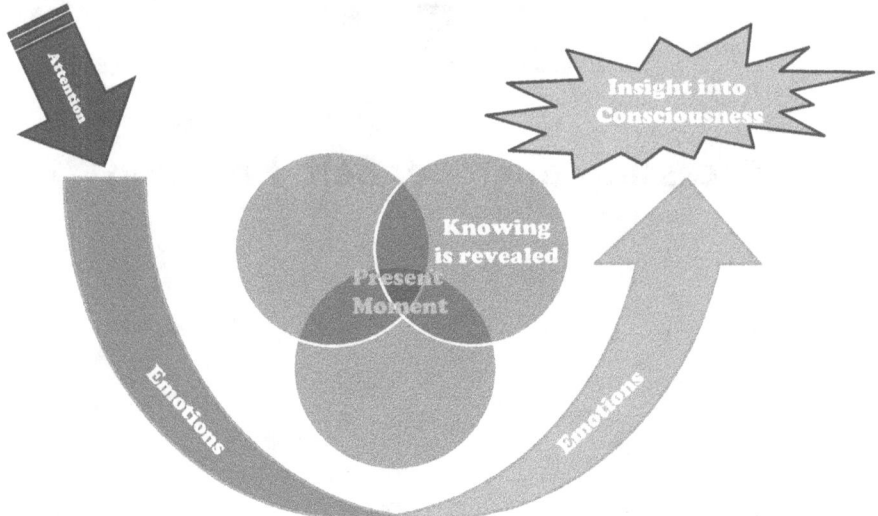

Fig. 5.1 Role of inner knowing in self-organizing

We then focus on describing the activity of *knowing*, which is of direct interest to coaches as we engage in the mutual dance of creation and understanding in our coaching conversations. Instead of seeing our clients and the process of coaching as "objects" of study, we explore ways of knowing that more genuinely reflect the interactive process and lived experience of coaching in which we are participants (Fig. 5.1).

What Is Knowledge?

We start by distinguishing the idea of knowledge from the act of knowing. Knowledge is the awareness, understanding or information obtained by experience or study that is either in a person's mind or possessed by people generally.[3] There is the everyday usage of knowledge that we are familiar with (e.g., I know it is raining outside) but also the scientific and philosophical notions of knowledge which influence us at a deep level (e.g., What is matter made of? Who am I?). As we ask ourselves questions, we naturally wonder how we come to know the things we do. To some extent it seems that what is real for us depends on how we come to know things given our perceptual, cognitive background.[4]

---

[3] Cambridge Dictionaries Online.
[4] Henriques (2013).

For example, we are born into a specific culture which has certain deeply embedded social customs and traditions. Our culture influences how we perceive and cognitively grasp the reality we are raised in. Travelling through different cultures is a great way to experience first hand how people exhibit different knowledge based on the world around them. Just asking for directions in a strange culture can bring up feelings of frustration and bewilderment as we discover that our familiar perceptions and ways of thinking are not adequate to grasp this different context—from the language barrier and confusing hand gestures to subtle styles of interaction (e.g., bowing vs. nodding, direct vs. indirect eye contact).

The Impact of Modern Theories of Knowledge on Coaching

Philosophy is one of the oldest traditions which still retains the most dominant conception of knowledge in Western society. The study of epistemology (the philosophy of knowledge) focuses on how humans know things, and ontology (the metaphysics of knowledge) focuses on the nature of reality and what can be acknowledged as really existing in the world. Historically, most theorists agree that philosophy generated science, but that in modern times they are mutually influential and closely intertwined.

Philosophy often provides justification for particular scientific theories. Why? Because philosophy characterizes knowledge as "justified true belief," meaning that whatever the representation it must be legitimized and justified by logical and empirical factors.[5] Thus the approach and practice of science (i.e., scientific method) are considered to have originated in philosophy, whose intellectual thought and rigorous reasoning continue to influence science by framing debates and bringing awareness to science's weaknesses.[6]

Paul King, a computational neuroscientist, pointed out how the objects that science has discovered over time were really there all along but were too small to see (cells, atoms, electrons), too far away to see (galaxies) or required a reorganization of available information to be able to see (genes, DNA structure).[7] He has been intrigued by the most recent example of philosophy and science working together: the close interaction of the philosophy of the mind and the scientific study of consciousness to resolve the centuries-old debate about the nature of the mind.

---

[5] Henriques (2013).
[6] King (2011).
[7] King (2011).

In the 1890s, William James, a founder of modern psychology, first legitimized the study of consciousness only to have it dismissed as a credible scientific object by the behavioural psychologists led by B. F. Skinner in the 1960s and 1970s. According to King, consciousness only began to return as a viable object of study in the 1990s due in part to Francis Crick, one of the discoverers of DNA. Crick lent his support to launch a neuroscience study of consciousness as a credible and precisely defined field of study. This has led to philosophers, psychologists and neuroscientists meeting together annually to debate approaches to explanations of what consciousness is and how the brain produces it.[8] At the same time there are parallel gatherings of philosophers and physicists debating the relationship of quantum mechanics to consciousness.[9] King has stated that he is hopeful of the result—a fresh range of viewpoints in philosophy which are informed by scientific discoveries, and more precise scientific definitions being informed by philosophical debate.[10]

This current interplay of philosophy and science in the arena of consciousness and neuroscience bestows further legitimacy to the field of coaching. More scholars and researchers are needed to discover the theoretical foundations or "bedrock" of coaching.[11] Concurrently, the efforts to inform the philosophy of coaching with scientific precision are leading practitioners to become more expert in "facilitating self-directed neuroplasticity."[12]

Impact of Postmodern Theories of Knowledge on Coaching

Historically, both Western philosophy and science have relied on two dominant approaches to acquiring knowledge: empiricism and rationalism. The distinction between the two approaches has resulted in differing perspectives of how knowledge is acquired between philosophy and science. The scientific method has been constructed primarily on empirical observation and began to separate from those philosophical traditions which were intent on building rational systems of knowledge (Table 5.1).[13]

The Age of Enlightenment, the philosophical movement which erupted in the late eighteenth century in Europe, brought an increase in empiricism,

---

[8] For example, the Association for the Study of Consciousness; Science of Consciousness conferences.
[9] For example, Topological Association of Quantum Mechanics and Consciousness.
[10] King (2011).
[11] Rock and Page (2009).
[12] Brann (2015).
[13] Henriques (2013).

Table 5.1 Distinctions between empiricism and rationalism

Empiricism	Rationalism
Knowledge is based on experience and experimentation.	Knowledge is based on the use of reason or logic.
Experimental science is the paradigm of knowledge.	Mathematics is the paradigm of knowledge.
Experience and experiment rarely, if ever, produce certainty.	Genuine knowledge is certain.
Some empiricists believe that mathematics can be certain.	Experience does not produce certainty and does not conform to reason. Thus experience is at best second-class knowledge.

scientific rigour, reductionism and questioning of religious orthodoxy.[14] This awakening ushered in the "modern" era of scientific method, that of scientific materialism, whose models of the world were conceived to accurately describe ontology (how the world is) in a way that was separate from subjective impressions.[15]

The Western world considered the scientific method to have made a significant contribution to how knowledge of the physical world and its phenomena are acquired. It was taken for granted that knowledge could only be possessed by humans. Even the idea of systematically studying the unconscious as a knowledge domain was disregarded until Freud's recognition that it held thinking processes hidden from awareness.[16]

Only recently has that "weakness" of science been amended to include the fact that conscious human minds are not the only "self-organized compilers of knowledge"; there are also biological systems, such as the immune system and the DNA of the genetic code that are purveyors of knowledge, according to physicist Robert Traill.[17] He has proposed that the basic physical element of thought dynamics is likely some kind of string-like coding and that synaptic mechanisms between nerve cells could be the basic elements of thought and cognition.[18] He has argued for extending the limited philosopher's view of knowledge to incorporate at least four different knowledge-gathering domains: the brain of the individual; scientific method as the "brain" of society; DNA

---

[14] Gay (1996).
[15] Henriques (2013).
[16] Traill (2008).
[17] Traill (2008).
[18] Traill (2008).

Fig. 5.2 Blatz Beer advertisement

and genetics as the "brain" of species survival; and the immune system as the intelligence of the body's defence system.[19]

The postmodern era has clarified for us how "science can only be a process of understanding our world and ourselves, rather than a fixed set of rules for all time."[20] With the rise of new scientific paradigms and philosophies, such as social constructionism, the idea that knowledge is an "objective map of one true reality" has been challenged.[21] Instead the postmodern view of reality is inherently contextual, partly based on the way our minds are organized and build perceptions, and partly due to how societies and cultures legitimize ideas within specific historical and political eras that cannot be separated from knowledge.[22] Figs. 5.2 and 5.3 show two vintage advertisements which appeared in the USA in the early twentieth century that would be considered highly inappropriate and even shocking to today's young parents. It appears that much of our reality is socially constructed for us and we either consciously or unwittingly participate in legitimizing it.

The influence of the postmodern philosophy of knowledge on coaching cannot be overstated. Rock and Page have pointed out that "coaching must tackle the question of what it means to be human."[23] We believe this necessarily involves an expanded science and philosophy of knowledge and knowing

---

[19] Traill (2008), p. 12.
[20] McTaggart (2002), p. xix.
[21] Henriques (2013).
[22] Henriques (2013).
[23] Rock and Page (2009), p. 54.

Fig. 5.3 Iver Johnson Revolvers advertisement

that can provide a theoretical foundation in the field of coaching for what Rock and Page have discerned as "a shift in emphasis from individualism to community and context."[24]

Somatic Knowledge and Coaching

We conclude this section with a brief exploration of somatic knowledge, which, according to Hanna (inventor of the somatic term in the 1970s) was the "unavoidable" next step of philosophy: the creation of a philosophy of change, adaptation, evolution, growth, learning, self-control, autonomy and hence freedom.[25] Somatics encompasses systems of study that view physical reality and specific bodily, and even cellular, awareness as sources of knowledge that can be accessed through touch, movement, imagery and embodiment.[26] Also included in this field is social somatic theory, which applies a broader definition of somatic knowledge beyond just inner experience to encompass the ways in which our inner experiences are sociocultural constructions. Don Hanlon Johnson, another founder of somatics, asserted that our bodies and bodily experiences are shaped by our background, experiences, history and sociocultural habits.[27]

---

[24] Rock and Page (2009), p. 54.
[25] Hanna (1986, 1991).
[26] Eddy (2000).
[27] Johnson (1992).

It is an interesting postmodern domain of knowledge for the field of coaching. Somatics is considered to be a life science based on what is active, changing and unpredictable over time. It describes the functions of human organisms, those which involve movement and change through time; and it describes the structures of human organisms, those which are stable and fixed in space.[28] These are complementary stances of observation that one can take regarding human change (i.e., both/and instead of either/or) which transcend the mind–body dualism of pre-quantum modern science. For Hanna, somatic study envisioned the body as an embodied process of internal awareness and communication (inner experience), not as an objective entity or mechanical instrument.[29]

What Is Knowing?

As coaches and clients, we have already accumulated large stores of knowledge over our lifetime, some of which we are consciously aware of and some of which form part of our non-conscious assumptions about the world around us. There is a key connection between the knowledge we acquire, and therefore believe, and how greatly it is influenced by the scientific, political, social, cultural and historical times we live in. How we acquire that knowledge—our ways of knowing—are of significance to us in the coaching profession because we are often unaware of how much we can influence or impact the delivery of new or reframed knowledge to our coaching clients.

As we expand our concept of what constitutes legitimate knowledge, we also need to broaden our understanding and acceptance of the many ways in which we "know" something. For example, having an insight or an *aha* moment is an event in which we participate but also an inner process which we experience. In addition, such ways of knowing are covert to us in that they arise unbidden or reveal themselves without a conscious summoning. How do we categorize that kind of knowing? All humans experience insight or *aha* moments. Still, there is no commonly accepted scientific explanation for what occurs. Traditional science, limited by its focus on phenomena only as objects of study from an external observer perspective, cannot account for unconscious forces at work. Postmodern quantum science, dynamic patterns of self-organization, phenomenology and constructivist theory, however, are better able to accommodate phenomena such as insights by describing them in terms of action, interaction, process, event and participation.

---

[28] Hanna (1976).
[29] Green (2002).

Tacit Knowing

Knowledge is something we acquire, but knowing is a function of our inner senses, including intelligence, emotions, body and even spirit. One of the first modern scientists to formally describe a different kind of knowing was chemist and philosopher Michael Polanyi, who developed his tacit knowledge concept in the 1950s and 1960s.[30] He recognized the importance of a personal, embodied kind of knowledge which he believed was where creative acts, especially acts of discovery, were imbued with strong personal feelings and commitments.[31] He argued that informed guesses, hunches and imaginings were all internal exploratory acts and that such *tacit knowing* comprised a range of conceptual and sensory information and images that could be used to make sense of things. He began to acknowledge the place of intuition in knowledge and informal education practice.[32] He believed that much of human discovery was the product of the integration of conscious and unconscious knowing which relies substantially on personal knowledge as opposed to formalized rules and propositions.[33] His notion of tacit knowing helped to contribute to a generation of new understandings and social/scientific discovery, especially relevant to educators.[34] He also had his detractors, who argued that tacit knowledge prohibited the advancement of artificial intelligence.[35]

Phenomenological Knowing

The science of phenomenology has a deep and rich history in studying the flow of consciousness within the context of accepting the reality of the outside world. Henri Bergson, a major French philosopher who was influential in the first part of the twentieth century, published his concept of duration, or *duree*, and posed a subjective mode of knowing that was for him the primary vehicle to intuition, which he considered to be the ultimate basis of knowing.[36] Like Bergson, William James developed a dynamic psychology of consciousness around the turn of the twentieth century based on a similar sense of inner duration or stream of thought that was holistic in how it incorporated tem-

---

[30] Polanyi (1958/1998).
[31] Smith (2003).
[32] Smith (2003).
[33] London School of Economics and Political Science (n.d.).
[34] Smith (2003).
[35] Fodor (1981).
[36] Bergson (1922/1965).

porality, reasoning and thinking *inside* the flow of consciousness.[37] He considered his notion of inner duration to be an alternative mode of knowing to that of scientific reasoning. James posited two ways of knowing things: knowing them immediately or intuitively and knowing them conceptually or representatively.[38] He believed that to know immediately (or intuitively), the mind and the object were one in that experience (i.e., non-dualistic). He used the example of looking at a piece of white paper in which the paper and the mind are actually two names given later to the one experience.

Philosopher Edmund Husserl, who established phenomenology in the early twentieth century, was influenced by James and made his life work the science of experience itself.[39] He focused on understanding a person's *lifeworld* or lived existence, which included time, intention and two different horizons of human experience: inner horizons, focused on intangible, elusive ideas, notions and fantasies considered to be a part of oneself; and outer horizons, focused on real objects in the outer world.[40] For Husserl, this lifeworld incorporated memory and expectation in the present moment, like listening to a melody where one actually only hears one note at a time. Consciousness, however, holds the previous notes in memory and anticipates the future notes because of a familiarity with the medium of music. In other words, the sensation of duration is being constructed of the raw material of memory, perception and expectation.

A philosopher and former student of Husserl, Martin Heidegger went beyond the intentional consciousness of his master to search for something more fundamental—an ontological concept of authentic human existence.[41] He broadened the notion of phenomenology to something more essential—understanding the meaning of being itself. Heidegger recognized that before anything else, such as knowledge, event or thing, the world existed, and his philosophy was concerned with the basic condition of existence he called "Being", the primordial condition or "ground" through which everything else comes into existence.[42] For Heidegger the meaning of Being was contextual and grounded in possibility. He gave the name *Dasein* to human Being, which can be interpreted as "being-there" and figuratively as meaning "the clearing in which beings can be manifest" in time.[43] Heidegger was concerned with the

---

[37] James (1890/1950).
[38] McDermott (1966).
[39] Husserl (1928/1964).
[40] Wagner (1983).
[41] Heidegger (1962).
[42] LeMay and Pitts (1994).
[43] Zimmerman (1981).

experience of being human in all its wholeness and he believed that humans are completely shaped by their culture so that no one is truly autonomous of culture. While there can be no existing without a world to exist in, he also believed in being responsible for one's own authentic existence. This meant reaching beyond just thinking, to opening up to all that one can authentically be. For Heidegger, Being was transcendent and beyond the control of humans. His mature concept of authenticity was compared to the Zen Buddhist idea of enlightenment.[44]

Of interest to coaching in Heidegger's work is shifting to a deeper knowing in which we can observe our lived experience (both coach and client) not as an "object" to be analysed but rather as phenomena that arise from "nowhere" through thoughts, feelings, perceptions, memories and projections which continually appear and disappear (e.g., a feeling appears, then disappears; a thought comes up, then fades away).[45] Thus life is a happening in which a revealing and bringing to light occurs not through rational thinking but through an appearance from a source beyond the control of conscious human thought. Heidegger suggests to us a broader perspective of knowing—that it is an experience or event that comes through us.

Enactive Knowing

Another interesting perspective on knowing comes from learning theory, primarily based on the work of cognitive psychologist Jerome Bruner in the 1960s and 1970s. In researching the cognitive development of children, he proposed three modes of representation or ways in which information or knowledge are stored and encoded in memory: enactive, 0–1 years (action-based); iconic, 1–6 years (image-based); and symbolic, 7 years up (language-based).[46] Enactive information is encoded first and stored in the memory, such as in the form of muscle memory when a baby shakes a rattle. Iconic information is stored visually as a mental picture in the mind. Symbolic information is stored as a code or symbol, like language, and is the most adaptable form. As adults, humans can perform many types of motor task (typing, sewing, operating machinery) that they would find difficult to describe in iconic (picture) or symbolic (word) form.[47] The purpose of education for Bruner was to facilitate thinking and problem-solving skills, not to impart knowledge.

---

[44] Zimmerman (1981).
[45] Zimmerman (1981).
[46] Bruner (1966).
[47] McLeod (2008).

He believed that students were active learners who constructed their own knowledge.

Bruner's model has been developed into an enactive approach to learning that encompasses the interaction between autonomous agents and their environments.[48] It is considered more natural than other forms of knowing because it is experiential (doing) and cultural (occurs in a context), and it is based on active participation—knowing by doing and by living rather than by thinking.[49] The enactive approach in cognitive psychology was further legitimized when Varela, Thompson and Rosch published their book, *The Embodied Mind: Cognitive Science and Human Experience*, in 1992. They argued that cognitive activity takes place not in a vacuum but in a world where someone (an autonomous agent) is trying to get something done (go to work, make a cup of coffee, write a book). In other words, there is an essential relationship with the experience of the individual and the meaningfulness of that experience; it isn't abstract thinking but really means something and feels like something.[50]

Cognitive psychologist Marek McGann has stated that enactive learning has implications for some of the studies that cognitive scientists often take for granted. He has noted that the typical assumption in cognitive psychology experiments is that subjects are essentially the same and act/react similarly in all situations. An enactive view, however, "sees the person as a tangle of skills and motivations which will be in a more or less unique combination in a given individual," and these individual differences need to be taken into account.[51]

In doing our literature review for this book, we read numerous articles on cognitive problem-solving experiments to induce *aha* moments of discovery in laboratory-type settings. From these experiments, researchers were viewing the phenomenon (*aha* moment) as an object to be studied, reduced and explained. We were struck by how different this experimental approach was to the moments of discovery that we experienced with our clients in real time in real-life contexts. Extensive research on enactive knowing and enactive interfaces can be found at the Enactive Network of Excellence, a European Community research project established in 2004 for the purpose of creating a new generation of human–computer interfaces.

---

[48] McGann (n.d.).
[49] Slee, Campbell and Spears (2012).
[50] McGann (n.d.).
[51] McGann (n.d.).

Transpersonal Knowing

Transpersonal psychology theorists have suggested that Western conceptions of culture and consciousness are in a time of transition and that one of the most fundamental of human activities is undergoing change: our understanding of "knowing."[52] The ways in which something comes to be known are now being questioned, as are the methodologies of modern science. In the postmodern era, "knowing has been greatly humbled by its self-acknowledged limits," and human consciousness appears to be transitioning through a significant knowledge shift in which "knowing is becoming increasingly aware of its own processes."[53] In their book *Transpersonal Knowing*, editors Tobin Hart, Peter Nelson and Kaisa Puhakka argued not only for multiple perspectives on knowing but also for multiple modes of knowing as we become more self-aware of these experiences. They suggested that certain basic themes seem to emerge in describing "authentic knowing": it is one's own knowing; there is immediacy with little to no conceptual mediation; a sense of connectedness dissolves boundaries and separateness from others; and transformative capacity arises as the knower is changed by the knowing while at the same time openness to change in one's sense of identity further opens a person to the knowing.[54]

Kaisa Puhakka has identified experiences of spiritual direct knowing not as altered states but rather as acts that can occur in various states, altered or ordinary, and which are actually a way of being. She has suggested that knowing is not a state of consciousness but an activity of awareness that is able to bring about shifts and integrate different states of consciousness.[55] She described knowing as "a moment of awareness in which contact occurs between the knower and the known," and which "is nonconceptual, nonimaginal, nondiscursive, and often extremely brief."[56] Such knowing connects and integrates experience across contexts, is often subtle, has presence, and may be accompanied or followed by mental images and thoughts. She also described the contact involved in direct knowing as the subject *becoming* the object (embodiment) as opposed to the scientific perspective of the subject *viewing* the object.

---

[52] Hart, Nelson and Puhakka (2000).
[53] Hart et al. (2000), p. 1.
[54] Hart et al. (2000), p. 5.
[55] Puhakka in Hart et al. (2000), pp. 12–13.
[56] Puhakka in Hart et al. (2000), p. 15.

Jorge Ferrer, faculty in the department of East-West Psychology at the California Institute of Integral Studies, has argued for a more pluralistic and participative perspective on transpersonal psychology integrating many levels (neuroscientific, cognitive and neuropsychological, psychodynamic and spiritual/mystical) in an approach to understanding the mind and process of transformation.[57] He has noted how modern Western education emphasizes developing rational and intellectual powers, with little attention being paid to learning other ways of knowing that include somatic, emotional, aesthetic, intuitive and spiritual intelligences.[58] He proposed that transpersonal phenomena are participatory and co-creative events that occur not just individually but also in relationship or community. He regarded humans "as vehicles for the creative self-unfolding of reality and the enaction (or 'bringing forth') of directly knowable spiritual worlds, realms, or domains of distinctions."[59]

Tobin Hart has focused on the concept of "interiority and education," noting that the greater the complexity and demands of the outer world, the greater the need for internal discernment, attention to values and ability to be present in the midst of streaming information. Developing *interiority* is a kind of internal spaciousness and depth to help us meet and take in the world we live in.[60] He supports an approach to knowing that involves looking not only at what he calls "outer data" but also closely into oneself—*knowledge by presence*.[61] According to Hart, knowledge by presence cultivates an interior life for navigating the complexities of life with wisdom, virtue and meaning.

The Bandwidth of Knowing

Have you ever had a time in your life when you found yourself doing something that you hadn't consciously intended? A time when something within you compelled you to take a certain action. Ann had an experience like that when backpacking in Europe in the mid-1970s. She was hitching a ride with a group of New Zealanders from Greece to Munich where she was going to find work and study German. The Volkswagen bus stopped in a parking lot in Vienna so that everyone could get out and stretch. She opened the rear door, stepped out and looked around. Suddenly she found herself saying to the others that she was going to stay

---

[57] Ferrer (2014).
[58] Ferrer (2014), p. 163.
[59] Ferrer (2014), p. 168.
[60] Hart (2007).
[61] Hart (2007), p. 1.

in Vienna and find a job. Her companions looked at her with a combination of puzzlement and astonishment. "We thought you were going to Munich with us? What are you talking about?" She again found herself saying with an even greater sense of certainty that, no, she was now going to stay in Vienna. She didn't know anyone in Vienna and up to that moment it had never crossed her mind to live in Austria. But stay she did, and as a result of that synchronous moment it set her on a path that changed the course of her life, from meeting the fellow American she eventually married (and still lives with in Montana) to establishing a new career for herself. It was an event of such powerful "inner knowing" that she followed it without conscious awareness.

That event, besides being a great story to tell at parties over the years, remained with Ann as an inexplicable, strange moment of deep connection. It was not until her research into pivotal moments years later that she encountered a written description by an author who narrated a personal event that had great similarity. In her book *Extraordinary Knowing*, psychoanalyst and researcher Elizabeth Lloyd Mayer wrote about "a strange dissociated moment" she had in looking for a gold watch that her husband had given her sister and which had gone missing.[62] She and her sister spent a few hours searching the house with no luck when Mayer found herself experiencing something she never had before. She walked into her husband's study "deliberately, intentionally, but with no awareness of volition on my part ... as though I was watching myself in a slow-motion film."[63] As she tells it, she walked straight to a closet in the corner of the room, bent down and reached in behind a row of shoes and boxes and pulled out a small leather case at the very back. When she looked inside she found the watch. At the time she couldn't find the words to explain to her sister how she had known it was there. Later her husband told her that he had found the watch in the bathroom and to teach her sister a lesson in responsibility had hidden it in his closet. Mayer described the strange experience: "I didn't *decide* to walk into my husband's study ... it feels more like I was *being* walked ... walked, somehow, by the experience."[64]

Ann was astounded to read this account because it described how she experienced that moment in the parking lot in Vienna. She didn't consciously decide to stay in Vienna but rather it seemed to be decided for her at some deeper level, which she then (apparently) completely trusted. She always knew it was some type of inner knowing guiding her, but without a scientific

---

[62] Mayer (2007).
[63] Mayer (2007), p. 58.
[64] Mayer (2007), p. 59.

explanation she categorized it as "that time something profound happened" and so placed it beyond the need to be figured out. Of course, it was not until years later, when living with her husband in Montana (where she had never imagined she would ever live), that she realized the true significance of that moment of knowing.

Inner Knowing as Frequency

We propose that inner knowing, being a different kind of knowing from the rational, relies on different, subtler signals to be detected and/or accessed. Mayer has pointed out that in order to account for these different kinds of data, science needs to take *feelings* into account—those gut feelings that tell us something has happened, those unique dissociative jolts or shock of body, emotion and idea erupting into consciousness in a way that feels completely different from ordinary knowing.[65] She observed that the feeling of what happens *is* part of the data. She used the analogy of seeing with "daytime" eyes versus "nighttime" eyes, two different ways of seeing and perceiving. Mayer has proposed that scientific models that explain what happens when we see with daytime eyes aren't able to explain what happens when we see with nighttime eyes.[66]

As a psychoanalyst, she had witnessed many patients having moments of insight that seemed to change everything for them. Yet the experience was paradoxical as well, according to Mayer, because most people experiencing an insight also felt a sense of *"I knew this—it's deeply familiar—I knew it all along."*[67] She described it as knowing something in a new way when it joins consciousness—that is, consciousness changes things. She offered an explanation that matched our experiences, both personally and professionally: humans shift between inner knowing and rational cognitive knowing according to different sets of figure–ground configurations.[68]

In Chapter 4 we carried out the Gestalt activity of shifting perceptions between figure and ground (seeing the old/young woman). The same principle can be applied to ways of knowing. Mayer has concluded, "The perceptions that characterize potentially anomalous experience appear to emerge from a state of mind that is, in the moment of perception, radically incompatible with the state of mind in which perceptions characterizing rational thought

---

[65] Mayer (2007).
[66] Mayer (2007).
[67] Mayer (2007), p. 116.
[68] Mayer (2007).

are possible."⁶⁹ This is the analogy of the daytime versus nighttime eyes. The paradoxical sense of familiarity that occurs with an insight is the result of a knowing at the non conscious level rising to the conscious level. The figure–ground shift explanation also matches the two ways of knowing proposed by William James:⁷⁰ knowing things immediately or intuitively and knowing things conceptually or representatively. James believed that, in knowing things immediately or intuitively, the mind and the object became one in that experience as opposed to the observer–observed configuration of conceptual knowing.

Mayer also pointed out that there may be a sense of loss when one switches from one mode of knowing to another. It's a giving up of "our habitual grounding in rational thought to see something else, even just for a moment—that's anything but easy for most of us."⁷¹ Like with the old/young woman visual, we cannot engage in both kinds of knowing at the same time but rather shift out of one to pick up the other. Intuition author Laura Day described this type of knowing or intuition as a non-linear process of gaining information which does not rely on senses, memory, experience, feelings or thoughts. It is another state of consciousness that just requires a slight shift in attention in order to access different information.⁷²

Here are seven types of inner knowing that we have discerned from the literature and our research learnings and experience. These are different "frequencies" that we can tune in to as we become alert and aware of more subtle ways of picking up information (or begin using nighttime eyes to see differently):

1. *Expert intuition and tacit knowledge*: intuition that draws on prior learning, experience and expertise; previous analyses frozen into habit or degrees of automaticity;
2. *Instinct*: reflexive responses for survival; premonitions, hunches;
3. *Creative intuition*: when knowledge and inner knowing are combined in novel ways to create insight;
4. *Social intuition*: rapid and automatic evaluation of other people's cognitive and affective state; empathic perception and judgement;
5. *Somatic knowing*: deep empathy or clairsentience; knowing arriving through a feeling, a sense or an image;

---

⁶⁹ Mayer (2007), p. 137.
⁷⁰ McDermott (1966).
⁷¹ Mayer (2007), p. 138.
⁷² Day (1996).

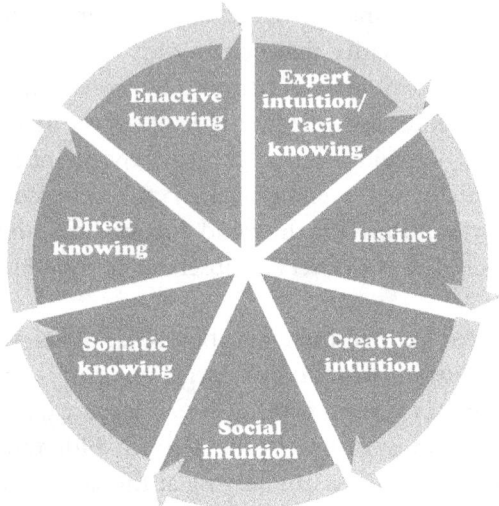

Fig. 5.4 Seven types of inner knowing

6. *Direct knowing*: understanding without use of conscious awareness or rational thinking; holistic and associative; spiritual knowing and awareness; paranormal, may include: clairvoyance, clairaudience, telepathy, precognition or embodiment;
7. *Enactive knowing*: actively constructing knowledge through a direct interface with the environment; experiential learning in a specific context; knowing by doing and living (Fig. 5.4).

Implications for Coaching

For those of us who have experienced some or all of the ways of knowing described above, we are often reluctant to share these stories or strategies. Mayer called this reluctance the "underlying cultural disinclination" to publicly acknowledge highly subjective or personal experiences that seem rationally indefensible.[73] In the exploration of philosophical and scientific theories of knowledge in this chapter, however, we have seen substantial support for accepting an openness and legitimacy towards different modes of knowing. As Mayer pointed out, these experiences of knowing *are* empirical data which,

---

[73] Mayer (2007), p. 25.

while they may feel chaotic and difficult to review, are what we have to work with; the challenge is to begin making scientific sense out of them.[74]

As coaches, therefore, we can learn to distinguish between knowledge acquired as an object (i.e., often programmed in the non conscious, externally derived) and the action of knowing, an internal constructive process that enables access to more authentic ways of being and taking action. When engaged in the process of coaching, we "live" more in the active process of exchanging levels of knowing and awareness with our clients; we are working in real time, in the present moment. If we listen/sense/feel closely, we can often detect when a client is focused on knowledge about themselves because it will be pattern-like, often from the past, and usually self-limiting. When we help them to shift out of this set knowledge about themselves to a focus on knowing themselves, they can experience a substantial shift.

We encourage coaches to reflect on the modes of knowing with an open mind; the majority of them are experiences that are innately human and that most of us have some familiarity with. We believe that coaching is a potent vehicle for helping others to recognize, listen for and attune to their inner knowing. What greater service can we render as coaches than to help our clients become more aware and adept at following their own inner guidance?

---

[74] Mayer (2007), p. 38.

6

Accessing the Inner Self: Memory

It is perfectly true, as philosophers say, that life must be understood backwards. But they forget the other proposition, that it must be lived forwards.
—Søren Kiekegaard

Accessing Our Inner Process

In terms of our consciousness, we don't exist without memory. It is the holder of who we are in the present. Memory is a crucial linchpin between our beliefs and ways of knowing. Our beliefs are lodged in memory but we often do not have direct access to what they are and why they motivate us. Likewise, we have large stores of knowledge in memory, some of which we are aware of and some of which form non-conscious assumptions about the world around us.

Yet consciousness relies on the capacity of memory to make links between our past, present and future selves. Our perceptions are funnelled by information laid down in the past, and our thinking relies on the short-term and long-term storage of information. Our memories are mental constructions that bring our lives into the present moment for review and consideration. Memories contribute to shaping our personality and character, and our social interactions. We take our memory abilities for granted until they do not function in some way—we can't find our keys or we forget an important appointment.

In coaching, our clients are a mysterious interplay of their beliefs (covert and overt), their capacity and openness for knowing more about themselves, and their construction of memories of who they think they are. Patterns

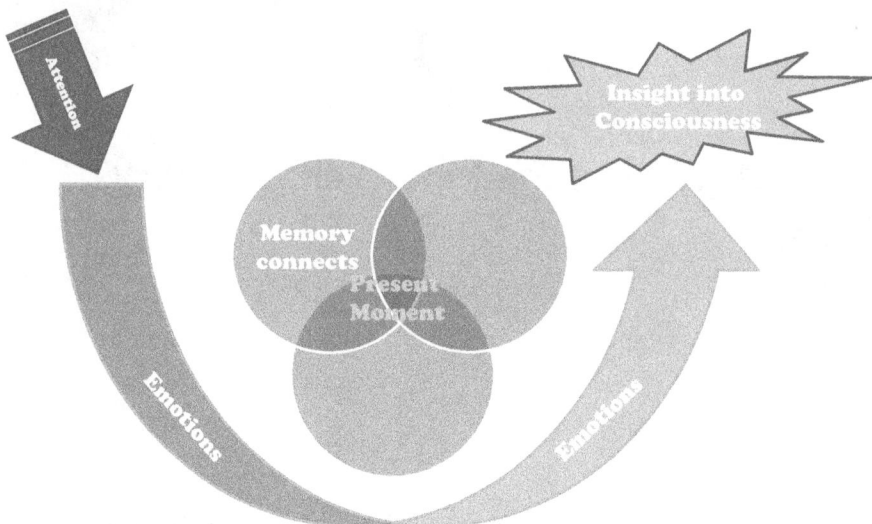

Fig. 6.1 Role of memory in self-organizing

abound, and we as coaches often play pivotal roles in helping our clients free themselves from their limited self-perceptions anchored in memory. In this chapter we explore fascinating new insights into what memory is, where it "resides" and what role it plays in supporting clients towards substantial change (Fig. 6.1).

The Predominant View of Memory

The study of memory has been of interest to philosophers, natural scientists, psychologists, biologists, neurologists, neuroscientists and learning theorists from ancient times to our postmodern era. In his textbook *Human Memory*, psychologist Gabriel Radvansky outlined a brief history of memory research beginning with Plato's thoughts as a rationalist philosopher describing memory as a bridge between the perceptual world and the rational world of idealized abstractions.[1] Aristotle's significant contribution was viewing memories as primarily composed of associations between various stimuli or experiences. In medieval times, St. Augustine looked at memory in a way that is similar to modern times. Charles Darwin in the late nineteenth century influenced sci-

---

[1] Radvansky (2016).

entific thinking about human memory with his notion that it has developed through evolution to capture major characteristics of the environment and to perform specific tasks.

At the turn of the twentieth century, early memory researchers in psychology, especially Hermann Ebbinghaus, engaged in detailed studies of memory. He used himself as both experimenter and subject, focusing on nonsense syllables to study memory in as pure a manner as possible. His research went on to greatly influence the study of memory for many years.[2] William James at the turn of the twentieth century articulated a distinction between primary and secondary memory, which closely parallels the difference between the modern-day understanding of short-term and long-term memory. Another major figure was Sir Fredrick Bartlett who, during the first half of the twentieth century, focused on how prior knowledge influences memory. Radvansky noted different movements in psychology. For example, Gestalt psychology emphasized memory as a whole being different from the sum of its parts. Behaviourism focused on conditioning and its impact on learning and memory.

Recent discoveries have drastically changed some traditional notions of how memories are made and retrieved. The predominant historical view of memory has been that of a singular concept: a more or less stable depiction of past events that a person possessed. Long-term memory was once thought to be formed, stored and retrieved in a singular, linear process. Memory was thought to be persistent through a lifetime. An event occurred, was experienced and was then recorded as a memory trace to be retrieved when summoned—as if it were a possession or were stored in a box in the mind. The past went away and life continued. The memory process was considered to be simple and straightforward.[3]

Psychologist Daniel Schacter, a pioneer in the field of memory, wrote that we tend to think of memories as we do pictures in a family album—that if we stored them properly, we could retrieve them in the same condition as when they were put away. He explained, however, that we do not record our experiences in the way that a camera does. Instead we extract key elements from our experiences, store them and then recreate or reconstruct them, sometimes adding feelings, beliefs or knowledge that we have gained since.[4]

---

[2] Radvansky (2016).
[3] See Tulving (2002), Nadel and Land (2000), Alberini and LeDoux (2013), Miller and Matzel (2000), Fernyhough (2012).
[4] Schacter (2001).

Research studies now show how complex memory actually is, and new theories are being proposed and debated to explain how memory works neurologically. This scientific process of achieving a deeper understanding of memory has not been without challenge. Endel Tulving, an eminent scholar and researcher in the field, admitted how his 1985 publication *Elements of Episodic Memory*[5] caused a controversy in the field when he proposed two types of memory (episodic and semantic) as two functionally different memory systems. Critics at the time considered the idea of episodic memory (unique memory of a specific event) to be vague and they claimed that it violated science's law of parsimony. Other critics believed that he was making up imaginary memory systems to account for facts and phenomena. Yet others did not like his apparent "metaphysics of identifying hidden systems."[6] Interestingly, Tulving noted that the suggestion for distinguishing between these two memories came well before him when, in 1958, J. M. Nielsen, a neurologist at University of California, Los Angeles, observed what he called two different pathways of memory: one centring on the person and the other on knowledge acquired by study.[7] Today the distinction between semantic (memory of common knowledge, not personal) and episodic memory is commonly accepted.

While it may seem "intuitive" that memory is a singular construct, research over the years has demonstrated that memory is multifaceted and complex. Generally stated, it is the record of experience that is represented in the brain, and multiple forms of memory support distinct brain systems.[8] Ways of mapping specific memory networks are characterized by whether they last for a short (*working memory*) or long period, whether they involve unique experiences (*episodic*) or accumulated knowledge (*semantic*), and whether memory is expressed *explicitly* through conscious remembering or *implicitly* by acquiring skills and habits without conscious recollection and making non-conscious associations.[9] And there is also emotional or affective memory response. Knowing more about these aspects of memory and their impact on thought, behaviour and emotion is certainly germane to the coaching process.

---

[5] Tulving (1985).
[6] Tulving (2002), p. 9.
[7] Nielsen (1958).
[8] Eichenbaum (2008).
[9] Eichenbaum (2008).

Memory: Conscious or Unconscious?

Is memory conscious or unconscious? The answer is both, and the distinction is a major one to remember (no pun intended) about memory. At one time, memory was seen as the process of bringing thoughts into consciousness.[10] Memory researchers assumed that thoughts could only influence action to the extent that they were perceived, registered, consciously processed, sent to long-term memory and then retrieved into short-term memory—that is, consciousness. Things have changed, however, and cognitive scientists today believe that memory involves two systems: conscious (explicit) and unconscious (implicit). The conscious level of memory is called explicit or declarative memory and describes those contents of memory that are accessible to consciousness, including autobiographical memories, both episodic and semantic. These memories can easily be verbalized. Implicit memory is non conscious and often involves memories about procedures and conditioned emotions. It is also referred to as non-declarative memory because we are unable to verbally declare these memories. Priming and implicit memory are bedmates.

A major breakthrough in understanding these two memory systems and their underlying brain mechanisms resulted from the study of a patient, Henry Molaison (1926–2008), known in the literature until his death as H. M. In 1953, Molaison had drastic experimental surgery for epilepsy in which his medial temporal lobe was removed. His seizures diminished but the operation left him with severe amnesia, as a result of which he could only remember a limited amount of information for a short time (up to a few minutes).[11] Despite the explicit (declarative) memory loss, Molaison retained forms of implicit memory, such as being able to learn new procedural skills (writing words upside down and backwards). He also continued to make new associations with emotion. Following a visit to his mother in hospital, of which later he had no memory, he was able to express a vague idea that something had happened to her.[12] Here was evidence that despite the loss of access to conscious memory, Molaison retained access to his non conscious memory.

Explicit memory is home to those memories that we are able to recall consciously, whereas implicit memories, being part of the non conscious, can only be observed or inferred from behaviour.[13] Both explicit and implicit memories

---

[10] Westen (1999).
[11] Eichenbaum (2008).
[12] Westen (1999).
[13] Westen (1999).

play a role in impacting our thoughts and behaviours. For our purposes, we look at the major components of memory which we find relevant for a coach to understand.

Procedural Memory: The Storehouse Model

Procedural memory is an aspect of non conscious (implicit) memory and its function is to hold the memory of how to do things, such as how to drive a car, swing a golf club or play a piece on the piano. Psychologist Stan Klein observed, "We are all much more expert unconsciously than consciously, because expertise implies automatization of processes that once required conscious attention."[14] Thus procedural memory, like much of the implicit memory function, is usually much faster than conscious retrieval. For example, people can type faster than they can make meaning of a passage, and they can play measures of music faster than they can interpret them.[15] Interestingly, in trying to bring this type of memory into consciousness (i.e., making it explicit), concentrating on each step of a process actually disrupts the ability to carry out the action.

Consider how Tiger Woods consciously changed his golf swing in 1997 as described by Butch Harmon, one of the USA's best golf-teaching professionals.[16] After winning the Masters Golf Tournament that year, Woods insisted on overhauling his entire swing to become more consistent and versatile. Despite Harmon's advice to make one small swing change at a time, Woods wanted to do it all at once. Harmon pointed out that it took Woods most of 1998 before he saw the results he wanted. Harmon said it took trust that it was the right decision and a lot of hard work on Woods' part. However, Woods' commitment paid off and he had a huge year in 1999. An important note about procedural memory is that when clients learn new behaviours, things will get worse for them before they get better. This is otherwise known as the "learning edge."

Training has often been defined as learning a new skill which uses procedural memory. It was once believed that the brain was a storehouse of images of the movements involved in a procedure. Thus each movement created a trace memory, which was then recalled for each succeeding movement, and which controlled the latter movement. This explanation was discarded as

---

[14] Weston (1999), p. 1097.
[15] Westen (1999).
[16] Harmon and Yokam (2009).

scientists came to understand that the storehouse notion of the brain was unwieldy, and it also demanded that each subsequent movement be exactly like the preceding one. It was not able to account for each movement in, say, pedalling a bike, when a person is producing something new, never repeating the same movement because of the changes in circumstances. The rote, imaging notion of procedural memory was discarded in favour of a theory of construction rather than reproduction.[17] The notion that memory is not simply a filing cabinet or computer storage of events is relevant to coaching, as will be seen when we discuss episodic memory (unique memory of a specific event) in the next section.

Memory has the amazing capacity to store and retrieve information whether after seconds or years. This ability is essential to daily life. We don't have to relearn each day how to prepare a meal for ourselves or find directions for getting to work. Memory, although closely linked to learning, is not the same process. For example, the muscle memory of learning a task, such as riding a bike, is understood as a product of learning; remembering a string of memorized numbers can be considered a learned response. "Few would argue with the idea that one can learn to remember or that one remembers what is learned."[18] However, learning is considered a process of acquiring new information, while memory is retaining information over a delay.[19] Biologists Jeffrey Stock and Sherry Zhang have reported that learning and memory are actually molecularly different processes.[20]

Remembering Our Lives

How often have you been driving along only to realize that you have no memory of what's happened in the past few minutes? Whatever you experienced was absorbed into some part of your brain separate from your conscious awareness. What about all the times you've encountered someone who looked familiar but without a context you couldn't remember who they were or how you knew them? These experiences embody the ebb and flow we continually engage in between consciousness and unconsciousness. Memory and consciousness are inextricably linked.

---

[17] Bartlett (1932/1995).
[18] Stock and Zhang (2013).
[19] Crystal and Glanzman (2013).
[20] Stock and Zhang (2013).

Our understanding of memory has evolved since Tulving's seminal work in the 1980s.[21] The field has moved beyond looking at memory as types to be linearly classified according to past, present or future, or even by what is being remembered. Episodic memory is now described as a neurocognitive (brain/mind) system which is unique among memory systems in that it enables humans to remember past experiences.[22] Tulving explained that it involves the ideas of self, subjective time and autonoetic consciousness, and he considered it to be a "marvel of nature."[23] The term "autonoetic" refers to the capacity to be aware of our own existence as an entity in time. It means that we are self-conscious of a memory being ours; we have a sense of living it no matter the timeframe.

Autonoetic consciousness in our episodic memory allows us to mentally time travel to the past or to the future to set goals, make plans and set expectations for our lives.[24] It allows us to be aware of our subjective time, whether travelling to the past or the future. We generally think of time as an arrow moving inexorably from the past through the present into the future. Yet Tulving describes how, "When one thinks today about what one did yesterday, time's arrow is bent into a loop."[25] In our minds we are able to travel to our past without feeling confused because we are looking at and experiencing the past from the present moment. This is also true of anticipating the future from the present moment. In fact, our autonoetic consciousness of the now moment "is made up of *both* memories of the past *and* of the future."[26] This self-awareness allows us to imagine our own experiences in different places at other times, such as through remembering, dreaming, imagining and even meditating. It represents the experiential "flavour" of our remembering or recollection, like a depiction or painting on the canvas of our lives that we can access. We remember our own lives because of autonoetic consciousness.

In contrast, noetic consciousness is simply having knowledge of a memory, a mental and internal representation. It is associated with semantic memory and allows us to be aware of objects and events, and their relationships.[27] This distinction was made clear in the case of patient R. B., who after a car accident could recount events from his life in great detail but could not experience the events—that is, he experienced them only from a third-person perspective.

---

[21] Tulving (1985).
[22] Tulving (2002).
[23] Tulving (2002), p. 2.
[24] Klein (2016).
[25] Tulving (2002), p. 2.
[26] Ingvar (1985), p. 130.
[27] Metcalfe and Son (2012).

In talking about his memories, he was recorded as saying, "When I recall memories from my past I intellectually know they are about me. It just does not feel like it."[28]

Semantic and episodic memories are the primary functions associated with the explicit (autobiographical) memories of our lives which include both the facts of who we are and what we did (semantic), and the memory of the events themselves (episodic). Semantic memory is remembering facts, such as places we've been or names of people we've met. Episodic memory allows us to consciously recollect personally experienced events. It is about the what, where and when of our lives.[29] It enables us to consciously re-experience our past. Remembering appears to be a conscious recollection that relies on episodic memory, whereas knowing something seems to be retrieved via a procedural memory perceptual process.[30] For example, we might know that we travelled to a certain country but we may not remember any particular events of the time when we were there with a sense of experiencing them. Semantic memory develops earlier in childhood than episodic memory—that is, children are capable of learning facts about the world before they remember their own experiences.[31]

Remembering Our Future Positively

We typically think of memory as only a view of the past, but it is also involved in imagining the future. Those individuals who have impairments that affect their episodic memory also lose the ability to look into the future.[32] A specific type of memory of the future is "prospective memory," which is remembering to remember, as in executing a delayed intention.[33] Common everyday examples include needing to remember to pick something up from the grocery store, to share some information with a friend and to complete some task at work. It is another aspect of Tulving's perspective of time, moving us to the future in our minds. This memory can be triggered in two ways: time-based prospective memory where time serves as the memory trigger (a 3:00 pm meeting), and event-based prospective memory (the grocery store, the friend).

---

[28] Klein (2016), p. 391.
[29] Nyberg, McIntosh, Cabeza, Habib and Tulving (1996).
[30] Rajaram (1993).
[31] Tulving (1993).
[32] Tulving (2002), p. 14.
[33] Crystal (2013).

What is interesting about prospective memory is that we encounter interruptions to our intentions to stop at the store, tell a friend or complete a task. Our intentions are temporarily put on hold (stored in memory), to be reactivated or retrieved at an appropriate time in the future.[34] Sometimes we remember to follow through, but sometimes we forget. So prospective memory also involves other aspects of cognition, such as attention, control of the executive mind, episodic memory and planning.[35] A great deal of theoretical and applied interest is focused on understanding what causes reactivation or retrieval of prospective memory.[36] Multiple proposals have been ventured: voluntary production (called back to consciousness by exertion of will), unconscious influences of prior states, and spontaneous appearance of a mental state recognized as previously experienced.[37] Other proposals include both monitoring (active, effortful detection) and spontaneous retrieval as being utilized in prospective remembering.[38] This type of memory is linked to cognitive decline, associated with normal ageing.

Of interest to coaching are studies of simulations of the future—that is, remembering the future. Researchers have learned that details of future events are more difficult to remember for negative simulations than positive or neutral ones.[39] This is in keeping with "studies showing that emotional reactions to negative life experiences fade more quickly than emotional reactions to positive life experiences do."[40] Healthy adults simply remember positive experiences better than negative ones and they tend to think about their future in an overly positive light. When we think about what may happen to us in the future, we tend to overestimate the likelihood of positive events happening and underestimate the negative.[41] For example, we tend to think we will have a better time on vacation or at a movie than we reportedly do, we expect to receive higher salaries and we expect our children to be especially talented. This optimism bias appears to be true for about 80 % of the population but it is not true for individuals who are depressed.

This optimistic bias has been a puzzle to scientists because we maintain this bias and are resistant to changing it even when faced with disconfirming evidence. "An optimism bias is maintained in the face of disconfirming evidence

---

[34] Crystal (2013).
[35] Crystal (2013).
[36] Crystal (2013).
[37] McDaniel and Einstein (2007).
[38] Crystal (2013), p. 750.
[39] Szpunar, Addis and Schacter (2012).
[40] Szpunar et al. (2012), p. 28.
[41] Sharot (2011).

because people update their beliefs more in response to positive information about the future than to negative information about the future."[42] Selectively updating beliefs in response to positive information produces optimism that is resistant to change. This selective bias and updating has been tied to the performance of the frontal lobe regions of the brain failing to code the new information that would reduce positive expectations.[43] It appears that other parts of the brain contribute to optimism "by biasing attention and vigilance towards positive associations and emotions when imaging the future."[44] Our belief about our control over future events also increases our level of optimism.

Our brains clearly have mechanisms to create optimistic beliefs, but it is not clear why they adapt to hold an optimistic bias. In economics and psychology, the classic belief is that correct beliefs maximize reward and minimize loss. This would lead us to come to the same conclusion regarding optimism. "The present data suggest that optimistic views of the future can be compounded by the effects of the fading-affect bias, such that the 'remembered future' is extremely rosy."[45] While extreme optimism may lead to unhealthy, damaging behaviour, such as smoking, unsafe sexual practices or overspending, overall it has been shown to be healthful. Optimistic people tend to be healthier and live longer, and to have greater financial success. The conclusion thus far, however, is that "optimistic illusions are the only group of misbeliefs that are adaptive," and the benefits appear to outweigh the hazards.[46]

The following coaching story exemplifies how memories of the past, present and future bend time's arrow as described by Tulving, and how a positive memory of the future can further the rewards of coaching.

Sylvia was in a profession she loved but in a job that diminished her spirit. She felt unsuited to the way the company related to clients, how they managed work and how employees associated with one another. The demands of the job prevented her from travelling to visit her ailing parents. When Jackie met her, she was discouraged and felt depressed and lost, wondering how to fix herself. In coaching, Sylvia began to reconnect to past memories of when she was at her best, doing work she loved and relating to others in productive, caring ways. Drawing on the strengths of these memories, she envisioned a future ideal job. Sylvia's picture became rich in detail, even describing the furniture in her office. When she had a

---

[42] Sharot (2011), p. 943.
[43] Sharot (2011), p. 943.
[44] Sharot (2011), p. 944.
[45] Szpunar et al. (2012), p. 28.
[46] Sharot (2011).

clearer image of her future, Jackie suggested that Sylvia should "name" the coming year, a name to help her remember to focus on her vision each day. Sylvia named her year as the time to "come into my own." This focus on the future helped her remember what she was creating in the present.

Less than a year after the coaching ended, Sylvia sat in her new office and called Jackie to tell her how her dream was now a reality. She was most excited to report that the evening before, her husband had turned to her and said: "You know, honey, you have really come into your own this year." She had never told him the name of her year.

Constructivist View: Memory Reconsolidation

In addition to the different types of memory we have, how memory actually functions is advantageous for coaches to understand. As we've seen, unlike popular belief, memory does not provide a stable picture but changes and shifts each time we retrieve it. Studies now show that memory is first formed by the information we encode at the time. When we retrieve the memory, it is mixed with the knowledge, expectations and beliefs we hold at the moment of recovery, which creates a lens through which we see the event and translate its meaning.[47] Memory is literally revised as we learn and grow. When we think of memory in this new way, it requires us to rethink the linear relationship between the notions of past, present and future that many of us still hold from traditional scientific theory.

Each time a memory is retrieved, it is susceptible to being changed in some way and is then restored through a process called reconsolidation, a discovery that is now widely accepted even though how it works is strongly debated.[48] The belief that memory is a stable process has been challenged by data that show memories to be susceptible to change each time they are retrieved. The process of when a memory is first stored is called memory consolidation. It was thought that after consolidation the memory became stable and insensitive to disruption. Studies now show that memories, when retrieved, can become vulnerable and susceptible to change before undergoing another consolidation process (i.e., reconsolidation). The process of reconsolidation occurs whether the memory is new or old, or whether the reactivation occurs implicitly or explicitly. It is unclear why some memories are more sensitive to reconsolidation than others.

---

[47] Bartlett (1932) in Fernyhough (2012).
[48] Alberini and LeDoux (2013).

A memory can undergo this dynamic process many times, with the result that memories can be weakened, disrupted or enhanced. While this may sound disturbing, there is a strong benefit to the process of reconsolidation. It provides us with "the ability to respond in a flexible and adaptive manner to continuously changing environments."[49] Learning experiences can enable memories to become labile, and over time they can be reconsolidated and changed.[50] A second advantage of the reconsolidation process is that the learning experience does not have to be a re-experiencing of the original learning situation or of painful memories. When we start to feel differently about an event, we also start to remember it differently.[51]

Going back and changing the memory trace that is stored is called "memory updating." What triggers this update is under debate. It can be re-exposure to an experience that was similar to the original one, or by new experiences that reactivate memories. This process is generalized across different memory types and neural systems: "reconsolidation occurs in aversive, appetitive, and neutral memories, in simple and complex tasks, in emotional, declarative, incidental, spatial, drug-paired, motor memories, and in hippocampal, amygdala and cortical-dependent memories."[52]

Scientists are attempting to understand "how systems undergoing constant change can nonetheless give rise to apparently permanent entities such as perceptions, memories and thoughts."[53] One suggestion is that memory is actually inaccurate when it comes to facts. As an example, most people do not remember a list of nonsense syllables or a string of numbers without mental training to do so. Brains are designed to retain meaning and encode relevant information.

Memory works between two opposing forces: correspondence, which represents our need to remain true to facts, and coherence, which represents our need to be congruent with our image and beliefs about ourselves.[54] These two forces are involved in the process of constantly changing our memories each time we retrieve them. In fact, researchers have shown that a memory is affected by our beliefs about the world and we change them to fit into our knowledge structures.

---

[49] Alberini and LeDoux (2013), p. 746.
[50] Albertini and LeDoux (2013), p. 746.
[51] Fernyhough (2012).
[52] Albertini and LeDoux (2013), p. 747.
[53] Nadel and Land (2000), p. 211.
[54] Fernyhough (2012)

Memory as a Social Process

Memory is not only important in shaping our individual personality and character; it is also critical to our social interactions. As seen in cases of individuals who have lost memory function, it has impeded their ability to interact with others. "Memory is not just about remembering the past or predicting the future; it is also a way of being with other people. If you lose memory, you lose that opportunity to connect."[55] This is apparent to those with family members who are experiencing dementia.

Our memories are also created in collaboration with other people.[56] We socialize and talk about our past and our hopes for the future as a way to get to know one another. We discuss our memories as a way to understand each other and to understand ourselves better. In sharing our memories, we tell stories of our lives and narratives about ourselves. We become characters in our own life novel. "What we remember is shaped by the people we were then—not just what happened to us, but what kind of individuals we were—as well as by the people we are now."[57]

Memory is even important in culture. Psychologists are demonstrating a growing appreciation for how culture can directly affect how memories are formed and recalled. Studies have shown that people from various cultural backgrounds vary in eye movement when viewing a scene, and vary in sensitivity to contextual information in visual cues serving as filters to what we perceive and thus remember.[58] Anybody who has ever driven or been driven in a country with a driving culture dissimilar from one's own marvels at how differently traffic can flow. For example, driving on the opposite side of the road is a startling experience that requires one's full attention until the body, mind and eye become accustomed (procedural memory) to how to position oneself safely and consistently in the correct lane. Cultures differ in adhering to traffic laws—some countries seem to view them as guidelines whereas other countries enforce strict observance. It is from social/cultural memory that this sense of familiarity and strangeness emanates. These are examples of how memory is linked to embodied cognition.

In writing this, we were taken back to a recent experience while travelling in Thailand with a friend who had never been in the country. In Bangkok, driving on the expressway for the first time can be a harrowing experience for Americans.

---

[55] Fernyhough (2012), p. 171.
[56] Fernyhough (2012).
[57] Fernyhough (2012), p. 209.
[58] Laland and Rendell (2013), p. 2013.

The lines on the road have very different meaning to the drivers of that country. Americans are careful to stay in their designated lanes, often honking if someone strays over the line. In Bangkok, our friend was amazed at how the lines on the road seemed to be only suggestions as drivers easily added an extra lane, or even two, unperturbed by how close they were coming to one another. She especially noticed how closely vehicles passed one another when travelling in southern Thailand in a type of truck called a songthaew, *which has two benches for open seating in the back.*

Psychologist Qi Wang at Cornell University conducted a study that showed how the way in which autobiographical memories are recalled can be affected by culture.[59] She has studied East–West differences in the functions and contents of biographical memory, making a link between culture and memory. To preserve a culture, according to Wang, group members must remember their values, customs, rituals and history. She cited studies showing that when recalling memories of past events, adults and children of Euro-American backgrounds frequently referred to their own roles, feelings and predilections. In contrast, those of Asian backgrounds would describe group activities and social interactions.

In Wang's study of how cultural differences could be seen in memories of Asian Americans, participants were each asked to complete ten sentences, five of which began with the prompt: "As an American, I am …" The other five began with: "As an Asian, I am …" The results indicated that when the prime was about the American self, it activated recall of more self-focused and less socially oriented memories. When the Asian self was made salient, more shared social experiences were remembered.[60] Such studies highlight the subtle and often hidden interplay between self and culture in the memory function.

Unconscious Associative Networks

Neuroscience has contributed to a new perspective on the question of where memories reside in the brain. In studying the remembering brain, scientists have turned to neuroimaging scans, EEG experiments and the interviewing of brain-damaged patients to discover that

---

[59] Wang (2008).
[60] Wang (2008).

Brain imaging shows activity in the frontal lobes, where the efforts to reconstitute a remembered experience are initiated, through the emotional circuits of the amygdala system and the associative centers of the neocortex, to the occipital lobe at the back of the brain, where the characteristically visual qualities of autobiographical memories are stored as sensory fragments.[61]

Biologically, memory is networked in the brain in associative neuroanatomical patterns. Visional memory operates in a similar manner, with bits stored in the visual cortex and only assembled when necessary in the hippocampus and its related structures.[62]

As an example of the memory's associative network, the hippocampus resides as the single most important structure for autobiographical memory. It is named from the Latin word for seahorse because of its similar shape. There are two hippocampi located near the centre portion of one's brain.[63] The hippocampus works with diverse psychological processes such as memory, spatial navigation and anxiety. In memory it is the central connector for other memory areas, including the amygdala which is crucial for learning the emotional significance of stimuli.[64] Memory is biologically anchored.

Not only does memory consist of associative networks but many memories also function at a non conscious level, and these can be stimulated by a variety of factors. Smell, for example, is known to trigger memories that can go back into childhood. Pictures, a spoken word and specific sounds can also trigger memories. These mechanisms demonstrate how our brain is wired so that different parts are interconnected and stimulate one another. These connections can even be involuntary when a past recollection shows up suddenly in our consciousness. Recall Ann's story with the handgun (Chap. 3). Such recollections can bring to mind small, fragmentary intrusions or much more meaningful events, as Ann experienced. Research on implicit memory suggests not only that a memory can be triggered outside our awareness but also that we can defend a memory without any conscious awareness of feelings about it.[65] In fact "there is no necessary correlation between behavior and conscious experience."[66] Here we have the intersection of neurobiology and psychology because so much of what we know, believe and remember is at the non conscious level.

---

[61] Fernyhough (2012), p. 14.
[62] Fernyhough (2012).
[63] Gross (2013)
[64] Fernyhough (2010), Weston (1999).
[65] Weston (1999).
[66] Tulving (2002, p. 4; 1989).

The literature on how our brains and minds work to activate these non conscious associations is long and fascinating.[67] In the field of psychotherapy, it began with Freud's assertion that unconscious processes and associations impact daily life. Drew Westen, professor in the departments of psychology and psychiatry at Emory University, has described the associative network of implicit memory as the forming of associations that guide mental processes and behaviour outside consciousness.[68] In his 1999 review entitled "The Scientific Status of Unconscious Processes: Is Freud Really Dead?" he reported substantial evidence to support the supposition that unconscious thoughts, feelings and motives exist, that they are linked in networks of associations, and that many different kinds of unconscious process serve different functions.[69] Westen pointed out that the associative networks of memory have been explored using priming experiments. The assumption underlying these experiments is that "priming can reveal the latent structure of associative networks by examining the impact of the prime on memory…"[70]

Memory, once believed to influence action only to the extent that it made thoughts conscious, is now seen to impact behaviour through unconscious associations and processes. In research on attitudes and prejudice, social psychologist Russell Fazio and his colleagues demonstrated that conscious and unconscious racial attitudes could actually be entirely independent of each other. Some study participants, in response to priming stimuli to measure their unconscious associations regarding blacks, revealed racist attitudes unconsciously in contrast to their conscious verbal responses that were non-racist in nature.[71]

Further studies have shown how negative unconscious racial associations can affect even the people who are targets. Social psychologist C. M. Steele, who is known for his work on stereotype threats, demonstrated that black students, when taking a test that they believed diagnosed their ability, experienced their own unconscious negative associations becoming active. They doubted their own performance ability (based on their own unconscious stereotype associations), which resulted in diminished performance in taking the test. His research brought to light the distinction between conscious

---

[67] There is much work on unconscious processes in the psychoanalytical field, especially how these unconscious processes relate to affective processes and motivation. Our discussion does not delve into these processes, but attempts to discuss those topics that are immediately useful to coaching as distinguished from therapy. We realize that this line may be blurry as some psychological constructs are very useful to the coach.

[68] Westen (1999).

[69] Westen (1999).

[70] Westen (1999), p. 1066.

[71] Fazio, Jackson, Dunton and Williams (1995).

and unconscious feelings that can reflect back on oneself—that is, one can hold unconscious negative beliefs about oneself that would, in turn, impact one's performance.[72]

According to Westen, "When people are attending to their conscious attitudes, these attitudes influence their behavior. When they are not, which is much of the time in everyday life, their unconscious affective associations may guide their actions."[73] This is in line with Argyris' theory-in-use and espoused theory (Chap. 4).

A groundbreaking study of priming methodology highlighting unconscious associations began in the 1960s with Lloyd Silverman, a psychologist and psychoanalyst at New York University. His innovative experiments took implicit memory associations beyond simple cognitive tasks to test whether subliminal priming would lead to measurable changes in adaptive functioning and sense of well-being in a variety of subject groups.[74] He exposed his subjects to subliminal verbal-pictorial messages that read: "Mommy and I are one" (MIO). Initially he recruited male schizophrenics as his subjects but he and other researchers later extended these priming experiments to include diverse groups: female schizophrenics; individuals with problematic behaviour to change, such as ceasing to smoke; subjects requiring help to reduce personality disorders and desensitize phobias; college students in group therapy; individuals with assertiveness difficulties; and subjects in educational settings.[75]

Details of the studies, actually sets of experiments, were compiled in a report that Silverman and colleague Joel Weinberger presented in a 1985 article, "Mommy and I Are One: Implications for Psychotherapy."[76] The work showed, overwhelmingly, that brief exposure to the prime resulted in many different kinds of subjects improving their adaptive functioning.[77] Mayer reported that while Silverman's work was widely accepted for its scientific merit, "its import was hotly contested" because it challenged the psychology of the time.[78] According to Mayer, in that period there were two worlds of psychology—behaviourism and psychoanalysis, grounded in unconscious mental processes. She stated that Silverman believed his data could inform both of these worlds about the power of unconscious mental processes, and

---

[72] Steele (1997).
[73] Weston (1999), p. 1076.
[74] Mayer (2007).
[75] Silverman and Weinberger (1985).
[76] Silverman and Weinberger (1985).
[77] Mayer (2007).
[78] Mayer (2007), p. 221.

that instead of focusing on personal individuality his results showed that powerful unconscious wishes for a state of oneness could enhance adaptation.[79]

The breadth of these studies showed how a prompt can have important lingering effects. Since these experiences, other researchers have continued to explore the reasons why the stimulation of MIO had such surprising effects, and they have posited that it's not from "psychoanalytic magic" but from unconscious associative networks, which include not only cognitive information but also moods and emotions.[80] Sohlberg and colleagues have suggested that future MIO research could be better informed by including the areas of social cognition, interpersonal theory and attachment.

Understanding how our memories work and the associations they may activate has caused researchers to delve further into the mysteries of how our brains and minds function. In the next section we look at priming and what may be useful for a coach to know in order to tap into these unconscious associations.

The Power of Priming

Ann is listening to the audiotape and reading the transcript of Jackie's fifth session with one of her research clients, Paul. He is moving to a new position in his firm, which will stretch his abilities as an engineer, requiring him to take on a central office role with no direct lines of authority. Paul's coaching focus has been on setting priorities and action plans to leave behind his old responsibilities and transition to the new ones. Jackie has a sense that part of Paul's concern is that the new position will require him to work by influencing others—something new and uncomfortable for him. In this telephone session the client starts off with low energy and asks Jackie for some suggestions to improve his planning process. The numbers indicated in Jackie's responses chronicle the priming strategies/tools she applied during the session.

P: *Wants to improve planning process.*

J: *Asks discovery questions (1) about what he has already accomplished, probing for strengths/skills he can transfer.*

P: *Says he feels he has no clear direction in starting his new job—it feels like a blank page.*

J: *Applies discovery questions (2), then shifts focus to discuss influence vs. authority vs. engagement (3).*

---

[79] Mayer (2007), p. 222.
[80] Sohlberg, Birgegard, Czartoryski, Ovefelt and Strömbom (2000).

P: *Listens.*
J: *Links to what he is already doing by asking about his current mentoring (4).*
P: *Responds favourably.*
J: *Widens context of conversation (5) by directing attention to his vision and role in moving forward.*
P: *Responds with ideas (still low energy and seems distracted).*
J: *Adds knowledge (6) about putting structures and process in place to guide behaviour.*
P: *Agrees and restates ideas.*
J: *Directs attention (7) to his replacement and asks about his level of enthusiasm.*
P: *Responds with concern about the individual being too busy, needs to backfill a position and that's not happening. Comes up with some ideas about that.*
J: *Summarizes and reflects (8) on what she heard client say in terms of where he is at with people, processes, structures and timeline of the transition; shares positive affect (9) about what he's accomplishing.*
P: *Agrees and notes he's lost some time.*
J: *Shifts attention (10) to a direct report needing to "learn his lesson" that they've talked about before.*
P: *Admits his approach is not working (he's been pointing out to direct report what he's not getting done, showing his displeasure with direct report).*
J: *Asks discovery questions (11).*
P: *Admits that the lack of compliance on the part of the direct report is a new experience for him.*
J: *Suggests reframing (12) the situation and provides some knowledge about how to do that using positive approach.*
P: *Responds favourably and fleshes out her ideas (energy level picks up).*
J: *Again brings focus back to positive of the situation (13).*
P: *Admits he could have focused more on the positive when working with the individual.*
J: *Reframes the situation again to what could be positive (14).*
P: *Suddenly realizes the impact that his negative approach has had on the individual and sees with new awareness that he has contributed, with his own negativity, to making the situation worse rather than better (burst of energy). Begins to use word "positive" as he talks about a new approach with direct report. Connects with possible motivations for moving the individual forward.*
J: *Probes for what different actions client could take in his new approach.*
P: *Responds with new ideas and expands it with Jackie's feedback (much more animated and expressing positive emotion).*

J: *Gives suggestions and talks about "experimenting" with new behaviours.*
P: *Expands concept/approach and sees the positive .*

Ann counted no fewer than 14 priming strategies/tools that Jackie used in this conversation until suddenly the client had a shift in perspective and experienced an insight or aha moment. His insight moment had all the characteristics that have been identified earlier. He ended the call in a very different emotional place. When he started the call he exuded low energy, distraction and uncertainty about whether anything was going to come from the coaching conversation. As the coaching began, Jackie had the sense that Paul was relying on her to keep him engaged, but she didn't feel it was appropriate at that point to say anything. The prime asking about the individual with the lesson to learn came up because Jackie intuited that there was a thread in their discussion around learning to lead through influence rather than control. From past sessions she knew that this individual was not responding as Paul typically experienced direct reports.

In following this interaction, what could we say about which prime(s) might have contributed to the insight that the client experienced? Were all the early primes superfluous and unrelated or did they build on each other to finally accumulate enough momentum to ignite a change? We don't have a concrete answer—it continues to be a mystery as to identifying any direct causal relationship between priming and pivoting. Did the client come to the coaching session internally ready for a change, ready to deal with what was really bothering him?

What Is Priming?

"Priming is a psychological process in which exposure to a stimulus activates a concept in memory that is then given increased weight in subsequent judgment tasks. Priming works by making the activated concept accessible so that it can be readily used in evaluating related objects."[81]

Imagine you hear disturbing news about the economy that gets you thinking about the current economic situation and how it impacts you personally and the nation in general. Now you see the US President on television and immediately start assessing his performance based on this newly stimulated concern for the economy. Why? Because you've just been primed. Economic concepts have been activated within you, made accessible to you and they

---

[81] Parkin (2008), p. 612.

presumably seem relevant to your evaluation of the President in this manner.[82] This is how priming works, "it affects the opinions that individuals express, not by changing their attitudes, but by causing them to alter the criteria they use to evaluate the object in question."[83]

Priming is a widely used construct in psychology, political science and communication. It is relevant to survey researchers who can inadvertently (or intentionally) prime with the kind of questions they ask, especially with wording and the order in which questions are presented. Well-intentioned survey researchers usually ask a general question before specific ones to ensure that the response to the initial open-ended question is perceived as the major topic and does not reflect a prime from a more specific question.[84]

In a meta-analysis of priming studies, German social psychologists Dirk Wentura and Klaus Rothermund found that priming studies fell into two broad categories: (1) short-term priming where the goal was to investigate cognitive structures or mental representations of concepts and their inter-relationships; and (2) long-term priming where the goal was to activate some broad knowledge structure (e.g., a mindset, emotion or goal).[85]

Short-term priming studies look at effects that occur in a maximum of a few seconds. These studies investigate how individuals respond to a prime. For example, a study may look at how someone who sees the word "yellow" will be slightly faster to recognize the word "banana" because yellow and banana are closely associated in memory. Long-term priming studies look at effects that range from minutes to hours, or even days or weeks. Social priming generally falls into the category of long-term priming; these are studies concerned with effects related to everyday behaviour of practical or applied interest. With long-term priming, participants are exposed to some type of experimental prime condition followed by part two of the experiment, after a delay, which includes measuring a behavioural outcome.[86]

In their analysis, Wentura and Rothermund concluded that short-term and long-term priming were distinctly different phenomena and must be interpreted differently.[87] Short-term priming effects likely indicate structural associations in semantic memory that determine the ease of switching between mental representations. Long-term priming most likely represents an enduring and context-dependent change in long-term memory related to the retrieval of previous processing episodes. Long-term priming involves at

---

[82] Parkin (2008), p. 612.
[83] Parkin (2008), p. 612.
[84] Parkin (2008).
[85] Wentura and Rothermund (2014).
[86] Wentura and Rothermund (2014), Molden (2014)
[87] Wentura and Rothermund (2014), p. 56.

least two different kinds of process: a fast process that connects semantically related elements, and a more enduring process that changes representational structures and leaves traces in memory.

Human judgement is often influenced by significant anchors.[88] Social psychologists Englich, Mussweiler and Strach conducted a long-term priming study focused on how human judgement is often shaped or anchored by irrelevant influences.[89] Judges and prosecutors who participated in a case-study review of a rape incident gave longer or shorter sentences based on how they were primed at the beginning of the case study.[90] As part of this study, participants were primed (low/high anchor) with the question: "Do you think that the sentence for the defendant in this case will be higher or lower than 1/3 year(s)?"[91] Those who were exposed to a higher anchor number gave significantly longer sentences than those who were primed with the lower anchor number. The researchers proposed that the anchor effect was based on the accessibility of relevant knowledge—that is, the participants retrieved relevant knowledge that was most compatible with the anchor.[92] In other words, the prime accessed the judges' internal knowledge which became "anchored" to the prime and influenced their judgement. This is described as activation of a self-generating mode of knowledge, which is considered distinct from standard (short-term) priming effects.[93]

Long-term *semantic* priming refers to priming experiments characterized by delays that are considerably longer than the usual short-term semantic priming studies. In this type of priming, more complex tasks are applied and thus must be processed more deeply than is typically the case in short-term priming experiments,[94] and there is usually a long lag between the prime and its effect.[95] Wentura and Rothermund presented a well-known experiment as an example of long-term priming.[96] The study of "automaticity of social behaviour" focused on priming stereotype behaviour of the elderly.[97] In this experiment, participants who were primed with an elderly stereotype later walked more slowly down the hallway when leaving the experiment

---

[88] Mussweiler (2001).
[89] Englich, Mussweiler and Strach (2006).
[90] Englich et al. (2006).
[91] Englich et al. (2006), p. 191.
[92] Wentura and Rothermund (2014), p. 56.
[93] Mussweiler (2001)
[94] Wentura and Rothermund (2014).
[95] Mussweiler (2001).
[96] Wentura and Rothermund (2014).
[97] Bargh, Chen and Burrows (1996).

than did control participants.[98] The results of the experiment confirmed that using a prime in an earlier situation carried over for a time to exert an unintended, passive influence on behaviour.[99] Social psychologist John Bargh and colleagues at New York University further proposed that attitudes and other affective (emotional) reactions can be triggered automatically "in the realm of direct, unmediated psychological effects of the environment."[100] Wentura and Rothermund have pointed out that the most intriguing features of these types of long-term priming studies is that "the link between the prime and the behavior is non-conscious."[101]

Social psychologists Kentaro Fujita of Ohio State University and Yaacov Trope at New York University have proposed an approach to priming that extends the long-term, or constructivist, model of priming even further.[102] They noted that the traditional (short-term) priming models often presented priming as if "people are out of control and at the mercy of their environments."[103] In contrast, constructivist models suggest that "priming results from very sophisticated self-regulation processes."[104] That is, people internally respond to the stimuli via different mechanisms. It is not just a matter of associations but involves a more complex process of meaning-making. They explained that priming research was based on the premise that "exposure to a stimulus makes some constructs or processes temporarily more accessible, which in turn enhances their influence on thoughts, feelings and behavior."[105] This is a finding that has a direct bearing on how coaches may influence or prime their clients. Researchers such as Fujita and Trope describe priming in terms of impacting process rather than content, such as the process of goal setting and attaining.

Fujita and Trope have also looked at the role of construal in priming—that is, how an individual understands or makes sense of the priming context. They have stressed that "more needs to be done to understand the active 'ingredients' in priming effects and how these ingredients operate and interact."[106]

Researcher Daniel Molden of Northwestern University has identified three challenges to be addressed in the study of priming: "(1) greater precision in

---

[98] Bargh et al. (1996).
[99] Bargh et al. (1996).
[100] Bargh et al. (1996), p. 230.
[101] Wentura and Rothermund (2014), p. 61.
[102] Fujita and Trope (2014).
[103] Fujita and Trope (2014), p. 82.
[104] Fujita and Trope (2014), p. 82.
[105] Fujita and Trope (2014), pp. 68–69.
[106] Fujita and Trope (2014), p. 69.

conceptualizing and communicating about priming effects, (2) greater attention to when these effects should occur (and when they should not), and (3) better understanding of the mechanisms for both the activation of social representations and the subsequent application of these representations during judgment and behavior."[107] Researchers E. Tory Higgins at Columbia University and Baruch Eitam of University of Haifa, Israel, would like the field to return to studying the psychological mechanisms that underlie what priming *does* (process approach) rather than focus on priming as an *object* of study.[108] They have noted that the study of priming goes beyond the understanding of memory alone and needs to include research on attention as well.

Social psychologists have distinctly broadened understanding beyond the cognitive associative model of how priming functions in our daily lives and how it works in our non conscious minds. The number of studies and volume of literature on the function of priming have exploded over the last decade, especially in the past few years. In looking at the literature on priming, we can see that scientists are striving for more complex constructs and environments to better explain this seemingly commonplace phenomenon.

At the beginning of our research project we had observed a connection between what the coach would prompt in the conversation and later effects on the clients' part. We believed that what we were seeing was some type of priming on the part of the coach and so began documenting what might constitute a priming action or strategy that could result in a client shift. We have been pleased to discover that our observations were well founded. This triangulation of what the clients were saying to us, our own observations and the results of new priming research gives us the confidence and legitimacy as coaches to believe in the value of priming.

Implications for Coaching

Memories are fascinating. Through them we tell the stories of our lives to others, thereby informing them who we are, what we believe and what we want in the future. Through memory we relate to each other, gathering together to remember family picnics, a football game, our experiences, our hopes and our fears. Memory aids us to create a sense of who we are in this world and to negotiate it with others.

---

[107] Molden (2014), pp. 243–244.
[108] Higgins and Eitam (2014).

Through the process of coaching we become acquainted with our clients' subjective quality of memory. We spend time getting to know the clients' individual stories and their "fragile and complex truths of memory."[109] In coaching, we are subtly aware that "to the extent that networks of associations operate unconsciously, and to the extent that pieces of those networks can be inaccessible to consciousness, the art of interpretation of the gaps becomes essential not only to clinical work but to the science of the mind."[110]

Below are updated facts about how memory can influence and shape the stories and perceptions that we and our clients have about ourselves:

- Memory is the repository of who we think/believe we are in the present.
- Beliefs reside in and affect our memories, some overtly but most covertly.
- Each time a memory is retrieved, it is susceptible to being changed in some way and is then re-stored through the process of reconsolidation.
- Memory has two opposing forces: remaining true to facts (correspondence) and representing one's need to be congruent with one's image and beliefs (internal coherence).
- Training and memory represent two different molecular processes.
- We mentally time travel easily and continually among the past, present and future.
- Implicit memory is closely linked to unconscious associative networks, and priming activates those networks.
- We can remember our future positively (e.g., name our year).
- We are biased to be optimistic about the future (thankfully).
- Memory is created as a social and cultural process and we are influenced by what we learn and remember.
- We are unconsciously primed as part of the human journey.
- We prime our clients (and they us), whether we are consciously aware or not.
- The field of priming research is rapidly expanding and worth following as coaches.

---

[109] Fernyhough (2012), p. 16.
[110] Weston (1999), p. 1094.

7

Turn of the Kaleidoscope

I don't see why a changeable man shouldn't get as much enjoyment out of his changes, and transformations and transfigurations as a steadfast man gets out of standing still and pegging at the same old monotonous thing all the time. That is to say, I don't see why a kaleidoscope shouldn't enjoy itself as much as a telescope, nor a grindstone have as good a time as a whetstone, nor a barometer as good a time as a yardstick.

—Mark Twain

A Kaleidoscope Story

Yesterday, I experienced a turn of the kaleidoscope—a moment when my understanding of my life and world shifted in a way that I felt changed. I went from feeling unhappy, dissatisfied and frustrated about my circumstances to feeling relieved and joyous that I was actually in a good place. It was like lancing a boil which brings forth both relief from the pressure and a clearing out of poisons so healing can occur.

What my coach said to me turned the kaleidoscope for me so I had a different image, a different perspective. She didn't say anything that I didn't already know (we coach each other); actually she brought my own words back to me, but it created a new pattern in me. She reminded me of the four levels of learning: unconscious incompetence, conscious incompetence, conscious competence and unconscious competence. I had told her a month ago how normal it was to feel the difficulty that the conscious competence phase can bring when she was struggling. Like a bolt, I understood that my difficulties were not caused by a lack in me but by the *circumstances I was living through, loss of my spouse. It was alright to be kind to myself. I could feel the grief of loss and confusion without judging myself. I couldn't understand how I wasn't able to make the decision to see my husband's death as a transition in spiritual life. Why wasn't I able to let go? I believed I had to practice what I preach and be congruent within myself or what kind of a coach was I?*

When my coach gently pointed out that I was in the phase of conscious competence, the kaleidoscope turned. After all, this phase is about practice and consciously making choices to create a new reality. Finally understanding I was making a new life for myself and it was difficult, the pressure immediately lifted. This feeling lingered on into the evening while I was out with friends. I felt the loss of my husband but I also experienced the joy of being with friends. I realized I could grieve but still feel good about each day.

Wielding the Kaleidoscope

We have focused in this book on finding deeper and broader levels of awareness and context around the coaching process so that coach and client make better sense together. The coaching process is ever evolving in real time with real people dealing with real situations. It's sometimes chaotic, scary and confounding, but also wildly rewarding, and it keeps us on the learning edge. The when, where, who and why of each unique pivotal moment remains a mystery, but we are facilitators and witnesses to its occurrence.

We like the kaleidoscope metaphor when pondering the nature and magic of pivotal moments—with one turn you can shift a complex array of coloured glass from one pattern into a captivating new one. What turns the kaleidoscope? We suspect the coach has a hand in helping to create new images and patterns for the client. Well-known pioneer in memory research Endel Tulving wrote, "It is difficult for an explorer to find something that he does not know exists."[1] Our clients do not always know what may exist for them. We are their intrepid co-explorers—believing in them, especially during those times when they can't do it for themselves.

The topics that we have covered so far (beliefs and guiding principles, context, levels of awareness, modes of knowing, domains of knowledge, associative networks of memory) all contribute to ways we can more skillfully wield the kaleidoscope in precipitating substantial change with clients. This chapter is filled with ideas, suggestions, examples and stories of ways to ignite substantial change.

---

[1] Tulving (2002), p. 11.

Coaching Awareness: Tuning into Fundamentals

Understanding the Role of Priming

We began our research with our curiosity about the Poetic Principle that states our "past, present and future are an endless resource for interpretation, inspiration, or learning."[2] We can create any number of new realities by reinterpreting our story. We saw evidence of this principle in play as we became more adept in our Appreciative Coaching practices. We were inspired to see clients make significant shifts yet did not fully understand what had prompted them. We began a coaching research project, asking ourselves: What are the characteristics of pivotal moments in coaching, and what roles do the coach and client play in bringing them about? (Fig. 7.1).

In reviewing our research transcripts and reflecting on our coaching experiences, we discovered numerous ways in which coaches prime their clients to form new understandings and perspectives. We organized them into two main categories of priming tools: comments, observations or reflections on what our clients say to us, and strategies for helping them broaden their perspective. The types of priming strategies or tools we observed in our sessions are listed in Table 7.1.

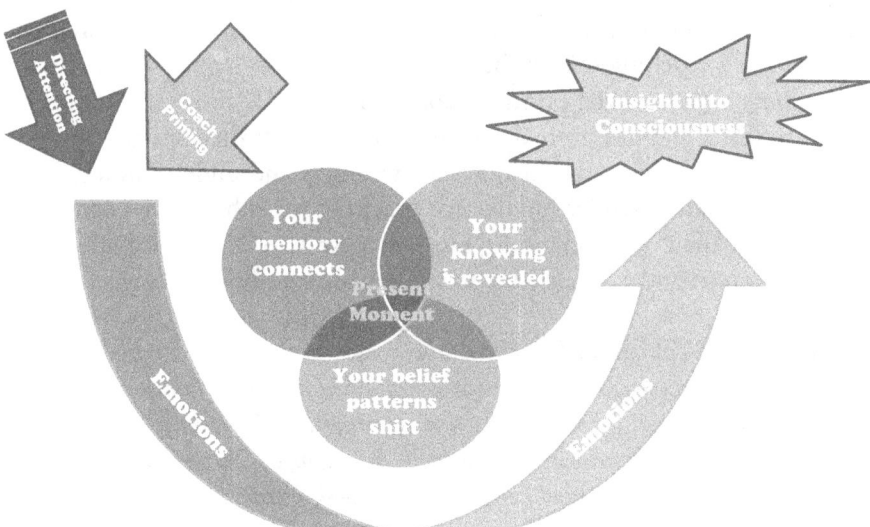

Fig. 7.1 Model of self-organizing pivotal moments

---

[2] Ricketts and Willis (2001).

Table 7.1 Priming strategies observed in initial research

Priming: commenting on observations:
- noticing their use of language;
- recognizing patterns;
- summarizing and reflecting;
- making connections;
- naming;
- acknowledging impasse.

Priming: broadening perspective:
- inquiring;
- clarifying context and intent;
- widening context;
- directing attention or focusing the client;
- furthering or challenging the client's ideas or thinking;
- discovering and transferring past or current strengths and successes;
- using positive affect;
- noticing and reminding the client of a shift;
- recognizing that emotions are contagious;
- sharing concept of neuroplasticity;
- making suggestions;
- offering knowledge or tools;
- using a generative metaphor;
- calling the client to action.

It became clear in our initial research that while pivotal moments sometimes occurred in an instant, like an *aha* moment, they also transpired over time during a coaching session, between sessions or even after the conclusion of coaching. We used the priming tools and strategies above to prompt our clients to think and feel more deeply or broadly about their situation so as to raise them to a greater level of internal awareness and understanding. These priming tools are essential to effective coaching for substantive change. We also felt that there was something more that we needed to learn about how coaches support and prime clients towards more significant change.

After some discussion with a client about how to sustain a learning after the conclusion of coaching, Jackie suggested a simplified approach to one of her client's ideas. She shared how when she was first learning the Appreciative approach she would focus on one element at a time (such as one of the Appreciative principles) and would keep it at the top of her mind for a week or two by putting sticky notes with the element in strategic places as reminders. Jackie suggested that her client should try something similar by picking an element from her coaching and putting a note in her car to focus on. She could set an intention for the day on her way to work or reflect on her drive back home. It would require no extra time in her day. When Jackie finished her thought, her client responded with excitement, "You don't know the epiphany I just had! I feel like such a weight has lifted off me, my whole body is vibrating!" She went on to explain how this idea cascaded through other life issues. Jackie was startled by her client's reaction. During the session, Jackie wondered whether to even bring the idea up as they were running out of time and it seemed so simple, but she was prompted to do so and followed her inner inclination. Who was to know it would have such a profound impact on her client?

It was not clear to Jackie whether it was the idea itself that was of great impact or if it was added pressure that caused the kaleidoscope image to shift for her client. Jackie and her client had been discussing the idea of taking a growth-focused approach in developing her subordinates for a number of coaching sessions, but for some reason something connected inside the client when she applied the idea to herself.

As we saw in Chapter 6, unconscious associative networks and the varied functions of priming have become a much studied phenomena and we are especially interested in those studies that explore the process of priming, using attention and memory to generate new networks of association in nonconsciousness. Research efforts are now focused on developing more complex constructs to explain priming, such as distinguishing between short- and long-term priming effects. Silverman's MIO priming experiments are noteworthy for coaching because the results of this type of positive priming raised the level of adaptive functioning across a diverse group of subjects and sought to transcend personal individuality by tapping into a state of oneness.

We also prime in a broader sense by the very way we present ourselves to our clients. We influence our clients by expanding their awareness, discerning the present moment and expanding understanding, much of that operating at the nonconscious level. This classic control–influence–concern model (Fig. 7.2)[3] demonstrates how little we control, even within ourselves, but how much greater our sphere of influence is than we know. We influence or prime our clients in multiple ways, both consciously and non-consciously. We simply cannot NOT influence our clients.

The Appreciative Stance

Coaches have a stance which reveals their bias to the world. The coaching stance that we assume with Appreciative Coaching incorporates a clear distinction between two functional categories of survival mechanisms: growth

---

[3] Adapted from Covey (1989).

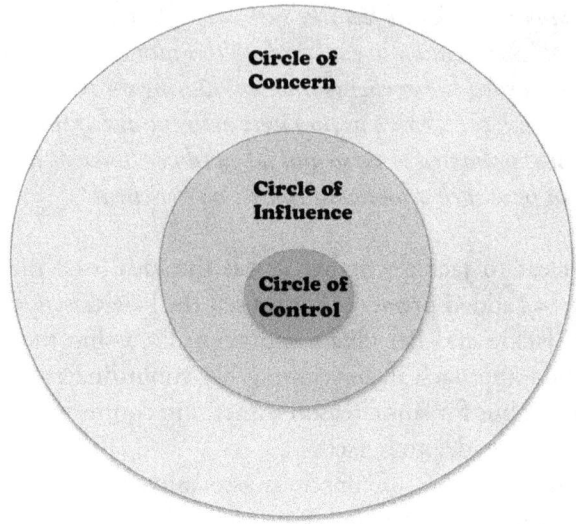

Fig. 7.2 Control-Influence-Concern Model

and protection.[4] When humans are in a protective mode, their perceptions narrow in focus and they are attentive to danger and how to avert it. Learning, of course, happens in these moments, but it is focused on survival and protection. When humans are more expansive and positive in their perspectives, they are more open to possibilities of growth. As coaches, we work to create these growth moments with our clients rather than enter the relationship with a perspective to fix clients or to repair their "deficits." Holding this perspective does not mean that we ignore problems, tough situations or, as is often a misperception, reality itself. We help our clients to accept the presenting situation or topic, but then we shift the perspective so that rather than needing to protect themselves they can look towards growing and learning.

The scaling question from Solution-Focused Brief Therapy[5] has evolved in our thinking from being a simple tool to a metaphor of how to approach a coaching engagement. Any situation can be scaled from 1 to 10, 10 being the ideal and 1 being the absence of what is needed. Usually an evaluation is made and assessed by designating a number, say 3. In a problem-solving or fix-it approach, the client's attention would be focused on the gap between 3 and 10, and the conversation would address how to reduce this gap. This means defining the problem, identifying root causes and putting a development plan in place. This approach works well with mechanisms and processes,

---

[4] Lipton (2005).
[5] A tool we have incorporated into the Appreciative Coaching approach.

What we pay attention to grows

Fig. 7.3 Growing vs. closing the gap

but with human beings the problem becomes the individual; the root causes become internal, personal defects; and a plan is developed to fix the person. This approach causes the individual to shift to a mode of *protection*. We choose to use the scale from a growth perspective. We ask clients to select a number on the scale, let's say a 3 again. With the Appreciative approach, attention is paid to what has already been successful to make it a 3 (i.e., it's not a 0 or 1). We query what resources are at hand in the situation that makes it a 3. Attention turns to *growing* the 3 to a 4 or 5 or 6, ever moving towards the stated desired outcome. In this approach the difficulties are still addressed but in a growth metaphor (Fig. 7.3).

In describing this stance to our clients, we help them to understand that the scale is a moment in time and that the assessment number is an ever-moving indicator. What one client identifies as a 10 today may at one time have been seen as an achievement to look for in the future or as an impossibility in the past. This perspective demonstrates that it is all about growth and it takes away embarrassment about any particular self-assessment. Using a generative approach such as Appreciative Coaching is typically met with relief and gratitude as clients perceive that they are moving forward in a positive way. In turn, they become more open and willing to explore their inner resources.

As an example of stance, we take an Appreciative perspective of positive growth and development. Adopting this approach then impacts the fundamentals of how we structure a coaching engagement, including creating a relationship, directing our client's attention and helping them to better discern a situation and receive feedback. Our stance defines our main strategy of influence and therefore impacts how we wield other coaching or priming tools.

Roberta was concerned about the challenges and tensions that her team was facing in working with difficult clients. Wanting to be a supportive supervisor, she would ask them to rate their stress level from one to five at each team meeting. After working with her coach in an Appreciative approach, she grasped that she was inadvertently focusing the attention of team members on the negative, on what stresses they felt, even those who were feeling little stress. After this realization she revised the question to read: *What do you appreciate in the work we're doing?* Her team members told her that they loved the new question because it helped them feel better about their work.

Feedback

Feedback is an important coaching tool and can be an effective priming mechanism. How we approach it is influenced by whether we hold a problem-solving or a generative stance. Some clients come to us wanting to develop and grow towards a new vision or dream. Others come to us with challenging feedback on performance correction or a situation that needs repair. While we respect the evaluation, we shift the client's attention as soon as we can from protection to growth. We want our clients to understand that others' opinions exist whether they are aware of them or not, and knowing those opinions gives them the opportunity to choose whether to do something about them or not. We also remind them that feedback says as much about the giver as it does about the person receiving the feedback. For example, if someone says, "You need to listen more," it may mean that the speaker values listening as a skill or wishes to be listened to more.

Often this type of growth perspective regarding feedback comes as something totally new to clients. They may find it mystifying. Personal stories from the coach often help in such situations. A personal story that Jackie has been known to tell focuses on feedback she received when she worked at Ford Motor Company as an internal consultant. She conducted many large-scale change interventions for Ford, such as those described by Bunker and Alban.[6]

Because of leading large-scale meetings, many people knew Jackie. In addition, her office was located by the building escalators across from the cafeteria, a place of much social interaction. One day, Jackie received feedback that she was a snob. It startled and hurt her, even confused her. Only by accepting that feedback did she subsequently learn how it came about. One of her signature strengths is organizing large amounts of information into meaningful frameworks of data requiring great concentration on her part. Being near the cafeteria, she would get up from her computer to fetch coffee while still ruminating on the data. As she was walking the hallway, she was turned inward, seeing no one and missing greetings coming her way. Once she understood the feedback, she recognized that it was not about

---

[6] Bunker and Alban (1997).

changing who she was but making a decision about how much she wanted a cup of coffee. Each trip to the cafeteria required her to disengage from her work so as to be fully present in the hallway.

Some coaching methodologies guard against the coach bringing in any personal stories to illuminate learnings. Our stance is that judicious use of such stories can be useful tools to exemplify concepts, especially for clients who learn better through examples than models. Stories of self-disclosure help to create relationship with clients, furthering connection, trust and positive emotions.[7] When Jackie shared this story, she saw the shift in her client's eyes to a new understanding of how to look at feedback. This new perspective shifted the client from a stance of protection to one of growth and provided her with choices regarding how to approach the feedback process.

In addition to 360° assessments, we use other feedback instruments to help provide clients with baseline self-awareness. The instruments we prefer to use are descriptive in design and adaptable as learning mechanisms. Not to promote but to share a couple of examples, we find the Thomas-Kilmann Conflict Inventory[8] and the Strengths Finder 2.0[9] suitable for this purpose. They are non-threatening, thereby not pushing the client into a protective mode. Descriptors in these instruments have both strengths and weaknesses, which provide talking points to open up exploratory conversations about what might be useful in a client's circumstances, rather than focusing on evaluation. In addition, they allow us to help to shift language from the connotation of "right or wrong" or "bad or good" to "working or not working" and "useful or not useful." Again, this non-accusatory language helps clients to accept where they are starting from (e.g., that "3") and be more open to a shift in internal understanding about themselves.

Creating Relationship

One of the master coaches we interviewed spoke at length about how creating strong relationships with clients builds trust, which is a prerequisite for enabling coaching to go beyond intellectualizing to visceral, emotional pivots. Research evidence both in the literature and in our own epistemological work supports this position. Self-disclosure involving the revealing and sharing of

---

[7] Jourard (1959), Collins and Miller (1994).
[8] Thomas and Kilmann (2007).
[9] Rath (2007).

personal information leads to feelings of warmth, trust and confidence,[10] and we tend to disclose more to people whom we initially like.[11]

> *The master coach related the story of a pivotal moment of a client he was coaching. The manager had been resisting feedback about the effect he was having on others owing to his micromanaging and dominant behaviour. The organizational culture was collegial and team-based, whereas the manager was sure that his perspective was right and that he outperformed others. From the beginning of the engagement, the master coach really focused on building connection and trust with the manager, doing a lot of empathic listening. He considered it a prerequisite that he establish a strong connection and relationship with the client. He wanted the manager to know that he was valued in the organization for the results he was getting, just not for how he was generating those results. The relationship-building paid off when the manager was brought into a feedback meeting with the company owner and division head. The master coach facilitated and said it felt almost like group coaching. When told that people were getting upset about the way he was treating them, the manager broke down in tears. He said that he would do what he needed to in order to be there for the organization.*
>
> *According to the master coach, it was like a switch went on for the manager. When asked what he thought helped to build the foundation for the manager to be more open in that meeting, the master coach responded, "The connection, the trust, the relationship, the genuine caring. I care about this guy, it's palpable, real and folks knew it." This statement by the master coach actually demonstrates one of his signature strengths—establishing relationship. When he meets with his clients and they begin talking about their situation, without conscious awareness on his part, he builds his clients up, raises their awareness about their capabilities and encourages their success—all in an absolutely sincere and grounded way. He simply cannot NOT interact with his clients in this way; it is his stance as he genuinely believes in the capabilities of every client he meets.*

With executive coaching it is not unusual for "chemistry meetings" to occur to ensure that coach and client are a good fit. While there may be a match between coach and client on paper, a face-to-face meeting or telephone discussion is held to see whether they can work together. This is a foundational step for developing a quality relationship. We make sure that clients understand that they have a choice in working with us, even when the organization may give them little choice to be in coaching.

---

[10] See, for example, Jourard (1959).
[11] Collins and Miller (1994).

Making sure that there was a positive emotional bond with clients was a lesson learned early in Jackie's career. A mentor, Kathy Dannemiller, who was a forerunner in the field of organizational development, would often say, "If you don't love your client, don't work with him." Years later, a finding from a longitudinal study by Cohn and Fredrickson showed that an early positive emotion reaction is a potential marker for long-term adherence to an intervention.[12] Fredrickson found that "micro-moments of positive emotional experience," while fleeting, do set people on trajectories for growth and help to build their resources.[13] These studies, and the experiences of the master coaches whom we interviewed, demonstrate the importance of setting up relationships with positive emotion.

In initial meetings, however, clients could be in any frame of mind or in any emotional state. Recalling that emotions are contagious and that the first meeting sets the stage, it is important for coaches to present themselves in a genuine and coherent manner. Master coaches have learned that this comes both from understanding the dynamics of coaching situations and from knowing oneself.

Jackie arrived at a contracting session with her new client and her coaching sponsor, who was also her supervisor. Jackie's three go-to questions for new clients are: What brings the client to coaching? What are the areas of focus for coaching? What does success look like? In discussing these questions, the supervisor during the meeting made it very clear that the client was too tough with her staff and not connecting well with them. She was very pointed in her feedback, providing clear examples. The client listened to the feedback, seemed to take it well, asking for elucidation and examples. She didn't argue with her supervisor about her behaviour or the results that her behaviour seemed to produce. Jackie facilitated somewhat during the meeting, but it was clear that this was a typical interchange between supervisor and direct report. Jackie stayed after for a one-to-one discussion with her client. When the supervisor left, Jackie said, "Well, that was a tough meeting. I'm not sure how I'd be feeling right now if I were you." Her client immediately broke down in tears of relief.

Jackie was able to stay calm, which in turn calmed her client. She was able to connect with her client in a manner that created a more positive effect in their interaction. This developed their relationship further as a positive effect generated in a shared activity will, in turn, increase the subjective quality of the relationship.[14]

---

[12] Cohn and Fredrickson (2010).
[13] Fredrickson (2013), p. 15.
[14] Strong and Aron (2006).

Directing Attention

Another fundamental coaching tool is directing client attention. The world is filled with sensory data to be filtered and sorted through. Attention clearly serves as a requisite tool to be functional in our lives, but it is also a limiting factor. In the words of Josiah Royce, an American philosopher, "Whatever we come to know, whatever opinions we come to hold, our attention is what makes all our knowing and all our believing possible; and the laws followed by this, our own activity of attention will thus determine what we are to know and what we are to believe."[15]

In our Appreciative Coaching workshops we demonstrate this capability in a series of three short exercises. First, we tell participants, "Don't think of a red truck!" Of course, that is what each person does because it is impossible to tell the mind *not* to do something. The mind goes to that thought whether the direction is stated in the positive or negative. Second, we ask our participants to imagine, "When you are driving to your next destination, say to yourselves as you drive along, 'Don't look for a red truck. Don't look for a red truck.'" Anyone trying this experiment will see more red trucks than they ever have simply by directing their minds not to do so. Our last experiment asks participants to count all the red objects they can see around them as quickly as they can as we time them for 20 seconds. As they come back curious to report their success, we ask them, "How many blue objects did you see?" Most are startled and admit to seeing at most one or two blue objects, if any at all. These three experiments demonstrate how attention expands to where it is directed—whether positive or negative—and creates tunnel vision away from other things in the field of vision.

This is an important dynamic to integrate. In our interactions with clients, we cause them to go down a path of attention. We prime them in some way to expand thinking on a topic, whether we are conscious of that or not. We prime them not only with their conscious attention but also with their nonconsciousness—like directing them to see red trucks. We do not know, nor do we have control over, what thoughts, ideas or feelings may arise. We touch or prime the internal mechanisms of belief, memory and inner knowing that then cause them to vibrate together, much like touching a child's mobile that hangs above the bed.

One of Jackie's clients was using a negative metaphor to describe her relationship and frustration with her boss. She described herself as "chafing at the bit," like a

---
[15] Royce (1885), p. 317.

wild horse being reined in unwillingly. This showed how she felt constrained and slowed down in doing her work, contrary to her natural spirit. Jackie asked her how she might change this metaphor to reflect how she wanted things to be. In thinking about a new description, her client realized that it was not in her nature to be a rule-breaker. Therefore, as long as she was not breaking the rules of the organization, she should be able to do what she wanted. With that knowledge, she changed her image to that of *a wild stallion running free but within the fences of a large, expansive ranch.*

Jackie shifted her client's attention from the limitations she felt in working with her boss to the freedom she had in doing her job while still staying within organizational boundaries. This was in alignment with what she wanted to do. The shift helped Jackie's client to interact in new ways with her boss because she had a different understanding about their interchanges and it expanded her thinking about what she could do. It also started to transform the emotional tone of her relationship with her boss.

Discernment

Another way to direct client attention is by touching on what is seen. To discern is "to perceive by the sight or some other sense or by the intellect."[16] How we perceive or discern is filtered by our beliefs, and it is closely linked to how we understand a situation and come to conclusions. This is a natural, mostly nonconscious capability which allows us to move through our day with some ease. Consider how paralysed we would be if every item in our day needed to be seen, understood and integrated in a conscious manner before any action could be taken. But this ability can be a challenge at those times when we need to remain open to possibilities. Sometimes it is helpful to not immediately judge situations but to allow them to present more fully. "For if you judge them, you have set the rules for how you should react to them."[17] By remaining open longer, it is possible to become more aware of choices and responses that are available. It also creates room for listening and learning to trust the internal voice (of knowing and embodiment).

A specific tool we use with our clients when discussing a conflict situation is the "cone in the box" (Fig. 7.4). This visual metaphor is a mental experiment to help clients broaden their perspective. Pretending that the cone is

---

[16] Stein (1975), p. 377.
[17] A Course in Miracles (2007), p. 625 (30, I, 3:5).

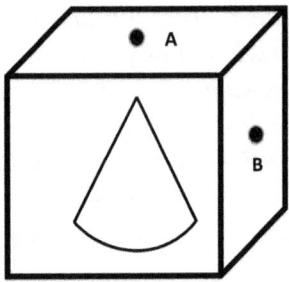

Fig. 7.4 Cone in the box visual metaphor

in an opaque brown box, an individual looking through peek hole A will see the shape of a circle, while an individual looking through peek hole B will see a triangle. The cone demonstrates visually how the perspective of seeing a circle is always right, and the perspective of seeing a triangle is always right; however, it is necessary to see both the circle and triangle together to grasp the larger perspective of the cone. Using this metaphor in a conflict situation demonstrates how one viewpoint can be put into a larger context by including the apparently opposing perspective. In a non-threatening manner it presents potentially contrasting views in a larger picture or context. This model helps clients to become more open to seeing situations from different perspectives, thus creating possibilities for mental shifts to occur.

Rachel had met numerous times with a business partner who loudly complained about the service he was receiving from Rachel's team. Hearing the criticisms and feeling pressured from the other demands of their jobs, her team members were demoralized. Rachel realized that she was irritated by the complaints but also knew that she needed to bring the two perspectives together. She met with the business partner, assuring him that his concerns were heard and promised resolution, but she also helped the partner to understand that his team needed to give her team a break and be more appreciative of what her team did. Two days later she heard from her team that they had received a thank you note signed by everyone on the partner's team along with other individual stories of appreciation. It turned the mood of her team around and inspired them to perform better.

We can help clients to learn to discern different aspects of their situation to gain greater perspective and meaning. For example, a client might decide to direct attention to the language used and make a choice to select language that is more in line with what she wants to create—like the client who chose the more generative metaphor of being a stallion free to roam. This metaphor created the potential for the client to experience her days in a new way, to see (discern) her work life more clearly. According to Frank Pajares, "All words begin as servants, eager to oblige and assume whatever function may be assigned to them, but, that accomplished, they become masters, imposing the will of their predefined intention and dominating the essence of human discourse."[18]

Present Moment

While we mentally time travel in our memories to the past and future, all of life happens in the present moment. Yet it is a challenge for most of us to stay in the present moment. Our ability to mentally time travel is, in part, how we create the fullness of our lives, but it also transports us away from the lived present. To stay in the present moment requires two components: the self-regulation of attention and the adoption of a particular orientation towards one's experience in the present moment.[19] Directing attention and discernment are thus important tools to help us live in the present. An orientation of acceptance of what is occurring in the present moment and a commitment to maintain an attitude of curiosity are also required. Staying in the present moment is not a passive process but an active one.

A characteristic of the human mind is wandering, and the mind wanders frequently no matter what we are doing. Curiously, we are less happy when our minds wander away from what we are doing in the moment, even when we wander to pleasant topics. Mind wandering is often the cause, not the consequence, of unhappiness and is a better predictor of happiness than what we are actually doing: "a human mind is a wandering mind, and a wandering mind is an unhappy mind."[20]

When our minds ruminate, we find ourselves caught in elaborate thinking about a situation and its origins, implications and associations. In this state we often find ourselves stuck in thoughts about personal goals or intentions that can be neither attained nor relinquished.[21] Mindfulness has been adopted into contemporary psychology from Buddhist spiritual practices as a useful approach for increasing awareness and responding skillfully to situations that cause emotional distress and maladaptive behaviour. "In a state of mindfulness, thoughts and feelings are observed as events in the mind, without

---

[18] Pajares (1992), p. 308.
[19] Bishop et al. (2004).
[20] Killingsworth and Gilbert (2010), p. 932.
[21] Teasdale, Segal, Williams and Mark (1995).

over-identifying with them and without reacting to them in an automatic, habitual pattern of reactivity."[22] In this story, the client benefited from practising mindfulness in a situation that had been repetitively troubling to her.

Sylvia, by ruminating on past experiences of how she felt fearful in executive meetings and interacting with senior leaders, often inhibited her ability to present herself as the professional she was in other, more comfortable circumstances. In one coaching session, anticipating an upcoming senior retreat, she and her coach discussed what she could do to prepare herself to feel more confident during the meeting. They brainstormed a number of ideas that Sylvia could use to feel more at ease. Her coach reminded her, "Above all, don't make yourself wrong about being nervous." Sylvia was to keep in mind that it was normal to be nervous in such meetings and was to allow the feeling to be. At their next coaching session she reported that the ideas that they had brainstormed were useful, but reminding herself that it was okay to be nervous helped the most. Paradoxically, being aware of the feeling and allowing herself to be nervous reduced her anxiety.

By making it okay to be anxious in a meeting that held stresses for her, this client was able to stay in the present moment's anxiety without expanding it to include the fearful experiences of the past. Mindfulness is not about thought suppression. Some anxiety stayed with her, but at a level that did not interfere with her feeling good about her presence at the meeting. This ability to stay mindfully in the moment resulted in a new experience and awareness of herself—one of greater acceptance—which in turn created the opening for a shift in how she experienced herself and others at the meeting.

By becoming mindful of what is and accepting of it, we can look at a situation with a beginner's mind, that is, from a perspective of curiosity, openness and learning. With mindfulness comes greater resources.[23] We become observers, rather than victims, opening up the possibility for new awareness or action. Mindfulness helps us to manage negative emotions and rumination,[24] as in Sylvia's case. She was able to observe herself as nervous as she interacted with new people or higher-level leaders, and she could be present with other people rather than withdraw into herself in fear. She was able to increase the information that was available to her in the moment which otherwise would have remained outside her awareness. This resulted in a wider perspective. This story exemplifies Rosch's observation that lives can "be improved by

---

[22] Bishop et al. (2004)
[23] Catalino and Fredrickson (2011).
[24] Coffey, Hartman and Fredrickson (2010).

changing the consciousness with which experience is perceived rather than the content of the experience."[25]

We coach our clients in the present moment even when we discuss the past or future. It is from this present perspective that we prime our clients to make pivots. One of the master coaches whom we interviewed described how a present moment expanded for her as she worked with one of her clients.

I began working with a leader who was described as visionary, intelligent, creative, passionate and even transformational, but his frustration with what he experienced as a slow, difficult corporate culture would come out in bursts of inappropriate temper. When he received feedback to this effect, he admitted that these outbursts happened frequently and he wasn't happy about them, but he also said that he was incapable of changing his behaviour because the emotion was too intense to control. I tried several tools to help him to see that he could change. After a number of failed attempts, I remember being internally, intensely looking for a way forward. I was very aware that he was losing faith in the possibility of his changing and I felt pressure to find something that would work for him. I was very aware of how I felt, what I was doing and what I sensed from my client. In that moment, inspiration struck to ask him whether he exhibited this behaviour with his daughter. Posing this question became the start of both shifting his understanding of himself and changing his behaviour.

Mindfulness and being in the present moment can give us, as coaches, "a greater capacity to see relationships between thoughts, feelings and actions and to discern the meanings and causes of experience and behavior."[26] It can help us to stay with our clients so that we respond from a greater perspective, as this master coach experienced.

Embodiment: Nexus of Mind, Body and Environment

In essence, we are hired as coaches because our clients want to have new experiences or new results in their lives or work. How are these new results created? We take new actions or behave in alternative ways from the past. But we must also consider that behaviours are impacted by feelings and in alignment with thoughts; therefore, for behaviours to change, so must emotions

---

[25] Rosch (2007), p. 263.
[26] Bishop et al. (2004), p. 234.

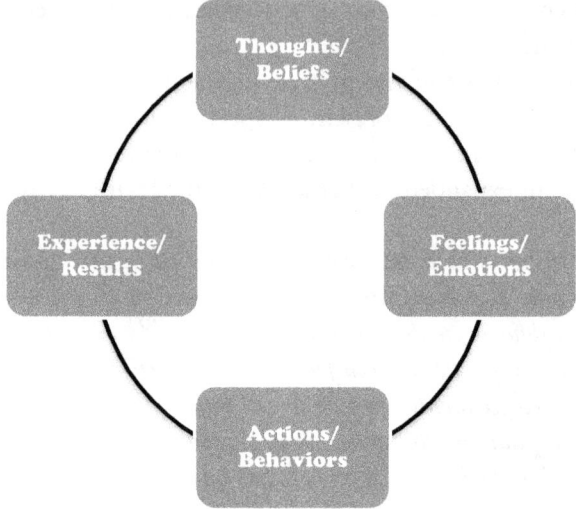

Fig. 7.5 Coaching cycle: The embodiment of mind, body and environment

and beliefs be changed. This describes the cycle of change as we see it in play in coaching (Fig. 7.5).

This dynamic cycle is best understood through the lens of embodiment. Traditionally, cognition has been identified solely with the brain, but in contemporary work the boundaries of cognition have expanded beyond the brain to include the body and environment as interacting elements. This new perspective breaks past the concept that what happens in our minds is isolated from our body. We see it now as distributed cognition—that is, what we traditionally attributed solely to the individual brain are actually accomplishments that transcend this boundary, taking into account our bodies and environment.[27] It is a dynamic interplay of how our brains think, how our bodies move and how we interact with environmental stimuli.[28]

In embodiment, perception and action are not separate systems. Perception is something we do as our bodies interact with our environment; it is not simply something that happens to us. To illustrate this with a simple example, if we are writing while riding in a vehicle that begins to move and our hand slips, we automatically shift to correct for the movement of the vehicle. We are not passive receivers of what is in our environment but active participants. As actors in our environment, what we experience is shaped by how we act. This process of creating our own experience through our actions is called

---

[27] Hutchins (2010).
[28] Hutchins (2010).

"enaction."[29] Embodiment and enaction are therefore closely linked as one system. In fact, "it is hard to imagine how abstract thinking could ever come about during an individual's lifetime without the body providing the proper sensory stimulation, the raw material for the body to process."[30]

This framework has exciting implications for coaching. It offers an interactive process model of human change which broadens and deepens our understanding of how we can help clients to effect change through their thoughts, feelings, actions and results, and it becomes a tool or way to approach clients to influence a pivotal shift. Our coaching cycle model, through the lens of embodiment, presents multiple entry points through which we can influence change with our clients: creating new thought and belief patterns; cultivating different feelings; experimenting with a range of actions and behaviours; and recognizing and building on positive results. Clients may respond better by beginning with one element over another. For example, one client may respond well to models that help to explain what is happening in the environment (thoughts/beliefs); another may need to be actively experimenting to see what results occur (actions/behaviours); and yet others may need to sort out their affect (feelings/emotions) about a situation in order to take action or to think strategically. In general, clients go through the entire cycle but their entry point for learning may differ.

This holistic embodiment model offers an explanation for why time between coaching sessions is critical as clients try out new ideas. In coaching conversations, interaction is often intellectual—that is, a discussion about what clients are doing or what they are thinking. The time between sessions provides opportunities for clients to interact with their environment. Coming back into the coaching conversation to reflect on the results of action completes the cycle. We interact with our clients by participating and co-creating events of change that help them to access their inner process through one or more of the four entry points.

Clients are often unaware of the energy that their physical presence exerts in a room. Jackie helped one client to learn that her physical presence impacted others and was a key part of her leadership presence, perhaps as important as how well she prepared herself or the language she used. She helped her client experience this in a couple of ways. First, her client came to understand that she could dominate a room simply by the way she held herself. This was not a positive or negative descriptor of the client but depended on the others in the room with her. She could either engage or intimidate others depending on how they experienced her. Becoming

---

[29] Hutchins (2010), p. 425.
[30] Pfeifer and Bongard (2007), p. 364.

aware of her presence helped her to consciously adjust how she interacted with others to create more productive interactions. Second, she learned about the impact of her presence in another way. She was asked to try an experiment with her boss. She changed nothing about their regular one-to-one meetings other than where she sat. Rather than sitting across from her boss she sat next to her, sharing a single document to review. She was very sceptical about whether her experiment would have any effect so she was startled by the positive change in the tone of their interaction. She came to understand herself in a new light.

Further, she unknowingly exemplified what is now recognized as "embodied rapport."[31] Rapport, traditionally defined by people's perceptions of positivity and mutuality, has been extended to include learnings from embodied cognition. It is now recognized that our perceptions and judgements are reflected in our motor and bodily experiences.

Coaching Context: The Client Internal Landscape

Role of Beliefs

How we interact with the world and create our lived experience is impacted by what we think or believe. Beliefs are interpretations of reality about ourselves, others, our environment and the spiritual domain. They are held explicitly and consciously but they also exist "beyond individual control or knowledge."[32] How to change beliefs remains a mysterious process.[33] As coaches, we have no manual to follow, but we can expand our awareness and knowledge of what is known and proposed about beliefs.

While beliefs are constructed by an individual, how this happens is mediated by the actions of others. Each of our individual actions creates some disturbance in the environment, which others then respond to and act. This is a constructive process where we each change and are changed by our environment. It is through this social process that we can experience a change in our beliefs; in fact, we often need outside influences to make changes in our belief systems.[34] We cannot simply will ourselves to believe something.[35] Outside input, as from a coach, may be needed.

---

[31] Vacharkulksemsuk and Fredrickson (2012).
[32] Mansour (2009).
[33] Mansour (2009), p. 37.
[34] Tobin and LaMaster (1995)
[35] Royce 1996/ (1920).

Some beliefs that clients change are more significant than others. Minor changes in beliefs are more easily assimilated, but the more central a belief (about the self), the more functional connections it will have and the more it will resist change.[36] Changing a central belief sends repercussions throughout the system, causing other beliefs to be examined. A change may therefore be experienced as a conversion or Gestalt shift.[37]

Beliefs are unlikely to be replaced unless they prove to be unsatisfactory—that is, when they are challenged or they cannot be assimilated into existing conceptions.[38] People operate in such a way as to maximize internal consistency, and they try to avoid internal dissonance. A belief may change when some anomalies are presented and the person is not able to accommodate the conflicting information as the master coach demonstrated in the story below.

I was coaching a young, divorced father working on his PhD. He was at the end of the dissertation process and it was a challenge for him to keep going. For several coaching sessions he complained about his struggles, until finally he declared that he was up to his eyeballs with all of it and was going to quit. I saw the pivotal moment occur when I said to him, 'Absolutely! I agree with you! I can see all the reasons why you don't want to go on. You really want this, but it's really too tough!' While saying this, I really believed in my heart of hearts that he very much wanted to finish. My client responded with a gigantic push back, 'I've always wanted this. It's something I've dreamed about. I have worked so hard, I can't believe you think I should quit…' After nearly 20 minutes I asked, 'Do you hear yourself?' When I asked the question he calmed down. The topic of quitting never came up again in our coaching, and he never went back to his negative style. Internally I felt a big smile when he pushed back.

The Genius of Metaphors

Metaphors are a rich tool for coaching. In terms of embodiment, they are created early in life through primary sensory experiences and they form a rich part of human language, as in expressions like "They greeted me warmly," "This movie stinks" and "Tomorrow is a big day." These "primary metaphors" link early childhood sensory experiences with conceptualizations about those experiences. In this regard, such metaphors are considered to be an embodied experience:

---

[36] Rokeach (1968).
[37] Pajares (1992).
[38] Pajares (1992).

- "They greeted me warmly" links the feeling of warmth to affection, like the early experience of feeling warm while being held by a parent.
- "This movie stinks" links the smell to the evaluation, as in the sensory experience of being repelled by a foul-smelling object.
- "Tomorrow is a big day" links size to importance, like a child finding big things such as parents exerting major forces on them or dominating visual experiences

These primary metaphors become part of our cognitive unconscious and part of our abstract thought process.[39] Cognitive linguist George Lakoff and philosopher Mark Johnson have gone so far as to claim that our conceptual system is largely metaphorical.[40] Metaphors are a means by which we conceptualize our world.[41] Some are so much a part of our language that we do not even recognize them as metaphors—for example, someone saying, "The odds are against us" or "We'll have to take our chances" are unlikely to be seen as speaking metaphorically.

"The essence of a metaphor is understanding and experiencing one kind of thing in terms of another."[42] A metaphor highlights features of an experience, connects to other features within the metaphor and helps create new meanings. In this way, metaphors help us to understand, guide action, justify inferences and set goals. Our beliefs can be seen in our metaphors.[43] Thus they give tacit knowledge voice and become a heuristic to express beliefs.[44] Creating a new metaphor with a new meaning "can have a feedback effect, guiding our future actions in accordance with the metaphor."[45] By changing a metaphor we change our conceptual system or beliefs, which in turn can change what is real for us and affect how we perceive the world and act on those perceptions. This effect can be seen in the story of one of the master coaches we interviewed.

Mitchell, a senior executive who aspired to a CEO position, was very interested in learning how he came across as a leader, even requesting extended leadership assessments as part of his coaching. He worked with his executive coach to apply for several CEO openings, failing in each attempt to secure the position. His coach

---

[39] Lakoff and Johnson (1999).
[40] Lakoff and Johnson (1980b).
[41] Lakoff and Johnson (1980a).
[42] Lakoff and Johnson (1980b), p. 124.
[43] Mansour (2009), p. 38.
[44] Martof (1996).
[45] Lakoff and Johnson (1980b), p. 130.

reflected that each disappointment brought with it an opportunity for Mitchell to learn more about himself. There were a series of what the master coach called "eco-spasm events" of the same tone that eventually, with coaching, amassed to a pivotal moment for Mitchell. The pivot came when Mitchell realized what it meant to be a public persona, and learned how to relax a little and not try so hard to be perfect. His coach saw this new understanding ignite when he offered the metaphor of orchestra leader to Mitchell as a lens to consider how a CEO leads. Mitchell came to realize that it didn't matter whether he was the best cello player in the orchestra. What mattered was how the orchestra director, the Leonard Bernstein, brought people together. This metaphor led Mitchell to a new understanding of his feedback data and provided him with an image of the leader he wanted to grow into. His coach supported him to deal with fears that came up as he tried new behaviours required of this image. With growing confidence, he did what he believed was important, eventually securing a CEO position.

The Associative Networks of Memory

Memory, as already described, is time travelling mentally to the past and to the future, from the present moment.[46] It is a subjective experience which differs from our conscious awareness of the present moment; we are unlikely to confuse what we remember with what we are experiencing. A memory is recreated in the present moment and is influenced by the present—that is, the past is constructed from present understanding and so is reconstructed. Memory is as much about the present as it is about the past.[47] This is important to coaching because it means that we can reinterpret the meaning of the past, and coaches can influence this reinterpretation.

Memory is stored in networks of association. In fact, cognitive models suggest that *all* thought, memory and perception, including complex cognitive processes, involve the activation of networks of association.[48] When these associations are activated, they may influence thought and feelings outside awareness and can lead to behaviour to approach or avoid situations or others.[49] Remembering is "more about recombining multiple sources of information than it is about calling to mind a fixed representation of an event."[50] When inconsistencies and distortions are exposed, interpretation can begin change.

---

[46] Tulving (2002).
[47] Fernyhough (2012).
[48] Westen (1999).
[49] Westen (1999).
[50] Fernyhough (2012), p. 122.

Coaches, in listening to a client's story, can bring together contrary facts that the client may not have seen but when presented and discussed make sense. How many of us have heard, "Oh, I never thought of it that way?" We help clients bring together new associations and create new interpretations.

Remembering is inherently a social process that happens in collaboration with others, and it is always contextual.[51] It is in sharing memories with others, as clients do with a coach, that they can relive and understand the past in a new way.

Gerald was encouraged to apply for a senior executive position but felt unsure whether to do so because of prior experiences on two major projects that he had led. He felt that each one could be looked at as failures because the organization had shifted direction on one and decided not to not move forward on the other. Reflecting on these experiences with his coach, he came to realize that they were also experiences where he had learned a great deal. He applied the skills that he had learned from these experiences to other successful projects, and they were requisite skills of the company's new leadership model.

Memory is not just about the past but also about the future. We use it to recall our aspirations, goals and plans for the future. The seeds of a desired future are in our memories of the past. In the discovery phase of Appreciative Coaching, we spend time helping our clients to achieve a more empowering perspective by recollecting their strengths, abilities, successes and aspirations. Through these they affirm a sense of the possible and look forward to possibilities.[52] The more imaginative effort our clients put into creating a future scenario, the more possible it seems.[53]

Modes of Inner Knowing

All humans experience a sense of knowing inside of them when something feels true. These "truths" may come from various modes, such as intuition, instinct, interaction with the environment, or deep empathy. Some of these kinds of knowing are culturally acceptable, such as trusting one's expert intuition, while others may be seen as inexplicable, such as clairvoyance. Which of these modes of knowing we use with our clients depends on our own comfort level and that of our clients. As we learned about the nonconscious, however, we are already

---

[51] Fernyhough (2012).
[52] Orem, Binkert and Clancy (2007).
[53] Fernyhough (2012).

using different sources of knowing without conscious awareness. As an example, research has shown that people tend to like a painting that they select at a gut level for longer than they do a picture that they analyse and then select.[54] Each of us has ways to internalize a sense of truth, and this sense of truth enters into our coaching conversations whether we explicitly acknowledge it or not.

Well-known author and intuitive Laura Day, in her book *Practical Intuition*, explained that every decision uses our intuition to some degree, as well as our knowledge, judgement and feelings.[55] For example, the question of "Should I go to Florida in February?" has us looking at the decision from multiple perspectives—tapping into what we know about Florida as a vacation place, how we feel about going there, and our inner knowing (the reason we can't put our finger on) for intuiting what the trip might be like. Day proposed that we evaluate situations in our lives according to four main sources of information:

1. What we *know* about them (our knowledge and memories);
2. What we *think* of them (our judgements and interpretations);
3. How we *feel* about them (our feelings and emotions);
4. What we *intuit* about them (our direct knowing).[56]

She considered emotions to be the least valid of the four sources. The strength of consciously employing the four sources, however, is that by incorporating all of them we provide a kind of check and balance process against concerns about over- or underusing any one of them. Well-known researchers such as Daniel Kahneman[57] have cautioned against the "biases of intuition" and feeling overconfident in intuitive beliefs and preferences which can result in errors of judgement. He has proposed that humans have two systems that drive our thinking: System 1 is fast, intuitive and emotional; System 2 is slower, more deliberative and more logical.[58] Kahneman referred to the "psychology of accurate intuition" as involving no magic[59] but rather representing the phenomenon of "expert intuition." While Day's perspective of intuition is that of a mode of direct knowing, Kahneman sees the core of his System 1 as associative memory, the automatic and unconscious processes that he says

---

[54] Westen (1999).
[55] Day (1996), p. 158.
[56] Day (1996), p. 158.
[57] Kahneman (2011).
[58] Kahneman (2011).
[59] Kahneman (2011), p. 11.

underlie intuitive thinking.[60] For him, intuition is a form of cognitive recognition, and acquired expertise.

Ann found herself conducting an experiment shortly after reading about the four sources of information proposed by Day. An unexpected event occurred on a beautiful autumn day when she was hiking in the mountains with Frank, a coaching colleague visiting from Germany.

> *We were walking to a waterfall at the foot of a steep hiking trail which was a short distance from the parking lot. On the way up we encountered a man who asked if we had seen his three children—two teenagers and a younger boy. We had not. The three children had preceded him down the trail and he had lost sight of them. We continued on our way. A short time later we descended to find the man, his wife and two other young people walking around and calling out names. They were upset because they could find no trace of the missing children in the forest and the day was waning. I was quite familiar with the area and knew there was another hiking trail that ran along the bottom of the mountain and came out about two miles down the road. I had this strong sense that I could really be of help in this situation. I thought about the four sources of information and began with the first one—my knowledge of the area. I knew there were only a few ways the children could have gone. I asked questions about where the children were last seen, gathered data and judged that they could easily have ended up on another trail, feeling lost and so kept walking. I then checked my feelings and did not pick up any fear or danger about the situation. If anything, I felt a kind of confidence and determination. Finally, I went to stand physically at the place where the children were last seen and asked for inner guidance. After a few minutes I got a strong sense that they had gone on a nearby path and that I should drive immediately to where the trail ended two miles away. Frank and I drove to the other trailhead where we found the children sitting on rocks, swinging their legs and waiting for someone to find them. They had arrived about 10 minutes earlier. Their cell phones didn't work in the area but they had followed good hiking rules by staying on the trail and waiting to be found. We drove the children back to their parents, who were elated. The father hugged me tightly with great thanks for the help. I felt euphoric—I had followed the four sources and the approach worked. Frank and I celebrated with champagne.*

Ann's story exemplifies the different ways in which coaches can learn to apply and get comfortable with new strategies and tools. This opportunity just appeared and Ann was spontaneously drawn to test the idea of using

---
[60] Kahneman (2011).

intuition in the context of the other sources of information. The learning was quite significant for her in that she applied a structured embodied process to the situation and in following it she allowed it to unfold without efforts to control it. It felt very affirming and raised her confidence level in listening to her inner process. As we encourage our clients to do, we also need to experiment with new strategies and tools so that we stay at our learning edge.

Tapping into the Nonconscious

Westen has reminded us that "We are much more expert unconsciously, because expertise implies automatization of processes that once required conscious attention."[61] Peter Block, a leader in the field of organization development, was known to ask clients who professed not to know an answer to a previous question, "If you pretended to know the answer, what would it be?" A form of this question has been a useful tool in coaching to help clients access their inner resources of knowing. Invariably, clients have an answer and the answer turns out to be insightful. The levels of learning model[62] has proved to be an effective tool in helping clients to tap into or trust a way of knowing that is unfamiliar to them. This is the model referred to in the story at the opening of this chapter. There are four levels or steps to learning:

1. *Unconscious incompetence*: We don't know that we don't know.
2. *Conscious incompetence*: We know that we don't know.
3. *Conscious competence*: We know that we know.
4. *Unconscious competence*: We don't know that we know.

In the fourth step, our expert knowledge or expert intuition is so familiar to us that it slips into unawareness. We may know how to do something but not be able to explain why or how we do it. This understanding has proved to be useful to some clients in learning to trust "with no proof" and have more faith in other ways of knowing.

> *Mary came to coaching because her manager was frustrated by her inability to do strategy in a strategy position. As an engineer, Mary was bewildered by how her manager seemed to capriciously select one goal over another when there was no apparent data to support the decision. She was frustrated that she was expected to*

---
[61] Westen (1999), p. 1097.
[62] The origin of this model is uncertain but we believe it to be Broadwell (1969). He presented it as the levels of teaching.

do the same. Her coach explained the levels of learning to her and she discovered how an expert level of intuition comes into play from unconscious competence. She then remembered how she also used that type of knowing to make decisions prior to her current position. The model resonated with Mary and helped her to reframe what she was being asked to do.

Nurturing Interiority and Inspiration

Deep learning requires that we include ourselves in the process—"knowledge by presence."[63] According to psychologist Tobin Hart, this involves looking not just at outer data but also closely into ourselves. Great texts of wisdom are often depicted as "living words," inviting readers to reconsider the words again and again in order to see what more will be revealed. Tobin described the process of deep learning in secular domains as being no different: "The world as a whole are [*sic*] living words—awaiting expansion in order to be fully understood" whether we are reading a biology text or the "text" of the situation or person in front of us.[64]

It is not the world that changes. The secret to grasping its meaning is to change the quality of how we encounter the world. We change by allowing ourselves to become open to it. *Knowledge by presence* is a reciprocal, interdependent revelation which requires valuing the development of interiority or creating internal spaciousness and depth to help us navigate the complexities of life. This form of learning contrasts with traditional ways of acquiring knowledge, like the studying of material for a test which involves external expectations, judgement, and anxiety to accumulate information. Life offers us the opportunity to go deeper by becoming the subject of learning. Interiority is creating a capacity within ourselves to take in the world. "The greater the complexity and demands of the outer world, the more essential is our internal discernment, our attention to values, our ability to be present in the midst of streaming information."[65]

Coaching can help clients to enhance interiority. It begins, of course, with how open our own interior space is. The more we accept the view that our clients are mysteries, the more this becomes important. We become curious about practices that quiet the mind to discern meaning and reveal possibilities. We realize how our questions can help to promote interiority. Deep questions can increase the capacity to open up to unexpected insight. For example,

---

[63] Hart (2007), p. 1.
[64] Hart (2007), p. 1.
[65] Hart (2007), p. 2.

the core questions we use as a tool in Appreciative Coaching ask clients to view their situation in a broader and deeper context:

1. What gives life to you now?
2. Describe a high point or peak experience in your life or work up to now.
3. What do you most value about yourself, your relationships and the nature of your work?
4. What one or two things do you want more of in your life?[66]

We have often found that asking these questions when a discussion seems steeped in a problem without resolution expands clients' thinking, reminding them of what is important, and creates a breakthrough. Interior expansion engages the imagination, which leads to discovery, synthesis and application.[67] Our minds slow down in contemplation and we gain deeper awareness. We develop our ability to trust ourselves and become better able to listen to the internal voice that guides us.

Inspiration

Inspiration is an activity of knowing.[68] We are inspired when we come to a deep sense of knowing and are invigorated. "These moments fill us and move us, providing a kind of psychological or spiritual sustenance."[69] When we are inspired, we can reach to the best in ourselves to expand what is possible in our lives. We enhance connections and feel greater love, acceptance, trust and appreciation, tapping into the resources of positive emotions. When this connection is intense enough, our boundaries of self seem to disappear and we experience fullness or a sense of awakening. Inspiration arises as a result of opening up our knowing in a way that is distinctly different from normal waking consciousness, whether we name that source as our unconscious, Self or God, or it remains a mystery.

With inspiration come clarity and vibrancy. We may see unexpected connections or a hidden layer of reality. Insight or deep clarity can shift us from a linear, rational mode of thinking to an intuitive mode. Clearly, the way we deal with our clients brings opportunities for us to inspire them, but they may come in unexpected ways.

---

[66] Orem et al. (2007), p. 18.
[67] Hart et al. (2000).
[68] Hart et al. (2000).
[69] Hart et al. (2000), p. 31.

Jackie was working with a coaching client who was a teacher, writer and consultant. The client had been stalled in writing. One day, Jackie read an article on teaching that she felt the client would greatly enjoy and sent it to her. She received the following reply, "What an insightful and thought-provoking article! Reading it I had so many ahas go off. The weirdest part is: I feel settled in a new way and I want to write ... go figure that one."

Positive Emotions

Positive emotions broaden and build an individual's internal resources. They broaden awareness by increasing the scope of attention, attentional flexibility and holistic processing, thus creating a form of consciousness that includes a wider array of thoughts, actions and perceptions.[70] Under the influence of positive emotions, people can have wider perceptual access, more inclusive and connected social perceptions, and more relaxed and expansive bodily comportment.[71] These resources can be cognitive (attending mindfully to the present moment), psychological (having a sense of mastery over a challenge), social (giving and receiving emotional support) and physical (a capacity to ward off illness).[72] Even small experiences of positive emotions have an impact over time. "Little-by-little, micromoments of positive emotional experience, although fleeting, reshape who people are by setting them on trajectories of growth and building their enduring resources for survival."[73]

As mentioned in Chapter 3, Barbara Fredrickson identified ten positive emotions as key contributors to broadening and building internal resources: love, joy, gratitude, serenity (or contentment), interest, hope, pride, amusement, inspiration and awe.[74] They are listed here in order of relative frequency. These ten are not an exhaustive list of positive emotions but they are experienced relatively frequently in our daily lives and they are targets of increasing research. In coaching we can benefit from research on ways to create positive emotions. Research has shown that participating in the following activities provides great benefit:

- *helping* or engaging in pro-social behaviour;
- *interacting* with others;
- *playing*;

---

[70] Johnson, Waugh and Fredrickson (2010), Fredrickson (2013).
[71] Fredrickson (2013), p. 24.
[72] Fredrickson et al. (2008).
[73] Fredrickson (2013), p. 15.
[74] Fredrickson (2013).

- *learning* something new;
- engaging in *spiritual activity*;
- *exercising*.[75]

This list offers us positive ideas and suggestions of daily activities that we can share with clients who are facing challenges or feeling confined by limiting patterns of behaviour. Interestingly, one need not be an optimist to gain the cognitive benefits of positive emotions.[76]

This is not to say that negative emotions can or should be avoided. They serve different functions and it is necessary to have an appropriate balance of positive emotions to negative emotions for generative thinking.[77] Negative emotions have been found to narrow attentional scope, decrease attentional flexibility and create attentional bias towards sources of threat.[78] However, trying to fight them off or repress them is not an effective technique to reduce their effects. Viktor Frankl, a psychotherapist and survivor of a Nazi death camp, got through his experience by searching for some meaning in his daily life. He found that feeling emotions to their fullest in the moment rather than reining them in was an effective therapy for their dissolution.

> *Sam was angry with his boss but he didn't want to discuss it with his coach because he believed that by acknowledging his feelings he would then inappropriately express them. He also didn't know what to do with these feelings. Since Sam had already brought the subject up, his coach gently moved the conversation forward, allowing Sam to express his feelings to her. Sam found that the conversation helped his feelings to dissipate. He realized that accepting the feelings didn't mean that he liked them, and, further, he realized that acknowledging them did not mean that he had to discuss his feelings with his boss. He gained greater freedom and choice in what to do.*

Creating New Habits

Habits are ways in which our minds work to save effort. They have a positive effect when they help us to engage in life efficiently, but they can also get in the way when they produce undesired results. Emotions are an important feature of our memory process. They colour the quality of a memory, become an integral part of it and facilitate its storage in long-term memory. Memories

---

[75] Catalino and Fredrickson (2011).
[76] Johnson et al. (2010).
[77] Fredrickson (2013).
[78] Johnson et al. (2010).

with emotions become Gestalts that are easily represented and remembered.[79] These memories have a signature feeling[80] associated with them—that is, an emotion that colors the quality of the memory and is a part of it. A signature feeling has three functions: it improves access to memory; acts as glue to hold elements of memory together for a long period of time; and fills in gaps or filters information that conflicts with feeling. These signature feelings become problematic when they keep an individual stuck in a pattern or assert themselves spontaneously in an inappropriate manner.

Donald did not like that he exploded in meetings when his direct reports failed to perform to expectations or when events didn't go as planned. He realized that his anger got in the way of his being the kind of truly strong leader that others wanted to work with. When he discussed this with his coach, she asked him, "What's your tell?" Not understanding the question, he learned that a "tell" was an unconscious physical act that disclosed one's thinking; what poker players seek to avoid. He asked a trusted colleague he thought would provide him with an answer. He was startled to discover that his friend had an immediate and easy response. Just before exploding, Donald would pull on his ear. Going forward, he used this knowledge to catch himself and consciously moved to a different response that he and his coach identified.

Ann has a rule of thumb that she coaches by: if she hears a client tell the same negative or self-limiting story of a troublesome experience more than three times, she stops the client and points out that the individual seems stuck. She also draws on paper the circular nature of the pattern. She helps her client to understand that the repetition of the story is a habit of thought—either of the past or future—which can be changed as any other habit can. She also asks her client if what they are feeling is familiar, checking to see if it is an old belief or pattern and discovering where it is signalled in the body. She tells them she is not interested in listening repeatedly to a self-limiting story because by doing so she inadvertently enables her clients in further telling their story, and each retelling solidifies its illusion of reality. She would rather ask them to tell a new story of what they want.

In these cases we help clients to develop new habits. We work with the understanding that it is more useful to create a new habit to replace an old one than to stop an undesired habit.[81] We support clients in creating new patterns

---

[79] Nespor (1987).
[80] Spiro (1982).
[81] Duhigg (2012).

so that attention is growing towards a desired result or future. We help clients to see that they have choice in how they feel.

Implications for Coaching

Our intent in this chapter has been to link the concepts and knowledge that we've gained from researching our model of self-organizing pivotal moments to actual ideas, suggestions, examples and stories of ways to ignite substantial change. We know that our readers have many more stories and experiences that will confirm and/or conflict with our findings and that will add to the storehouse of knowledge/knowing for the advancement of our profession. Our stance as coaches is to continue to be seekers of higher levels of awareness and to engage in developing our own interiority. We didn't know to call it that: we just felt compelled. At this point along our hermeneutic journey, we are glad we took the path less travelled.

8

Finding Coherence

You are not a drop in the ocean. You are the entire ocean, in a drop.

—Rumi

Alchemical Moments

Sometimes I feel the pivotal moment in clients before they do. For me it's often chills, or some kind of physical response. It may be butterflies in my stomach or some kind of wave that comes over me. When this happens, I'll share it with my client and might say, "Whoa, you just said something really big" or "Boy, I just got a big chill from that, let's stop a minute. What's that about?" When I first started coaching, I wondered if I was making it about me, and I would say, "I may be in left field about this, but I don't think it's about me." Over time I realized that, more often than not, I was right about it, and I'm not shy any more about sharing my own personal take on what might be their pivotal moment. I'm confident that something will come out of it for them. It is exciting to so viscerally share a pivotal moment in that way.

These words of a master coach reveal so clearly how pivotal moments are shared embodied experiences between client and coach. As we mature in our role as coaches, we learn to trust our inner knowing and to anticipate these internal experiences that bring with them a sense of coherence to our work. There were numerous times in writing this book that we penned the observation "There is no shared definition" for a particular construct or concept. The reality of our profession is that we seek to inspire and work with clients while still searching for philosophical and scientific roots to guide us on the path. We are like a sorcerer's apprentice searching for the formula to create alchemical, golden moments of change.

A New Science of Change

As incredulous as this may sound, one of the insights we had towards the close of our hermeneutic journey was that we were really searching for a new science of change that would help to explain or describe what dynamics were at play when pivotal moments occurred. At the beginning, our intentions were modest—how do we better understand this phenomenon of substantial change? We didn't know where this question would lead us. We hoped to gather knowledge about this issue so we could get better at helping our clients have more such moments. It was an inner agitation that we needed to quell because we had our own ideas and experiences about what was going on that seemed to work but we had little external verification.

From our research we began to find words to describe the phenomenological experience of living through or witnessing the act of pivoting: movement, process, interactive, holistic, eventful, embodied and, at times, spiritual (transpersonal). We were amazed to find studies, research and case studies that seemed to confirm what we were experiencing. In other words, we have been through our own slow or liminal pivotal moment. To use a metaphor, it feels like a veil has been lifted for us on what's really happening. What we are exploring is concrete, valuable and shared by many other curious individuals. We rejoice that well-intentioned, hard-working professionals, researchers, scientists and practitioners around the world are finding new ways to describe the complexity and chaos of human and social development. We actually found that the path less travelled turns out to be heavily trafficked with inquiry from fields as diverse as robotics, somatics, biology, molecular biology, psychology, social psychology, transpersonal psychology, neuroscience, business, organizational development and phenomenology. We are finding coherence in understanding what pivoting truly means.

Like Darwin's theory of evolution, which revolutionized science at the time and spawned numerous cultural and social metaphors (survival of the fittest, competition, control, structure), there is a new science of change emerging that describes the world as flow, interconnectedness, uncertainty, mystery, creativity, flux of patterns, self-organization and order in chaos.[1] This new

---

[1] Briggs and Peat (1999).

science weaves together constructivism, phenomenology, complexity theory, chaos theory, self-organization and quantum physics to see *human* change as dynamic movement that is holistic in nature. New cultural and social metaphors are emerging to highlight this basic shift from describing the world as an object to interacting with it as an ever-changing process. Coaching at its essence is a creative, mutual process of discovery.

Authors John Briggs and David Peat proposed that "chaos is nature's creativity" and noted how "the brain self-organizes by changing its subtle connections with every act of perception."[2] For them, moments of insight occur "when the flux of the creator's perception shifts and the chaos begins to self-organize," and these moments "seem to set in motion a significant change in our perception, to get to the 'truth' of our perception, the authenticity of our experience of life."[3] They defined creativity as getting beyond the conditioning by society to find the "truth" of the moment, not an absolute truth but truth as the expression of a person's connection to the whole, a moment of true self. As we've seen in previous chapters, the genius of metaphors is that our beliefs can be seen in them. When we change metaphors, we change our beliefs. Here are some elements of the new emerging metaphors from the writings of Briggs and Peat:

- There exists an underlying interconnectedness in apparently random events (hidden patterns, nuances).
- Like the turbulence of a mountain stream, apparent disorder masks underlying patterns that are simultaneously stable and ever-changing.
- Our sense of "self" is in perpetual flux; we are both the same person we were ten years ago and a substantially new person.
- We are interconnected with many other systems that surround and flow through us.
- Everything is connected to everything else through positive and negative feedback loops which result in self-organizing (think of a flock of birds taking off or pinball machines).
- We are shaped by what passes through us (influences from the social, cultural, historical, biological and emotional environments we reside in).
- Subtle, even tiny, influences can transform a system (ancient Chinese proverb: the power of a butterfly's wings can be felt on the other side of the world[4]).

---

[2] Briggs and Peat (1999), p. 19.
[3] Briggs and Peat (1999), p. 25.
[4] Briggs and Peat (1999), p. 31.

Table 8.1 Emerging Holistic Model

Traditional scientific model	Emerging holistic model
externally directed	internally directed
scientific paradigm	social constructionism
consciousness	non consciousness
linear time	expanded concept of time
planned change	self-organization
negative bias	emotional equilibrium

- In human development, each stage demands its own time.
- There will always be "missing information" and uncertainty (mystery, blind spots).

We find all of these elements in play when coaching others. As Briggs and Peat so succinctly stated, "Creativity can occur in a conversation when the turbulence of questioning and exchange gives birth to a subtle, new understanding or a true way of expressing something."[5] To so clearly articulate the essence of a coaching conversation, one would think they have experienced it.

Conditions for Igniting Substantial Change

Partway through our path of inquiry, we brainstormed six conditions that we thought were necessary for substantial change to occur and compared them to six more or less opposite conditions that we thought impeded or could not account for substantial change (Table 8.1).

We are pleased to report that we found each of the six conditions of the Emerging Holistic Model to be substantiated by many of the scientific and philosophical studies that we explored. We invite you to make your own assessment as you've accompanied us through the chapters of the book. We summarize our thoughts on these conditions below.

Externally Directed vs. Internally Driven

Deep and substantial change is a phenomenon of inner process. Research supports the premise that people are at their best when in alignment with their pure and natural behavioural nature and purpose, being the person they were born to be.[6] Humans are also subject to conditioned programming from

---
[5] Briggs and Peat (1999), p. 23.
[6] Bunnell (2011), p. 11.

the external world that often masks or suppresses their authentic self. Even though the true self is always present, it's often concealed behind external conditioning and individuals feel self-dislike when they fail to fulfill the layers of expectations they have taken on or that have been placed on them.[7]

To date, the business of changing humans has been thought to be a manageable, predetermined, measured and even controllable process. This belief has led to a deficit, fix-it perspective of humans, one that says that parents, educators, managers and employers can better identify what is wrong with someone and seek to fix them from the outside. This perspective of external, manageable change is still accepted at all levels of organizations, institutions and homes around the world.

The concept of self-organization tells us that an individual's inner process is growing all the time. Inner change may be anticipated or even transformational, but fundamentally it cannot be planned as was thought possible by Newtonian standards. We are capable of having moments of insight which can cause significant shifts in perception and allow for experiences of authenticity. The new organic metaphor of human change is that of a "garden" continually growing (generative approach).

Scientific Paradigm vs. Social Constructionism

Social constructionists say that we are moving from a fixed, seemingly objective idea of the capacities of human potential to a more open exploration of possibilities. Constructionist theory is an approach to human science and practice that "replaces the individual with the relationship as the locus of knowledge."[8] The key to the construction of social meaning is language.[9] This means that how we humans communicate, interact, create symbols and construct metaphors with one another creates our sense of reality. While we may be able to define the physical world in objective terms, our social and psychic worlds are subjective—that is, we create meaning and reality through human communication and language.[10]

---

[7] Bunnell (2011), p. 11.
[8] Cooperrider and Whitney (2001), p. 15.
[9] Berger and Luckmann (1966).
[10] Sociologists Berger and Luckmann initially introduced this view in their work, *Social Construction of Reality*. More recently, AI theorists such as Cooperrider, Srivastva and Whitney have drawn heavily on the work of Kenneth Gergen who believed that social actions get their meaning from a community of agreement. Recognition and acceptance of this view legitimizes much of the current research and practice in this area and has resulted in much innovation and creativity in organizational change.

What we know about ourselves and how we know it is fateful or full of destiny because it is the only way we know how to understand and relate to ourselves, our past and the potential of our future.[11] In other words, knowing (our strengths, abilities, dreams and desires) is at the centre of every attempt we make to change. Knowing what is best about ourselves gives us the base to be able to change in a positive, life-enhancing way. The philosophy and methodology of the coaching process are firmly anchored in social constructionism.

Consciousness vs. Nonconsciousness

Phenomena such as insights, epiphanies, *aha* moments and internal transformations seem to arise from a nonconscious, even direct, mode of knowing. These phenomena cannot be measured or quantified according to traditional scientific methods. Nevertheless, some aspect of direct knowing appears to play a key role in enabling individuals to shift their perceptions. The research studies on intuition and insights[12] acknowledge this ability as being innate to human beings. However, understanding this form of knowing requires scientists and researchers to account for data that they are not used to considering: feelings.[13] In lay terms, intuition and direct knowing are often experienced as "gut feelings" or as a strong feeling of knowing that "erupts" into consciousness.[14] Most theorists agree on the following explanations:

- Intuitive events originate beyond consciousness.
- Information is processed holistically.
- Intuitive perceptions are frequently accompanied by emotions.
- Intuition occurs almost instantaneously (with no verbal or conscious awareness).

There is also common recognition that there are two levels of direct knowing: everyday hunches and gut feelings, and something like a higher-level sense that is innate in humans to connect to a spiritual level (or quantum field). Intuition appears to be part of an individual's inner process, the "mysterious you" aspect of being human, and therefore plays a key role in coaching.

---

[11] Chaffee (2004).

[12] A literature review on the concept of intuition across fields related to human development yields a range of perspectives that do not agree on one clear definition with the exception that it appears to generate from a non conscious level and is innate to humans.

[13] Mayer (2007).

[14] Mayer (2007).

Linear vs. Expanded Time

Our clients' perspective on time and the way they think about the past, present and future exert an influence on their everyday behaviour. Clinical psychologists agree that this orientation is central to people's well-being and their ability to cope with life's difficulties (and opportunities).[15] Is there hope for the future? Can the past be overcome? What actions and decisions can be made now?

Substantial change requires a different perspective of time than that of an external linearity in which the present is only a brief moment between the past and the future, with the past holding supremacy. Newton's linear absolute time, which he described as an unchanging physical reality, is considered to be independent of human consciousness or choice.[16] His conception shifted the understanding of time from being a subjective, lived experience to being a mental construct. Newton's absolute time is still the primary, even exclusive, way we view time in Western society.[17] As Newtonian time became synonymous with clock time, it no longer accounted for other temporal experiences, such as intuition, sudden leaps of insight or discontinuous (abrupt) change.

The acceptance of Newtonian time in clinical and social psychology contributed to a predominantly deterministic, externally oriented view of change in individuals and groups.[18] As a result, the locus of control was almost exclusively outside the individual, and the individual was largely considered to be the sum total of his past. Historically, however, some psychological theorists and natural philosophers (e.g. Heidegger, Piaget, May, Husserl, Whitrow, James, McGrath and Kelly) focused on ways to account for the lived experience of time in everyday life which could not be explained by the external time of Newtonian science.[19] In the new sciences, the mind and the environment are understood as simultaneous parts of a greater Gestalt or life-space.[20] The past is only one possible influencer of action and change. The present and future are equally valid influencers. Change can be discontinuous—that

---

[15] Boltz (2006).

[16] Newton (1687/1990).

[17] The acceptance of Newton's absolute time was supported by the rise of industrialism and its need for scheduling and controlling factory workers, the transportation of goods and the resulting manufacture of cheap watches. Western societies settled on Newton's linear time as the only interpretation or construction of time.

[18] Clancy (1996).

[19] Clancy (1996).

[20] Lewin (1948).

is, abrupt, sudden and qualitative in nature. The past does not determine the present or the future; in fact, deep change only occurs in the present.

Planned Change vs. Self-organization

Instead of seeing the objective, predictable and controllable universe of Newtonian physics, scientists in the twenty-first century describe a vastly different world based on quantum physics and the new sciences of constructionism, systems theory, chaos theory, self-organizing change and complexity theory. The human brain is seen as a "pattern-forming self-organized system" that "dwells" for short times in phases of transition in which old ideas break up and something new is created.[21] In fact, this ability to be "poised on the brink of instability where it can switch flexibly and quickly" is what enables the brain to anticipate the future, not just react to the present.[22] This perspective of human change allows for transformational moments to occur. We are now aware of our ability to reframe our perceptions and choose to leave patterns of limited thoughts and action. We have the capacity and knowledge to bring out the best in our clients.

Negative Bias vs. Emotional Equilibrium

Imagine that you have been looking at the world around you but with one eye covered. In fact, you had no idea there was something covering your eye until it was ripped away, metaphorically, and you could suddenly see the totality of life around you, the positive in the world as well as the negative, in equal measure. Scholars have recently noted that because of the past imbalance of attention to the challenges, deficits and limitations of human existence, we have understudied, overlooked and even ignored what is positive, life-enhancing and resilient about human change.

This shift to a more balanced perspective of human change has been supported by neuroscience. As a result of technologies such as fMRI, scientists have detected factors which seem to show a mental and emotional bias towards a negative perception of human capacity. The brain appears to have a bias towards negativity for good reason: physical survival. Here are some factors that scientists have concluded operate at a non-conscious level:

---

[21] Kelso (1995).
[22] Kelso (1995), p. 26.

- We are primed to avoid danger.
- We detect negative information faster than positive.
- We perceive fearful faces more rapidly than happy or neutral ones.
- Negative events are carefully stored in our brain for future reference.
- Negative events generally have more impact than positive events, and they leave an indelible trace.
- Negative experiences can create vicious cycles, making us pessimistic, overreactive and inclined to become negative.[23]

Despite these nonconscious factors that influence the action of negative emotions, we also have unconscious factors that impact the expression of position emotions. As we've mentioned before, humans have an optimistic bias that specifically influences us to look to the future with optimism. We also have positive emotions whose role is to build capacity, connection and well-being. Striving for emotional equilibrium involves an acceptance that humans experience a range of emotions on a continuum of positive to negative, from joy and freedom to despair and fear. On life's journey, we visit the whole range of emotions as we process and experience the "stuff of life" from births to deaths and successes to failures. As practitioners, we need to be alert as to whether we or our clients are "living" in a negative emotion, such as boredom, pessimism, frustration, doubt, worry, anger, revenge or guilt. "Living" in a negative emotion means that we are unable to move ourselves to a more positive sense of being, which greatly affects our emotional equilibrium and therefore our freedom of thought and knowing.

Implications for Coaching

At the close of this hermeneutic circle, we have come to some conclusions and observations that we share in this chapter. But first we highly recommend and sincerely suggest that doing your own hermeneutic circle of research would be profoundly rewarding and insightful. It would also contribute to the great need we have for more research in our field. We invite you to engage in coaching research so that we all benefit from more deeply penetrating the mystery of being human. We share a quote from philosopher of science Sir Karl Popper, who in his famous work, *Logic of Scientific Discovery*, said, "There is no such thing as a logical method of having new ideas, or a logical reconstruction of

---

[23] Hanson and Mendius (2009), Yang, Zald and Blake (2007), Jiang and He (2006).

this process ... every discovery contains 'an irrational element,' or 'a creative intuition.'[24]

Most experienced coaches would agree that clients are unique in so many ways that the short journey we make with them is a mysterious one indeed. We show up, try to be prepared, witty, humble yet confident, and feign to be in charge. But some of us know from much experience that no one is really "in charge" in terms of being completely conscious about what unfolds in coaching. Thus we find the conditions for igniting substantial change to be comforting, reliable, and a good mental and emotional structure to have in mind while coaching. Some areas of learning that we have encountered and that we believe have implications for coaching are social context and influence, embodied knowing, finding coherence and the nature of insight. These are discussed below.

Social Context and Influence in Coaching

What surprised us from the extensive research we undertook was how socially wired we are as human beings to influence and to be influenced. Some researchers have proposed that social connection is necessary for human survival and that our beliefs, emotions and even ways of knowing are all socially, culturally and historically formed. As individuals we are a network of social connections that motivate us consciously but even more powerfully subconsciously. It helps to explain the aura of mystery surrounding the human condition—that we are programmed with cognitive, affective, physiological and biological patterns but also have moments of autonomy and authenticity. We realized how impactful this knowledge was for coaches. In all likelihood, we show up with attitudes, biases and emotional energy that are blind to us. Likewise, we may discern in our clients limiting beliefs, concerns and emotions that they are not aware of. Both parties are taking in information at levels of awareness that they have not brought to consciousness.

Mihaly Csikszenetmihalyi and Keith Sawyer wrote in *Creative Insight: The Social Dimension of a Solitary Moment* how all insights are embedded in the social milieu in which they occur.[25] Social, cultural and environmental influences play a role even if the moment of insight is experienced when an individual is alone. Why? Because creative insight is embedded in the stages of the creative process. They explained how the lifespan of creative insight

---

[24] Popper (1968) in Sternberg and Davidson (1995), p. 71.
[25] Csikszentmihalyi and Sawyer (1995).

(e.g., eureka moments) appears as a quick flash but occurs within a complex, time-consuming and fundamentally social process. Usually hard work goes on before and after the insight as part of an ongoing experience that is social and would be meaningless out of context. They used the example of Darwin's creative process in developing his theory of evolution, which was a long-term discovery process involving much social interaction.

We propose that coaching insights are similarly embedded in longer, more complex social processes that may include not only multiple coaching sessions but also organizational expectations and interventions, as well as the social and cultural context of the client's work setting. Thus the experience of coaching and any resulting insights or pivotal moments from that process are socially embedded and do not occur in isolation. We realized that this was another significant component of coaching to be aware of, especially in terms of what might help in leading up to a pivotal moment and what can ensure the integration of an insight into successful actions and behaviours.

Embodied Knowing

Another finding that surprised us was the notion of embodied knowing. We were aware of different modes of knowing as we believed we were making use of some of them in our coaching, but we did not realize there was a vast cross-disciplinary field of study on the concept of embodiment and enactive knowing. It gave us a new lens to understand our own coaching: that embodied cognition and a bandwidth of different modes of knowing were in play whether we consciously applied them or not. It also showed us that what we chose to believe about embodiment would impact whether we could apply these modes of knowing in a deliberative way. For example, if we didn't believe in a form of direct knowing, such as intuition, we would not recognize it in play or be able to capitalize on it strategically. We might inadvertently close off an avenue of expression or access with a client who displayed or was open to these experiences.

Many coaches engage in ways of somatic knowing, such as deep empathy, that express themselves through feelings and bodily sensations. All experienced and master coaches take advantage of expert intuition that they have built up based on years of working with volumes of clients in diverse work settings. Some of us get a feeling of knowing in terms of timing, language, energy and expression with our clients—we "know" when to hold back and when to thrust a point home, and sometimes we can be very creative with our use of metaphors and analogies. It was comforting for us to learn that these modes of knowing are part of the rapidly growing body of knowledge and study engaged by scientists and researchers from diverse fields. Perhaps we no longer need to be reluctant to share our stories and strategies around experiences that do not fit the traditional scientific paradigm but are more openly acknowledged in the emerging holistic paradigm.

Finding Coherence

From our bias we view coaching in its essence as calling for a phenomenological and hermeneutic lens of understanding. Coaching is therefore considered to be an interactive process, not an object of study. We have emphasized repeatedly that pivotal moments cannot be managed, controlled, planned or conjured up externally. On the other hand, we have learned that they *can* be anticipated, seeded, sensed, primed and even inspired. Insight has been defined as both a state of understanding (e.g., gaining insight into something) and an experience involving the sudden emergence of an idea into conscious awareness (*aha*).[26] Both of these are applicable to the discovery process of coaching in which we guide clients to greater levels of coherence in their lives.

As with an out-of-focus picture that can be instantly recognized once some clue is given, we can help our clients to find clarity in a problem situation or unwanted pattern through priming. The aim of priming is to create opportunities for potential sources of coherence to emerge. Gestalt psychologists called this experience of coherence a *Gestalt*; other psychologists call these moments of recognizing coherent patterns of information in the environment.[27] Of interest to coaches is realizing that one coherent pattern can be substituted for another in which elements are seen as one unity at one moment, and the next moment a different unity appears but with the same elements,[28] like what happens with the turn of a kaleidoscope. We have seen this experience occur repeatedly when we help to pivot a client from seeing a situation negatively to seeing it as a learning opportunity.

---

[26] Schooler, Fallshore and Fiore (1995).
[27] Schooler et al. (1995).
[28] Schooler et al. (1995).

The Nature of Insight

From research into what underlies pivotal moments and what role we might play as coaches, we have gleaned some core concepts and actions regarding the nature of insight[29] which can inform ways to prime clients to change. These represent common findings from the cognitive insight field that match our own experiences with pivotal moments. They may already be familiar but it is still reassuring to know *why* they work:

- Often clients are not looking at their problem situation from the "right" angle (think figure–ground illusion) so they fail to recognize a resolution that seems obvious to the coach.
- Clients can put too much focus on specifics and fail to see the big picture, or they can't recognize the available cues that are there.
- Sometimes clients need to move to a completely different vantage point to reduce redundant ways of looking at their situation.
- Coaches can distract clients from focusing on unimportant or inappropriate details so they don't waste time revisiting the same story.
- Often just "forgetting" or letting a passage of time go by can help to prepare the way for an insight. When a person "forgets" for a while they leave the old mental ruts behind and allow space for a fresh perspective to emerge.
- Helping clients to change the context (physical, psychological, social, etc.) can allow for more information to flow in and reduces the impact of the negative thoughts and feelings embedded in the unhappy situation. Sometimes previous successful contexts can be recalled. Often just changing everyday routines can open up space for an insight.
- At times, all clients need is a single word, image, metaphor or analogy from the environment to help them instantly reconfigure a situation. As coaches we are part of the client's environment.
- Helping clients to recognize that they are "lost" or "stuck" can be an important first step in encouraging them to search for something different.
- Encouraging clients to explore alternative approaches to their situation can help them to envision new approaches or directions. Coaches can encourage perseverance and a certain level of risk-taking in finding the "right" approach, as well as playfulness in looking at different options ("What if…?").

---

[29] Schooler et al. (1995).

- Recognizing and using analogies or metaphors is considered to be one of the most important tools that coaches can use to promote insight. Metaphors and analogies enable clients to conceptualize better, transfer knowledge and make unconscious connections.

Movement, Problem and Paradox

For theoretical physicist David Bohm, life was movement, a dynamic wholeness-in-motion in which humans sought to solve the problems and paradoxes of their lives. He was concerned with understanding consciousness as a coherent whole (which to him was an unending process of movement and unfoldment).[30] We were struck by Bohm's distinction between "the problem and the paradox" as it relates to coaching.[31]

He articulated a common denominator that he saw among all of the contradictions and confusion of modern life: that most people seem to agree that the world is faced with a set of *problems*.[32] He suggested that actually addressing modern difficulties as problems may paradoxically be the source of the problems. He explained that the root of the word comes from the Greek, meaning "to put forward". He agreed that the essential significance of the word was "to put forward for discussion or questioning an idea that is suggested toward the resolution of certain difficulties or inadequacies."[33] He cautioned, however, that putting forth an idea as a problem implied certain tacit and implicit presuppositions which must be satisfied for things to make sense.

One of the core assumptions is that the questions or problems raised are rational and free of contradiction. He noted that in the practical and technical realm, this is worked out and irrational ideas are eventually discarded. He asked, but what about psychological problems and problems of human relationships? People are not always rational and they are filled with contradictory needs and desires. Bohm defined the paradox in this way: "whereas one is treating his own thinking and feeling as something separate from and independent of the thought that is thinking about them, it is evident that in fact there is, and can be, no such separation and independence."[34] He pointed out that since most human disorders are actually the outcome of hidden paradoxes, no attempt to

---

[30] Bohm (1980).
[31] Bohm (1997).
[32] Bohm (1997), p. 61.
[33] Bohm (1997), p. 61.
[34] Bohm (1997), pp. 65–66.

treat them as problems can bring them to an end. He proposed that the very feelings and ideas which we identify with our "innermost self" are involved in paradox, through and through.[35] This sentiment thus calls for a new science of change and therefore new social and cultural metaphors to successfully navigate the constant flux of human and social change, fraught with uncertainty and mystery. Coaching seems uniquely designed to support this endeavour.

Handling Internal Doubt

It may be daunting, especially for newer coaches, to view clients not as problems to be solved but rather as mysteries and paradoxes to be appreciated. Research indicates that inexperienced coaches with doubts about their abilities account for the overriding form of tension during coaching engagements.[36] New coaches must experience new conditions, try new tools and become familiar with the coaching process in its entirety. With experience, however, coaches do not become doubt free. In fact, some level of doubt keeps us from presuming and assuming, and allows us to stay open to learning. As we mature, we become accustomed to letting ourselves "simmer" with feelings of anxiety that may be prompted in a coaching conversation, and we turn to inner guidance for clues.

Experienced coaches have learned to trust their own expert intuition because there is rarely a rationale for the diversity of ways in which they coach, according to Erik de Haan, Professor of Organisation Development and Coaching at the University of Amsterdam.[37] As a coach researcher, he has observed that "Coaching will remain a largely intuitive area of work until it can be demonstrated conclusively what works in what circumstances."[38]

Jackie's client was a leader who struggled to understand the consistent feedback he was receiving about not listening to others and pushing his own agenda. This feedback was keeping his career from progressing and is what brought him to coaching. Through a number of sessions, Jackie used many coaching tools to help shift the client's view of his situation. Nothing seemed to penetrate until one session when Jackie made a comment that clicked for him. In previous conversations he had complained how others were hurtful to him and how their behaviours were not any better than his own yet they were not being called on for their poor behaviour. Jackie's response was, "George, it doesn't matter how they behaved. What matters is that you want to

---

[35] Bohm (1997), p. 67.
[36] de Haan (2008a).
[37] de Haan (2008b).
[38] de Haan (2008b), p. 124.

be a strong leader of a high-performing team. What matters is how you show up." In that moment, for whatever reason, something connected for George. He realized that while he had needed to vent with his coach and get her empathy and understanding, she still had to help him move on. In subsequent sessions, he demonstrated much greater openness in how he understood situations from a true leadership perspective of what others needed from him. He was able to separate his personal needs from the business situation, and his leadership abilities grew. He admitted that he didn't always have to be right. Surprisingly to him, others around him seemed to change too. Coaching George was a challenge for Jackie in that he did not respond in the way that many previous clients with similar needs and goals had. Between sessions, Jackie prepared, but before each session, she centred herself to remain present for George to respond as seemed appropriate in the moment.

It is gratifying when we mutually experience or share a pivotal moment with our clients. In his research, de Haan found that experienced coaches described critical moments as turning points, breakthroughs or shifts.[39] These moments were associated with periods of radical change in the coaching to which clients often referred back. We can use these awe-inspiring moments to energize us to be more competent in supporting their occurrence. De Haan noted how novice coaches begin by questioning whether they are good enough to call themselves coaches,[40] and then continue with the realization that they cannot take coaching for granted.[41] We take inspiration from our clients, who share these pivotal moments with us, realizing that as we have more and more of them we begin to feel as the ocean in a drop, not a drop in the ocean.

Final Thoughts

As we complete this part of our journey, we can say with surety that we have found a greater sense of coherence for what we do and how we do it as coaches. The path we travelled was well worth the efforts, the detours and the unintended stops along the way. We have truly deepened our interiority with this knowledge and knowing; we better understand the concept of *knowledge by presence*. We certainly admit that there were paths we missed, blind spots we overlooked and areas we did not venture into. We invite our readers to launch future explorations for the benefit of all.

---

[39] de Haan (2008b).
[40] de Haan (2008a).
[41] de Haan (2008b).

References

Adams, M. G. (2004). *Change your questions, change your life: 7 powerful tools for life and work*. San Francisco: Berrett-Koehler Publishers, Inc.

Alberini, C. M., & LeDoux, J. E. (2013). Memory reconsolidation. *Current Biology, 23*(17), 746–750.

Andow, J. (2015). How "intuition" exploded. *Metaphilosophy, 46*(2), 189–212.

Argyris, C. (1976). Theories of action that inhibit individual learning. *American Psychologist, 31*(9), 638–654.

Argyris, C. (1983). Action science and intervention. *Journal of Applied Behavioral Science, 19*(2), 115–135.

Ash, I. K., Jee, B. D., & Wiley, J. (2011). Investigating insight as sudden learning. *Journal of Problem Solving, 4*(2), 1–27.

Ball, L. J., & Stevens, A. (2009). Evidence for a verbally-based analytic component to insight problem solving. Retrieved from http://csjarchive.cogsci.rpi.edu/proceedings/2009/papers/251/paper251.pdf

Bargh, J. A., Chen, M., & Burrows, L. (1996). Automaticity of social behavior: Direct effects of trait construct and stereotype activation on action. *Personality and Social Psychology, 71*(2), 230–244.

Bartlett, Sir F. C. (1932/1995). *Remembering: A study in experimental and social psychology*. New York: Cambridge University Press.

Barton, S. (1994). Chaos, self-organization, and psychology. *American Psychologist, 49*(1), 5–14.

Baumann, E., & Hill, C. E. (2008). The attainment of insight in the insight stage of the Hill Dream Model: The influence of client reactance and therapist interventions. *Dreaming, 18*(2), 127–137.

Belief. (n.d.). *In Oxford English Dictionary Online*. Retrieved from http://dictionary.oed.com

References

Berger, P. L., & Luckmann, T. (1966). *The social construction of reality.* New York: Doubleday.

Bergson, H. (1922/1965). *Duration and simultaneity.* Indianapolis, IN: Bobbs-Merrill.

Biess, F., Frevert, U., Jensen, U., Saxer, D., Roper, L., & Confino, A. (2010). Forum: History of emotions. *German History, 28*(1), 67–80.

Bishop, S. R., Lau, M., Shapiro, S., Carlson, L., Anderson, N. D., Carmody, J., et al. (2004). Mindfulness: A proposed operational definition. *Clinical Psychology: Science and Practice, 11*(3), 230–241.

Bohm, D. (1980). *Wholeness and the implicate order.* New York, NY: Routledge.

Bohm, D. (1997). *On dialogue.* (L. Nichol, Ed.) New York, NY: Routledge.

Boltz, M. (2006). The psychology of time. Retrieved from www.haverford.edu/psych/courses/p220%20syllabus.htm

Bowden, E. M., Jung-Beeman, J., Fleck, J., & Kounios, J. (2005). New approaches for demystifying insight. *Trends in Cognitive Science, 9*(7), 322–328.

Boyastzis, R., & McKee, A. (2005). *Resonant leadership: Renewing yourself and connecting with others through mindfulness, hope and compassion.* Cambridge, MA: Harvard Business Review Press.

Braithwaite, R. B. (1975). *An empiricist's view of the nature of religious belief.* Norwood, PA: Norwood Editions.

Brann, A. (2015). *Neuroscience for coaches: How to use the latest insights for the benefit of your clients.* London: Kogan Page.

Briggs, J., & Peat, D. (1999). *Seven life lessons of chaos: Spiritual wisdom from the science of change.* New York, NY: HarperPerennial.

Broadwell, M. M. (1969). Teaching for learning (XVI.). *The Gospel Guardian, 20*(41), 1–3.

Broudry, M., & Baeckman, J. (2012). How convenient! The epistemic rationale of self-validating belief systems. *Philosophical Psychology, 25*(3), 341–364.

Bruner, J. S. (1966). *Toward a theory of instruction.* Cambridge, MA: Belknap Press.

Bunker, B. B., & Alban, B. T. (1997). *Large group interventions: Engaging the whole system for rapid change.* San Francisco: Jossey-Bass.

Bunnell, L. (2011). *The definitive book of human design: The science of differentiation.* Carlsbad, CA: HDC Publishing.

Cameron, C. D., & Fredrickson, B. (2015). Mindfulness facets predict helping behavior and distinct helping-related emotions. *Mindfulness, 6,* 1211–1218.

Campbell, J. (1949). *Hero with a thousand faces.* New York: Princeton University Press.

Camus, A. (1961). *Resistance, rebellion and death.* New York: Albert A. Knopf.

Catalino, L. I., & Fredrickson, B. L. (2011). A Tuesday in the life of a flourisher: The role of positive emotional reactivity in optimal mental health. *Emotion, 11*(4), 938–950.

Chaffee, P. (2004). *Claiming the light: Appreciative Inquiry and congregational transformation.* Retrieved from www.congregationalresources.org/Appreciative/Introduction.asp

Chodron, P. (2004). *Start where you are: A guide to compassionate living.* Boston: Shambhala.

Chu, Y., & MacGregor, J. (2011). Human performance on insight problem solving: A review. *Journal of Problem Solving, 3*(2), 119–150.

Clancy, A. L. (1996). *Toward a holistic concept of time: Exploring the link between internal and external temporal experiences.* Doctoral dissertation, Fielding Graduate University, Santa Barbara, CA.

Coffey, K. A., Hartman, M., & Fredrickson, B. L. (2010). Deconstructing mindfulness and constructing mental health: Understanding mindfulness and its mechanisms of action. *Mindfulness, 1,* 235–253.

Cohn, M., & Fredrickson, B. L. (2010). In search of durable positive psychology interventions: Predictors and consequences of long-term positive behaviour change. *Journal of Positive Psychology, 5*(5), 355–366.

Collins, N. L., & Miller, L. C. (1994). Self-disclosure and liking: A meta-analytic review. *Psychological Bulletin, 116*(3), 457–475.

Cooperrider, D. L., & Srivastva, S. (1987). Appreciative Inquiry in organization life. In R. W. Woodman & E. Passmore (Eds.), *Research in organization change and development: An annual series featuring advances in theory* (Vol. 1, pp. 129–169). Greenwich, CT: JAI Press.

Cooperrider, D. L., & Whitney, D. (2001). A positive revolution in change. In D. L. Cooperrider, P. F. Sorensen, D. Whitney, & T. F. Yaeger (Eds.), *Appreciative Inquiry: An emerging direction for organization development* (pp. 9–29). Champaign, IL: Stipes.

Cosmelli, D., & Preiss, D. D. (2014). On the temporality of creative insight: A psychological and phenomenological perspective. *Frontiers in Psychology, 5*(article 1184), 1–5. doi:10.3389/fpsyg.2014.01184.

Covey, S. R. (1989). *The 7 habits of highly effective people: Powerful lessons in personal change.* New York: Simon & Schuster.

Crystal, J. D. (2013). Prospective memory. *Current Biology, 23*(17), 750–751.

Crystal, J. D., & Glanzman, D. L. (2013). A biological perspective on memory. *Current Biology, 23*(17), 728–731.

Csikszentmihalyi, M., & Sawyer, K. (1995). Creative insight: The social dimension of a solitary moment. In R. J. Sternberg & J. E. Davidson (Eds.), *The nature of insight* (pp. 329–364). Cambridge, MA: MIT Press.

Day, L. (1996). *Practical intuition.* New York, NY: Broadway Books.

Day, L. (2009). *The circle.* New York, NY: Atria Paperback.

de Haan, E. (2008a). I doubt therefore I coach: Critical moments in coaching practice. *Consulting Psychology Journal: Practice and Research, 60*(1), 91–105.

de Haan, E. (2008b). I struggle and emerge: Critical moments of experienced coaches. *Consulting Psychology Journal: Practice and Research, 60*(1), 106–131.

de Sola Pool, I., & Kochen, M. (1978). Contacts and influence. *Social Networks, 1*, 5–51.

Dennett, D. (1991). *Consciousness explained*. London: Penguin Books.

Descartes, R. (1637/1986). *Discourse on method and meditations* (D. A. Cress, Trans.). Indianapolis, IN: Hackett Publ. Co.

Devine, C., & Sparks, W. L. (2014). Defining moments: Toward a comprehensive theory of personal transformation. *International Journal of Humanities and Social Science, 4*(5.1), 31–39.

Dilts, R. (1990). *Changing beliefs systems with NLP*. Cupertino, CA: Meta Publications.

Dilts, R. (1996). *Belief change cycle*. Retrieved from http://nlpu.com/Articles/artic3.htm.

Dilts, R. (1998). *NLP and self organization theory*. Retrieved from http://www.nlpu.com/Articles/artic23.htm.

Duhigg, C. (2012). *The power of habit: Why we do what we do in life and business*. New York: Random House.

Eddy, M. (2000). Access to somatic theory and applications: Socio-political concerns. Retrieved from www.wellnessCKE.net

Eichenbaum, H. (2008). Memory. *Scholarpedia, 3*(3):1747. doi:10.4249/scholarpedia.1747. Revision #137659.

Englich, B., Mussweiler, T., & Strach, F. (2006). Playing dice with criminal sentences: The influence of irrelevant anchors on experts' judicial decision making. *Personality and Social Psychology Bulletin, 32*, 188–200.

Epstein, R. M. (2003). Mindful practice in action (I): Technical competence, evidence-based medicine, and relationship-centered care. *Families, Systems & Health, 21*(1), 1–9.

Fazio, R. H., Jackson, J. R., Dunton, B. C., & Williams, C. J. (1995). Variability in automatic activation as an unobtrusive measure of racial attitudes: A bona fide pipeline? *Journal of Personality and Social Psychology, 69*(6), 1013–1027.

Febvre, L. (1941/1973). Sensibility and history: How to reconstitute the emotional life of the past. In P. Burke (Ed.), *A new kind of history* (pp. 12–26). London: Harper Row.

Fernyhough, C. (2012). *Pieces of light: How the new science of memory illuminates the stories we tell about our pasts*. New York: HarperCollins.

Ferrer, J. (2014). Transpersonal psychology, science and the supernatural. *Journal of Transpersonal Psychology, 46*(2), 152–186.

Fodor, J. A. (1981). The appeal to tacit knowledge in psychological explanation. In J. A. Fordor (Ed.), *Representations: Philosophical essays on the foundations of cognitive science*. Cambridge, MA: Bradford/MIT Press. (Original work published 1968).

Folger, T. (2007, June 12). Time may not exist. Retrieved from http://discovermagainze.com/2007/jun/in-no-time

Foundation for Inner Peace. (2007). *A course in miracles (Combined Vol., 3rd Ed.)*. Mill Valley, CA: Foundation for Inner Peace.

Fredrickson, B. L. (1998). What good are positive emotions? *Review of General Psychology, 2*(3), 300–319.

Fredrickson, B. L. (2003). Positive emotions and upward spirals in organizations. In K. S. Camerson, J. E. Dutton, & R. E. Quinn (Eds.), *Positive Organizational Scholarship: Foundations of a new discipline* (pp. 163–175). San Francisco: Berrett-Koehler.

Fredrickson, B. L. (2013). Positive emotions broaden and build. In P. Devine & A. Plant (Eds.), *Advances in experimental social psychology* (Vol. 47, pp. 1–54). Amsterdam: Elsevier.

Fredrickson, B. L., & Branigan, C. (2005). Positive emotions broaden the scope of attention and thought-action repertoires. *Cognition and Emotion, 19*(3), 313–332.

Fredrickson, B. L., Cohn, M. A., Coffey, K. A., Pek, J., & Finkel, S. M. (2008). Open hearts build lives: Positive emotions, induced through loving-kindness meditation, build consequential personal resources. *Journal of Personality and Social Psychology, 95*(5), 1045–1062.

Fredrickson, B. L., & Levenson, R. W. (1998). Positive emotions speed recovery from the cardiovascular sequelae of negative emotions. *Cognition and Emotion, 12*(2), 191–220.

Fridja, N. H. (1986). *The emotions*. Cambridge, UK: Cambridge University Press.

Fujita, K., & Trope, Y. (2014). Structured versus unstructured regulation: On procedural mindsets and the mechanisms of priming effects. *Social Cognition, 32*, 68–87.

Gadamer, H. G. (1960/1997). *Truth and method* (2nd Rev. ed., J. Weinsheimer & D. G. Marshall, Trans. Rev.). New York: Continuum.

Gay, P. (1996). *The enlightenment: An interpretation*. New York: W. W. Norton & Company.

Gergen, K. J. (1978). Toward generative theory. *Journal of Personality and Social Psychology, 36*(11), 1344–1360. doi:10.1037/0022-3514.36.11.1344.

Gergen, K. J. (1994). *Toward transformation in social knowledge* (2nd ed.). Thousand Oaks, CA: Sage.

German History Society. (2010). Forum history of emotions. *German History, 28*(1), 67–80.

Gilhooly, K. J., & Fioratou, E. (2009). Executive functions in insight versus non-insight problem solving: An individual differences approach. *Thinking & Reasoning, 15*(4), 355–376. doi:10.1080/13546780903178615.

Green, J. (2002). Somatic knowledge: The body as content and methodology in dance education. *Journal of Dance Education, 2*(4), 114–118.

Gross, M. (2013). Are memories just ripples in time? *Current Biology, 23*(17), 734–736.

Haken, M. (2008). Self-organization. *Scholarpedia*, 3(8), 1401. Retrieved from http://www.scholarpedia.org/article/Self-organization

Hanna, T. (1976). The field of somatics. *Somatics*, 1(1). Retrieved from http://somatics.org/library/htl-fieldofsomatics

Hanna, T. (1986). Selections from ... Somatology: Somatic philosophy and psychology. *Somatics, VIII*(2), 14–19 Retrieved from http://somatics.org/library/htl-somatology.

Hanson, R., & Mendius, R. (2009). *Buddha's brain: The practical neuroscience of happiness, love, & wisdom*. Oakland, CA: New Harbinger Publications.

Harle, R. (2007). Disembodied consciousness and the transcendence of the limitations of the biological body. *Janus Head, 9*(2), 589–603.

Harmon, B. & Yokam, G. (2009, February). Ten rules for making a swing change. *Golf Digest*. Retrieved from http://www.golfdigest.com/story/harmonrules

Hart, T. (2007). Reciprocal revelation: Toward a pedagogy of interiority. *Journal of Cognitive Affective Learning, 3*(2), 1–10.

Hart, T. (2008). Interiority and education: Exploring the neuro-phenomenology of contemplation and its potential role in learning. *Journal of Transformative Education, 6*(4), 235–250.

Hart, T., Nelson, P., & Puhakka, K. (Eds.). (2000). *Transpersonal knowing: Exploring the horizon of consciousness*. Albany, NY: State University of New York Press.

Hawkes, S. L. (2003). *Development and assessment of personal belief system scales: Dimensionality, reliability, and preliminary construct value*. Unpublished doctoral dissertation, Kansas State University, Manhattan, KS.

Heidegger, M. (1962). *Being and time* (J. Macquarrie & E. Robinson, Trans.). San Francisco: Harper & Row.

Henriques, G. (2013). What is knowledge? A brief primer in the theory of knowledge. Retrieved from www.psychologytoday.com/blog/theory-knowledge/201312/

Higgins, E. T., & Eitam, B. (2014). Priming…shmiming: It's about knowing *when* and *why* stimulated memory representations become active. *Social Cognition, 32*, 225–242.

Hill, C. E. (2009). *Helping skills: Facilitating exploration, insight, and action* (3rd ed.). Washington, DC: American Psychological Association.

Hill, C. E., Crook-Lyon, R. E., Hess, S. A., Goates-Jones, M., Roffman, M., Stahl, J., Sim, W., & Johnson, M. (2006). Prediction of session process and outcome in the Hill Dream Model: Contribution of client characteristics and the process of the three stages. *Dreaming, 16*(3), 159–185.

Hill, C. E., Knox, S., Hess, S., Crook-Lyon, R., Goates-Jones, M., & Sim, W. (2007). The attainment of insight in the Hill Dream Model: A single case study. In L. G. Castonguay & C. E. Hill (Eds.), *Insight in psychotherapy* (pp. 207–230). Washington, DC: American Psychological Association.

Hockenbury, D. H., & Hockenbury, S. E. (2007). *Discovering psychology*. New York: Worth Publishers.

Housley, K. (2009). Seeing the thunder: Insight and intuition in science, mathematics and religion. Retrieved from http://www.metanexus.net/magazine/tabid/68/id/10941/Default.aspx

Husserl, E. (1928/1964). *The phenomenology of internal time-consciousness* (J. S. Churchill, Trans.; M. Heidegger, Ed.). Bloomington, IN: Indiana University Press.

Hutcherson, C. A., Seppala, E. M., & Gross, J. J. (2008). Loving-kindness meditation increases social connectedness. *Emotion, 8*(5), 720–724.

Hutchins, E. (2010). Enaction, imagination, and insight. In J. R. Stewart, O. Gapenne, & E. A. DiPaolo (Eds.), *Enaction: Toward a new paradigm for cognitive science* (pp. 425–450). Cambridge, MA: MIT Press.

Ingvar, D. H. (1985). "Memories of the future": An essay on the temporal organization of conscious awareness. *Human Biology, 4*, 127–136.

James, W. (1890/1950). *The principles of psychology* (Vol. 1). New York: Dover Publications.

Jiang, Y., & He, S. (2006). Cortical responses to invisible faces: Dissociating subsytems for facial-information processing. *Current Biology, 16*, 2023–2029.

Johnson, D. (1992). *Body: Recovering our sensual wisdom*. Berkeley, CA: North Atlantic Books and Somatic Resources.

Johnson, K., Waugh, C., & Fredrickson, B. (2010). Smile to see the forest: Facially expressed positive emotions broaden cognition. *Cognition and Emotion, 24*(2), 299–321.

Jones, G. (2003). Testing two cognitive theories of insight. *Journal of Experimental Psychology: Learning, Memory, and Cognition, 29*(5), 1017–1027.

Jourard, S. M. (1959). Self-disclosure and other-cathexis. *Journal of Abnormal and Social Psychology, 59*, 428–431.

Jung, C.G. (1965). *Memories, dreams, reflections* (R. Winston & C. Winston, Trans.; A. Jaffe, Rec. & Ed.). New York, NY: Vintage Books.

Kabat-Zinn, J. (1990). *Full catastrophe living: Using the wisdom of your mind to face stress, pain and illness*. New York: Dell.

Kahneman, D. (2011). *Thinking, fast and slow*. New York, NY: Farrar, Straus and Giroux.

Kaplan, C. A., & Simon, H. A. (1990). In search of insight. *Cognitive Psychology, 22*, 374–419.

Kegan, R. (1979). The evolving self: A process conception for ego psychology. *Counseling Psychologist, 8*(2), 5–23.

Kegan, R. (1982). *The evolving self: Problems and processes in human development*. Cambridge: Harvard University Press.

Kelso, J. A. S. (1995). *Dynamic patterns: The self-organization of brain and behavior*. Cambridge, MA: The MIT Press.

Keyes, C., & Haidt, J. (Eds.). (2003). *Flourishing: Positive psychology and the life well-lived*. Washington, DC: American Psychological Association.

Killingsworth, M. A., & Gilbert, D. T. (2010). A wandering mind is an unhappy mind. *Science, 330*, 932.

King, P. (2011). What is the relationship between science and philosophy? Retrieved from www.quora.com

Kitchenham, A. (2008). The evolution of John Mezirow's transformative learning theory. *Journal of Transformative Education, 2*(6), 104–123.

Klein, S. B. (2016). Autonoetic consciousness: Reconsidering the role of episodic memory in future-oriented self-projection. *The Quarterly Journal of Experimental Psychology, 69*(2), 381–401.

Knox, S., Hill, C. E., Hess, S., & Crook-Lyon, R. (2008). The attainment of insight in the Hill Dream Model: Replication and extension. *Psychotherapy Research, 18*, 200–215.

Köhler, W. (1956). *Mentality of apes*. London: Routledge & Kegan Paul Ltd.

Köhler, W. (1959). Gestalt psychology today. *American Psychologist, 14*, 727–734.

Kounios, J., & Beeman, M. (2009). The *Aha*! Moment: The cognitive neuroscience of insight. *Current Directions in Psychological Science, 18*(4), 210–216.

Kuhn, T. (1970). *The structure of scientific revolutions*. Chicago: University of Chicago Press.

Kurakin, A. (2011, March 29). The self-organizing fractal theory as a universal discovery method: The phenomenon of life. *Theoretical Biology and Medical Modelling*. doi:10.1186/1742-4682-8-4.

Lai, C. Y., Zauszniewski, J. A., Tang, T. C., Hou, S. Y., Su, S. F., & Lai, P. Y. (2014). Person beliefs, learned resourcefulness and adaptive functioning in depressed adults. *Journal of Psychiatric and Mental Health Nursing, 21*, 280–287.

Lakoff, G., & Johnson, M. (1980a). The metaphorical structure of the human conceptual system. *Cognitive Science, 4*, 195–208.

Lakoff, G., & Johnson, M. (1980b). *Metaphors we live by*. Chicago, IL: University of Chicago Press.

Lakoff, G., & Johnson, M. (1999). *Philosophy in the flesh: The embodied mind and its challenge in Western thought*. New York: Basic Books.

Laland, K. N., & Rendell, L. (2013). Cultural memory. *Current Biology, 23*(17), 736–740.

Langer, E. J. (2000). Mindful learning. *Current Directions in Psychological Science, 9*(6), 220–223.

Lazarus, R. S. (1991). *Emotion and adaptation*. New York: Oxford University Press.

Lehrer, J. (2009). *How we decide*. New York: Houghton Mifflin Harcourt.

LeMay, E., & Pitts, J. (1994). *Heidegger for beginners*. New York: Writers and Readers Publishing.

Levenson, H. (1995). *Time-limited dynamic psychotherapy: A guide to clinical practice*. New York: Basic Books.

Lewin, K. (1948). *Resolving social conflicts: Selected papers on group dynamics*. New York: Harper & Brothers Publishers.

Lieberman, M. (2013). *Social: Why our brains are wired to connect*. New York: Crown Publishers.

Lipton, B. H. (2005). *The biology of belief: Unleashing the power of consciousness, matter and miracles*. Santa Rosa, CA: Mountain of Love/Elite Books.

Lipton, B. (2009). *Spontaneous evolution: Our positive future*. New York: Hay House, Inc.

London School of Economics & Political Science. (n.d.). Tacit knowledge: Making it explicit. (Toolkit for travelling facts). Retrieved from www.lse.ac.uk/economicHistory/Research/facts/tacit.pdf

Lonergan, B. (1957). *Insight: A study of human understanding*. Toronto: University of Toronto Press.

Longhurst, L. (2006). The 'Aha' moment in Co-active Coaching and its effects on belief and behavioural changes. *International Journal of Evidence Based Coaching and Mentoring, 4*(2), 61–73.

Lundgren, H., & Poell, R. (2016). On critical reflection: A review of Mezirow's theory and its operationalization. *Human Resource Development Review, 15*(1), 3–28.

Luo, L., & Niki, K. (2003). Function of hippocampus in "insight" of problem solving. *Hippocampus, 13*, 316–323.

Mansour, N. (2009). Science teachers' beliefs and practices: Issues, implications and research agenda. *International Journal of Environmental & Science Education, 4*(1), 25–48.

Margolis, J. (2010). *Pragmatism's advantage: American and European philosophy at the end of the twentieth century*. Stanford, CA: Stanford University Press.

Martof, N. M. (1996). *How does the personal belief system of novice and veteran biology teachers play out in practice?* Unpublished doctoral dissertation, University of Maryland, College Park, MD.

Maslow, A. H. (1971). *The farther reaches of human nature*. New York: Viking Compass.

Mayer, E. L. (2007). *Extraordinary knowing: Science, scepticism, and the inexplicable powers of the human mind*. New York: Bantam Books.

McCraty, R. (2015). Heart-brain neurodynamics: The making of emotions. In M. Dahlitz & G. Hall (Eds.), *Issues of the heart: The neuropsychotherapist* (pp. 76–110). Brisbane: Dahlitz Media.

McDaniel, M. A., & Einstein, G. O. (2007). Spontaneous retrieval in prospective memory. In J. S. Nairne (Ed.), *The foundations of remembering: Essays in honor of Henry L. Roediger, III*. New York, NY: Psychology Press, Routledge.

McDermott, J. (Ed.). (1966). *The writings of William James: A comprehensive edition*. New York: The Modern Library.

McGann, M. (n.d.). *Enactive cognition: A cognition briefing*. euCognition. Retrieved from http://www.vernon.edu/euCognition/cognition_briefing_enactive_cognition.htm

McGregor, D. (1967). *The professional manager*. New York: McGraw-Hill.

McLeod, S.A. (2008). Bruner. Retrieved from www.simplypsychology.org/bruner.html

McTaggart, L. (2002). *The field: The quest for the secret force of the universe*. New York, NY: HarperCollins Publishers.

McWilliams, S. (2016). Cultivating constructivism: Inspiring intuition & promoting process & pragmatism. *Journal of Constructivist Psychology, 29*(1), 1–29.

Merleau-Ponty, M. (1962/1996). *Phenomenology of perception* (C. Smith, Trans.). New York: Routledge.

Metcalfe, J. (1995). Foreward. In R. J. Sternberg & J. E. Davidson (Eds.), *The nature of insight* (pp. ix–xiv). Cambridge, MA: MIT Press.

Metcalfe, J., & Son, L. (2012). Anoetic, noetic and autonoetic metacognition. In M. Beran, J. R. Brandl, J. Perner, & J. Proust (Eds.), *The foundations of metcognition*. Oxford, UK: Oxford University Press.

Mezirow, J. (1997). Transformative learning: Theory to practice. *New Directions for Adult and Continuing Education, 74*, 5–12. doi:10.1002/ace.7401.

Mezirow, J. (2000). *Learning as transformation: Critical perspectives on a theory in progress*. San Francisco: Jossey-Bass.

Milgram, S. (1967). The small world problem. *Psychology Today, 2*, 60–67.

Miller, W. R. (2004). The phenomenon of quantum change. *Journal of Clinical Psychology, 60*(5), 453–460.

Miller, W. R., & C'de Baca, J. (2001). *Quantum change: When epiphanies and sudden insights transform ordinary lives*. New York, NY: Guilford Press.

Miller, R. R., & Matzel, L. D. (2000). Memory involves far more than 'consolidation'. *Nature Reviews: Neuroscience, 1*(3), 214–216.

Mills, D. H. (2002). *The hero and the sea: Patterns of chaos in ancient myth*. Wauconda, IL: Bolchazy-Carducci Publishers.

Molden, D. C. (2014). Understanding priming effects in social psychology: An overview and integration. *Social Cognition: Special Issue, 32*, 243–249.

Moravec, H. (1988). *Mind children: The future of robot and human intelligence*. Cambridge, MA: Harvard University Press.

Mussweiler, T. (2001). The durability of anchoring effects. *European Journal of Social Psychology, 31*(4), 431–442. doi:10.1002/ejsp.v31:4/issuetoc.

Myers, D. (2002). *Intuition: Its powers and perils*. London: Yale University Press.

Myss, C. (1996). *Anatomy of spirit: The seven stages of power and healing*. New York: Three Rivers Press.

Nadel, L., & Land, C. (2000). Memory traces revisited. *Nature Reviews: Neuroscience, 1*(3), 209–212.

Napoli, M., Krech, P., & Holley, L. (2005). Mindfulness training for elementary school students: The attention academy. *Journal of Applied School Psychology, 21*(1), 99–125.

Nespor, J. (1987). The role of beliefs in the practice of teaching. *Journal of Curriculum Studies, 19*(4), 317–328.

Newton, I. (1687/1990). *Mathematical principles of natural philosophy* (A. Motte, Trans.; F. Cajori, Rev.). Chicago: University of Chicago Press.

Nielsen, J. M. (1958). *Memory and amnesia*. Los Angeles: San Lucas Press.

Novicevic, M., Hench, T., & Wren, D. (2002). Playing by ear…in an incessant din of reasons: Chester Barnard and the history of intuition in management thought. *Management Decision, 40*(10), 992–1002.

Nyberg, L., McIntosh, A.R., Cabeza, R., Habib, R., & Tulving E. (1996). General and specific brain regions involved in encoding and retrieval of events: What, where, and when. *Proceedings of the National Academy of Science USA, 93*, 11280–11285.

Odman, P. J. (1988). Hermeneutics. In J. P. Keeves (Ed.), *Educational research methodology and measurement: An international handbook* (pp. 63–70). New York: Pergamon Press.

Ollinger, M., Jones, G., & Knoblich, G. (2008). Investigating the effect of mental set on insight problem solving. *Experimental Psychology, 55*(4), 269–282.

Orem, S. L., Binkert, J., & Clancy, A. L. (2007). *Appreciative Coaching: A positive process for change.* San Francisco: Jossey-Bass/Wiley.

Pajares, M. F. (1992). Teachers' beliefs and educational research: Cleaning up a messy construct. *Review of Educational Research, 62*(3), 307–332.

Pardi, P. (2015, January). What is truth? *Philosophy News.* Retrieved from http://www.philosophynews.com/post/2015/01/29/What-is-Truth.aspx

Parkin, M. (2008). Priming. In P. J. Lavrakas (Ed.), *Encyclopedia of survey research methods* (pp. 612–613). Thousand Oaks: Sage Publications, Inc. doi:10.4135/9781412963947.n399.

Passmore, J., & Marianetti, O. (2013). The role of mindfulness in coaching. *Coaching Psychologist, 3*(3), 131–138.

Peirce, P. (2013). *Leap of perception: The transforming power of your attention.* New York: Atria Books.

Perkins, D. N. (1995). Insight in minds and genes. In R. J. Sternberg & J. E. Davidson (Eds.), *The nature of insight* (pp. 495–534). Cambridge, MA: MIT Press.

Pfeifer, R., & Bongard, J. (2007). *How the body shapes the way we think: A new view of intelligence.* Cambridge, MA: The MIT Press.

Polanyi, M. (1958/1998). *Personal knowledge towards a post critical philosophy.* London: Routledge.

Popper, K. (1968). *Logic of scientific discovery.* New York: Harper & Row.

Radvansky, G. (2016). *Human memory* (2nd ed.). NY: Routledge.

Rajaram, S. (1993). Remembering and knowing: Two means of access to the personal past. *Memory and Cognition, 21*(1), 89–102.

Rath, T. (2007). *StrengthsFinder 2.0.* New York: Gallup Press.

Richardson, V. (1996). The role of attitudes and beliefs in learning to teach. In J. Sikula (Ed.), *The handbook of research in teacher education* (2nd ed., pp. 102–119). New York: Macmillan.

Ricketts, M. W., & Willis, J. E. (2001). *Experience AI: A practitioner's guide to integrating Appreciative Inquiry with experiential learning.* Chagrin Falls, OH: Taos Institute.

Riddle, D. (2012). Three keys to mindful leadership coaching. *Forbes Online.* Retrieved from http://www.forbes.com/sites/ccl/2012/01/23/three-keys-to-mindful-leadership-coaching/#5fab3431743f

Rock, D., & Page, L. J. (2009). *Coaching with the brain in mind: Foundations for practice*. Hoboken, NJ: John Wiley & Sons.

Rogers, C. R. (1942). *Counselling and psychotherapy*. Boston: Houghton Mifflin.

Rokeach, M. (1960). *The open and closed mind*. New York, NY: Basic Books, Inc.

Rokeach, M. (1968). *Beliefs, attitudes and values: A theory of organization and change*. San Francisco, CA: Jossey-Bass.

Rorty, R. (1999). *Philosophy and social hope*. New York, NY: Penguin.

Rosch, E. (2007). More than mindfulness: When you have a tiger by the tail, let it eat you. *Psychological Inquiry, 18*(4), 258–264.

Rosch, E., Thompson, E., & Varela, F. J. (1991). *The embodied mind: Cognitive science and human experience*. Cambridge, MA: MIT Press.

Royce, J. (1885). *The religious aspect of philosophy: A critique of the bases of conduct and of faith*. Boston: Houghton Mifflin Co.

Royce, J. (1920/1996). *Fugitive essays*. Cambridge: Harvard University Press.

Savasci-Acikalin, F. (2009). Teacher beliefs and practice in science education. *Asia-Pacific Forumon Science Learning and Teaching, 10*(1), Article 12. Retrieved from https://www.ied.edu.hk/apfslt/v10_issue1/funda/

Schacter, D. L. (2001). *The seven sins of memory: How the mind forgets and remembers*. Boston: Houghton Mifflin Co.

Scharmer, C. O. (2009). *Theory U: Leading from the future as it emerges*. San Francisco: Berrett-Koehler Publishers, Inc.

Schein, E. H. (1985). *Organizational culture and leadership*. San Francisco: Jossey-Bass.

Schilling, M. (2005). A small-world network model of cognitive insight. *Creativity Research Journal, 17*(2&3), 131–154.

Schooler, J. W., Fallshore, M., & Fiore, S. M. (1995). Epilogue: Putting insight into perspective. In R. J. Sternberg & J. E. Davidson (Eds.), *The nature of insight*. Cambridge, MA: The MIT Press.

Seelasettho, A. J. (2013). *Under the bodhi tree: A Dhamma talk on practicing the middle way*. Thailand: Light of Buddhadharma Foundation International, Mahasati Retreat Association.

Seligman, M. E. P. (2002). *Authentic happiness: Using the new positive psychology to realize your potential for lasting fulfilment*. New York: Free Press.

Sharot, T. (2011). The optimism bias. *Current Biology, 21*(23), 941–945.

Shotter, J. (2010). Adopting a process orientation…in practice: Chiasmic relations, language and embodiment in a living world. In T. Hernes & S. Maitlis (Eds.), *Process, sensemaking, and organizing* (pp. 70–101). New York, NY: Oxford University Press.

Silverman, L. H., & Weinberger, J. (1985). Mommy and I are one: Implications for psychotherapy. *American Psychologist, 40*(2), 1296–1308.

Simmons, A. (2009). *Quantum skills for coaches: A handbook for working with energy and the body-mind in coaching*. UK: Hot Hive Books.

Sinclair, M., & Ashkanasy, N. (2005). Intuition: Myth or a decision-making tool? *Management Learning, 36*(3), 353–370.

Slee, P. T., Campbell, M., & Spears, B. (2012). *Enactive representation in child, adolescent and family development.* Cambridge, UK: Cambridge University Press.

Slife, B. (1993). *Time and psychological explanation.* New York: State University of New York Press.

Smith, M.K. (2003). Michael Polanyi and tacit knowledge, the encyclopedia of informal education. Retrieved from http://infed.org/mobi/michaell-polanyi-and-tacit-knowledge/

Snyder, M. (1984). When belief creates reality. In L. Berkowitz (Ed.), *Advances in experimental social psychology* (Vol. 18, pp. 247–305). Orlando, FL: Academic Press.

Sohlberg, S., Birgegard, A., Czartoryski, W., Ovefelt, K., & Strömbom, Y. (2000). Symbiotic oneness and defensive autonomy: Yet another experiment demystifying Silverman's findings using "Mommy and I are one". *Journal of Research in Personality, 34*, 108–126.

Spence, G., Cavanagh, M., & Grant, A. (2008). The integration of mindfulness training and health coaching: An exploratory study. *Coaching: An International Journal of Theory, Research and Practice, 1*(2), 145–163.

Spiro, R. J. (1982). Subjectivity and memory. In J.-F. Le Ny & W. Rintsch (Eds.), *Language and comprehension* (pp. 29–34). New York: North-Holland.

Stapp, H. P. (2007). Mindful universe: Quantum mechanics and the participating observer. In A. C. Elitzur, M. P. Silverman, J. Tuszynski, R. Vaas, & H. D. Zeh (Eds.), *The frontiers collection.* Berlin: Springer-Verlag.

Stapp, H. (2011). *Mindful universe: Quantum mechanics and the participating observer.* New York: Springer.

Steele, C. (1997). A threat in the air: How stereotypes shape intellectual identity and performance. *American Psychologist, 52*, 613–629.

Stein, J. (Editor in Chief). (1975). *The random house college dictionary* (Rev. ed.). New York: Random House.

Sternberg, R. J., & Davidson, J. E. (1995). *The nature of insight.* Cambridge, MA: MIT Press.

Stock, J. B., & Zhang, S. (2013). The biochemistry of memory. *Current Biology, 23*(17), 741–745.

Strong, G., & Aron, A. (2006). The effect of shared participation in novel and challenging activities on experienced relationship quality: Is it mediated by high positive affect? In K. D. Vohs & E. J. Findel (Eds.), *Self and relationships: Connecting intrapersonal and interpersonal processes* (pp. 342–359). New York: Guildford Press.

Sullivan, E. (2013). The history of emotions: Past, present, future. (Review article). *Cultural History, 2*(1), 93–102. Retrieved from www.euppublishing.com/cult. doi:10.3366/cult.2013.0034.

Szpunar, K. K., Addis, D. R., & Schacter, D. L. (2012). Memory for emotional simulations: Remembering a rosy future. *Psychological Science, 23*(1), 24–19.

Tang, Y., et al. (2007). Short-term meditation training improves attention and self-regulation. *Proceedings of National Academy of Science, 104*(43), 17152–17156.

Teasdale, J. D., Segal, Z. V., Williams, J. M. G., & Mark, G. (1995). How does cognitive therapy prevent depressive relapse and why should attentional control (mindfulness) training help? *Behavior Research and Therapy, 33*, 25–39.

Thomas, K. W., & Kilmann, R. H. (2007). *Thomas-Kilmann conflict mode instrument*. Sunnyvale, CA: CPP, Inc.

Tobin, K., & LaMaster, S. U. (1995). Relationships between metaphors, beliefs, and actions in a context of science curriculum change. *Journal of Research in Science Teaching, 32*(3), 225–242.

Topolinski, S., & Reber, R. (2010). Gaining insight into the "Aha" experience. *Current Directions in Psychological Science, 19*(6), 402–405.

Traill, R. (2008, February 29). *Thinking by molecule, synapse or both?—From Piaget's schema, to the selecting/editing of ncRNA*. Ondwelle short-monograph, no. 2, General Science Journal and Ondwelle Publications, Victoria, Australia. Retrieved from http://www.ondwelle.com/OSM02.pdf

Tulving, E. (1985). *Elements of episodic memory*. Oxford, UK: Oxford University Press.

Tulving, E. (1989). Memory: Performance, knowledge, and experience. *European Journal of Cognitive Psychology, 1*(1), 3–26.

Tulving, E. (1993). What is episodic memory? *Current Directions in Psychological Science, 2*(3), 67–70.

Tulving, E. (2002). Episodic memory: From mind to brain. *Annual Review of Psychology, 53*, 1–25.

Turner, V. (1967). *The forest of symbols: Aspects of Ndembu ritual*. Ithaca, NY & London: Cornell University Press.

Usó-Doménech, J. L., & Nescolarde-Selva, J. (2015, January 14). What are belief systems? *Found Science*. doi:10.1007/s10699-015-9409-z.

Vacharkulsemsuk, T., & Fredrickson, B. L. (2012). Strangers in sync: Achieving embodied rapport through shared movements. *Journal of Experimental Social Psychology, 48*, 399–402.

Veltrop, B. (2002, Spring). Generative change. *The chaordic commons quarterly*. (Adapted version). Retrieved from http://www.theinfinitegames.org

Wagemans, J. (2015). Historical and conceptual background: Gestalt theory. In J. Wagemans (Ed.), *Oxford handbook of perceptual organization* (pp. 3–20). Oxford: Oxford University Press. doi:10.1093/oxfordhb/9780199686858.013.026.

Wagner, H. (1983). *Phenomenology of consciousness and sociology of life-world*. Alberta, CA: The University of Alberta Press.

Wang, Q. (2008). Being American, being Asian: The bicultural self and autobiographical memory in Asian Americans. *Cognition, 107*, 743–751.

Wasylyshyn, K. M. (2005). The reluctant president. *Consulting Psychology Journal, 57*(1), 57–70.

Wasylyshyn, K. M., Gronsky, B., & Haas, J. W. (2006). Tigers, stripes, and behavior change: Survey results of a commissioned coaching program. *Consulting Psychology Journal, 58*(2), 65–81.

Watkins, J. M., & Mohr, B. J. (2001). *Appreciative Inquiry: Change at the speed of imagination.* San Francisco: Jossey-Bass.

Weisberg, R. W. (2006). *Creativity.* Hoboken, NJ: Wiley.

Welling, H. (2005). The intuitive process: The case of psychotherapy. *Journal of Psychotherapy Integration, 15*(1), 19–47.

Wentura, D., & Rothermund, K. (2014). Priming is not priming is not priming. *Social Cognition, 32*(Special Issue), 47–67.

Westen, D. (1999). The scientific status of unconscious processes: Is Freud really dead? *Journal of the American Psychoanalytic Association, 47*(4), 1061–1106. doi:10.1177/000306519904700414.

White, W. L. (2004). Transformational change: A historical review. *Journal of Clinical Psychology, 60*(5), 461–470.

Whitworth, L., Kimsey-House, H., & Sandahl, P. (1998). *Co-active coaching: New skills for coaching people toward success in work and life.* Palo Alto, CA: Davies-Black Publishing.

Whyte, D. (1994). *The heart aroused: Poetry and the preservation of the soul in corporate America.* New York: Currency/Doubleday.

Wilbur, K. (1989). *Spectrum of consciousness.* Wheaton, IL: Quest Books.

Wilcock, D. (2013). *The synchronicity key.* New York: Dutton.

Wilson, J. (2014). *Mindful America: The mutual transformation of Buddhist meditation and American culture.* Oxford: Oxford University Press.

Wilson, V. E., Peper, E., & Gibney, K. H. (2004). The 'Aha' experience with somatics: Demonstrating mind and body unity. *Somatics, XIV*(2), 4–7.

Wood, D. (2006). Book review: Quantum change: When epiphanies and sudden insights transform ordinary lives, by Miller, W.R. & C'de Baca, J. *Journal of Transpersonal Psychology, 38*(2), 256–258.

Wussweiler, T. (2001). The durability of anchoring effects. *European Journal of Social Psychology, 31*, 431–442.

Yang, E., Zald, D. H., & Blake, R. (2007). Fearful expressions gain preferential access to awareness during continuous flash suppression. *Emotion, 7*(4), 882–886.

Zimmerman, M. E. (1981). *Eclipse of the self: The development of Heidegger's concept of authenticity.* Athens, OH: Ohio University Press.

Index

A

access, 10, 16, 31, 46–8, 50–3, 57, 60, 73–107, 109–34, 153, 161, 164, 166, 179
adaptive systems, 23, 24
   complex, 24
affect. *See* emotions
aha moments
   breakthroughs, 19
   characteristics of, 36, 37
   critical moments, 184
   triggers of, 37
   turning points, 184
Anticipatory Principle, 13
anticipatory theory, 6
Appreciative Coaching
   coaching tool: growing *vs.* closing the gap, 141
   core questions, 163
   discovery phase, 158
   principles, 12, 40, 41, 138
Appreciative Inquiry, 6, 7, 12

Archimedes, 20, 21
Argyris, Chris, 87, 126
Aristotle, 110
artificial intelligence, 69, 71, 97
Ash, Ivan, 21n5, 22, 25–7
assessments
   360, 143
   StrengthsFinder 2.0, 143
   Thomas-Kilmann Conflict Inventory, 143
attention
   directing of, 37, 48, 54–60, 128, 138, 146–7, 149
   and positive emotions, 67
   Seeing the Star, 54–5
awareness, 2, 9, 11, 13–17, 23, 29, 31, 37, 39, 43, 44, 48, 50, 52, 55–7, 59–72, 83–4, 90, 91, 93, 95, 96, 101, 103, 106, 107, 115, 116, 124, 128, 136–51, 154, 157, 159, 161, 163, 164, 174, 178, 180

Note: Page numbers followed by "n" denote notes.

B

Bain, Alexander, 26
Baker, Lynne Rudder, 82
Bargh, John, 131n97, 132, 132n98–100
Barlett, Fredrick, 131
Baumann, Ellen, 29, 29n50
behaviorism, 4, 13, 17, 26–9, 32–7, 44, 49–52, 59, 60, 64, 65, 68, 69, 71, 75, 76, 78–80, 83, 86–7, 92, 111, 112, 114, 119, 124–4, 130–3, 144, 145, 149, 151, 153, 157, 164, 165, 172, 175, 179, 183
being-in-the-world, 11
belief
  affective, 75, 126, 178
  attractors for, 16, 45
  behavioral, 126, 151
  belief systems, 20, 39, 74, 76, 78, 84, 86, 88, 154
  cognitive, 20, 21, 31, 36, 42, 73, 75, 79, 81, 82, 84, 90, 91, 126, 156, 159, 178
  core, vi, 17, 35, 36, 52, 75, 77, 80, 83, 86, 159
  cultural, 6, 76–78, 84, 134, 171, 178
  espoused, 87, 126
  faith, 75, 151
  knowledge, 6, 9, 14–16, 50, 73, 75–78, 81, 83, 91, 109, 111, 120, 121, 136, 147, 154, 156, 159, 166, 173, 178
  metaphor, 6, 35, 136, 146, 147, 156, 173
  neural basis for, 80
  nonconscious, 16, 45, 50, 73, 82–4, 87, 88, 109, 134, 146, 147
  opinions, 81, 146
  personal, vi, 5, 6, 9, 16, 35, 46, 50, 51, 74, 76–78, 80, 83, 88, 109, 126
  philosophical definition of, 81
  quantum, 3, 5, 31, 52, 79, 82, 85–6, 88, 171
  role of, 74, 83, 154–5
  scientific, vi, 6, 14–16, 20, 52, 74, 77, 78, 82, 85, 88, 91, 112, 120, 126, 173–4, 177
  self-organization, 4n3, 15, 16, 45, 47–51, 53, 72, 77, 79, 86–87, 171, 173
  social system of, 79
  societal, 77
  theory-in-use, 87, 126
  truth, 5, 9, 14, 15, 76, 81, 134, 159, 171
Bergson, Henri, 97, 97n36
Besso, Michele, 52
Bishop, Scott, 59, 59n20, 60n25, 149n19, 149n22, 151n26
Block, Peter, 161
body/mind
  connection, 31–2
  research, vi, 6, 20, 31, 32, 34, 52, 62, 65, 69, 70, 77, 103, 111, 124, 127, 133, 138, 177
Bohm, David, 182, 182n30–4, 183n35
Boyatzis, Richard, 60, 60n28
brain
  amygdala, 121, 124
  associative networks, 123–5, 127
  executive function, 71
  frontal lobes, 124
  hippocampal, 121
  hippocampus, 124
  metastable states of, 51
  negativity bias, 65
  neo-cortex, 124
  neuroanatomical patterns, 124
  occipital lobe, 124
  priming, 113, 125, 127, 180
Briggs, John, 171, 171n1–3, 172, 172n4, 172n5

Brooks, Rodney, 71
Bruner, Jerome, 99, 99n46, 100

C

Camus, Albert, 13
catalyst, 3, 45
Cavanagh, Michael, 60
C'de Baca, Janet, 33
change
 new science of, 17, 170–7, 183
 quantum, 19, 32–4, 39
 transformational, 32–4, 40
chaos theory
 non-linear dynamics, 86
 self-organization, 79
Churchland, Paul and Patricia, 82
Clark, W. H., 33
coaching
 creating relationship, 143
 executive, 3, 11, 34, 35, 41, 144
 influence, 6, 7, 12–14, 16, 17, 36, 39, 45, 53, 63, 69, 70, 72, 74, 78, 83, 84, 88, 90, 91, 94, 96, 118, 127, 129, 134, 139, 141, 142, 153, 154, 157, 164, 171, 172, 175, 178, 179
 insight-oriented, 34–6
 life, 20, 34
 phenomenological, 20, 34, 37, 41, 52, 180
 process of discovery, 171
 social context, 17, 178–9
 stance, 14, 139
 studies, 20, 34–6
Co-Active life coaching, 34
cognition
 creative, 19
 distributed, 17, 152
 embodied, 16, 69, 70, 72, 122, 154, 179–80
cognitive insight problem solving, 20
coherence

insight, 17, 24, 39, 42, 170, 171, 173–5, 177–82
Cohn, M., 67n63, 68n69, 145
complex systems, 51
complexity theory, 4n3, 171, 176
conditions for transformation/ substantial change
 consciousness *vs.* nonconsciousness, 174
 externally directed *vs.* internally directed, 172–3
 linear time *vs.* expanded concept of time, 175–6
 negative bias *vs.* emotional equilibrium, 178–7
 planned change *vs.* self-organization, 176
 scientific paradigm *vs.* social constructionism, 173–4
Confine, Alono, 64
consciousness
 autonoetic, 116
 noetic, 116
 stream of, 5
Constructionist Principle, 12
constructivism
 approach, 50, 171
 constructivist perspective, 13, 82–5
context
 cultural, 70, 179
 social, 17, 65, 178–9
Cooperrider, David, 6, 173n8, 173n10
Cosmelli, Diego, 36, 37n67, 37n68
Crick, Francis, 92
Csikszenetmihalyi, Mihaly, 21n3, 178, 178n25

D

Dannemiller, Kathy, 145
Darwin, Charles, 110, 170, 179
Day, Laura, 72n83, 105
defining moments, 32, 33, 42

de Haan, Erik, 183, 184
Dennett, Daniel, 82, 82n33
Descartes, Rene, 69
Devine, CaSondra, 33
Dewey, John, 10n22
Dilts, Robert, 42, 75, 87
discernment, 147–9
   cone-in-the-box, 147

E

Ebbinghaus, Hermann, 111
Einstein, Albert, 20, 52, 118n37
Eitam, Baruch, 133, 133n108
embodiment
   embodied knowing, 17, 178–9
   embodied rapport, 154
   enaction, 102, 153
   Model: Coaching Cycle, 152, 153
   social, 69, 95, 105, 179
emergent properties, 51
emotions
   action, 61, 65
   broaden-and-build theory, 66–8
   contagious, 62, 138, 145
   intelligence, 32, 97
   memory, 16, 46, 48, 61, 62, 64, 113–14, 119, 127, 159, 165
   mindfulness, 60, 67, 150, 151
   negative, 31, 33, 48, 62, 65–7, 150, 165, 177
   optimism bias, 69, 118
   positive, 16, 49, 65–9, 143, 163–5, 177
   representative positive, 66
   resources for change, 13
   social, 63, 65
   studies, 29, 32, 60, 66–8, 127, 145, 174
   undo effect of positive, 66
   upward spiral theory of lifestyle change, 68

empathy, 46, 63, 80, 105, 158, 179, 184
   deep, 46, 105, 158, 179
empiricism, 92, 93
   empirical approach, 5
Enactive Network of Excellence, 100
Englich, B., 131, 131n89–91
epiphany, 19, 25, 32–5, 38, 39, 43, 139
epistemology, 77, 81, 91
eureka moment, 19, 20, 179
experience
   embodied, 17, 36, 70, 72, 96, 100, 122, 154, 155, 169, 170, 178–9
   lived, 10, 13, 34, 40, 46, 53, 65, 90, 98, 99, 149, 154, 175
   tip-of-the-tongue, 37
expression, 1, 47, 48, 63, 66, 68, 82, 171, 177, 179

F

Fazio, Russell, 125
Febvre, Lucien, 62
feedback
   negative loops, 171
   positive loops, 171
   priming mechanism, 142
   self-organizing, 171
feelings, 1, 3, 4, 10–12, 17, 21, 28, 29, 33, 38, 41, 47–9, 51, 54, 58, 59, 61–3, 72, 73, 79, 80, 82, 84, 91, 97, 99, 104–6, 111, 116, 123–4, 132, 135, 136, 142, 144–4, 148–53, 155, 157, 160, 165, 166, 174, 175, 179–83
Ferrer, Jorge, 102
flourishing, 5, 6, 68
Fredrickson, Barbara, 60n27, 65n53, 66–8, 145, 164
Freud, Sigmund, 73, 93, 125
Frevert, Ute, 63, 64
Fujita, Kentaro, 132

G

Gadamer, Hans-Georg, 10
Gallup's StrengthsFinder, 68
generative approach
   capacity, 6, 7
   change, 7, 173
   theory, 6
Gergen, Kenneth, 6, 173n10
Gestalt, 20, 25–8, 34, 37, 53, 55, 104, 111, 155, 166, 175, 180
goal, 9, 10, 13, 21, 48, 68, 89, 116, 130, 132, 149, 156, 158, 161, 184
Gödel, Kurt, 30, 31
Grant, Anthony, 60
graph theory, 24
grounded theory, 34, 41
GROW model, v
Guare, John, 25

H

Hanna, Thomas, 36, 89, 89n1, 89n2, 95, 95n25, 96, 96n28
Harmon, Butch, 114, 114n16
Hart, Tobin, 101, 101n52–6, 102, 102n60, 102n61, 150n24, 162, 162n63–5, 163n67–9
Heidegger, Martin, 10, 11, 11n28, 53n7, 98, 98n41, 99, 175
   being-in-the-world, 11
Heidke, John, vii
Hemming, Betsy, vii
hermeneutics
   hermeneutic circle, 17, 40, 41, 177
   hermeneutic journey, 17, 167, 170
   hermeneutic phenomenology, 9–11, 50
Hero's Journey, 3
Higgins, E. Tory, 133, 133n108
Hill, Clara, 28, 29, 29n49, 29n50, 66
holistic paradigm, 15, 16, 20–1, 28, 77–79, 180
   assumptions, 12, 84, 87, 96, 182
   body-mind, 31–2, 35, 72
   perspective, 15, 16, 20, 28, 181
   process, 15, 16, 28, 79, 180
Housley, Kathleen, 29–31, 39
Husserl, Edmund, 11, 53n7, 98, 98n39, 175

I

identity, 11, 33, 38, 42, 80, 101
igniting substantial change, 2, 3, 13, 15–17, 45, 47–9, 59, 84, 136, 172–7, 178
immune system, 60, 68, 93, 94
   DNA genetic code, 93
impasse, 23, 24, 27, 30, 37, 138
influence
   cultural, 64, 65, 70, 78, 96, 178
   environmental, 178
   social, 64
inner knowing, 4n4, 15–17, 29, 35, 37, 46–8, 50, 58, 72, 89, 90, 103–7, 146, 158–61, 169
inner process, 3, 4, 7, 12, 15, 16, 47–50, 59, 73–, 89, 90, 96, 109, 110, 153, 161, 173, 174
insight
   cognitive, 21
   creative, 19
   learning, 26, 27
   nature of, 17, 178, 181–2
   network model of cognitive, 23–5, 25n34
inspiration, 2, 3, 23, 48, 50, 62, 66, 137, 151, 162–4, 184
Institute of HeartMath, 68
interiority, 102, 162–4, 167, 184
   knowledge by presence, 102, 162, 184
internal landscape, 17, 154–61
International Coach Federation, 52

interpretation, 9–12, 15, 29, 34, 40, 41, 50, 53, 58, 84, 134, 137, 154, 157, 159, 175n17
intuition
  biases of, 159
  creative, 105, 178
  direct knowing, 28, 106, 159, 174, 179
  expert, 46, 49, 105, 158, 159, 161, 180, 183
  instinct, 105, 158
  social, 97, 105, 158, 173, 174, 178

J

James, William, 1, 4, 5, 10n22, 54, 73, 92, 98, 105, 111
Jensen, Uffa, 63n43, 64
Johnson, Don Hanlon, 95
Johnson, Mark, 156
Jung, Carl, 73

K

Kabat-Zinn, Jon, 58
Kahneman, Daniel, 159
kaleidoscope, 17, 135–67, 180
Kegan, Robert, 39
Kelso, Scott, 50n1, 51
Keyes, Corey, 5
King, Paul, 91, 92
Klein, Stan, 114
knowing
  authentic, 101
  awareness of, 48, 72, 103
  bandwidth of, 16, 102–6
  being, 104
  creative intuition, 105, 178
  Dasein, 98
  daytime eyes, 104
  direct, 28, 101, 102, 106, 159, 174, 179
  embodied, 17, 178–9
  emotional, 22, 52, 72, 102, 112, 145, 159, 177, 178
  enactive, 99–101, 106, 179
  expert intuition, 46, 105, 158, 159, 179
  figure-ground configurations of, 104
  four sources of, 161
  frequency of, 104–6
  iconic, 99
  inner, 4n4, 16, 29, 35, 37, 46–8, 50, 51, 58, 72, 89, 90, 103–7, 146, 159–61, 169
  inner duration, 98
  insight, 16, 17, 22, 28–30, 33, 39, 48–51, 72, 90, 96, 104, 105, 110, 161, 163, 174, 178
  inspiration, 48, 137, 163
  instinct, 105, 158
  interiority, 102, 162, 167, 184
  intuitive, 69, 98, 102, 105, 112, 159, 163, 174
  modes of, 16, 28, 101, 106, 107, 136, 159–61, 179, 180
  nighttime eyes, 104, 105
  participatory, 102
  phenomenological, 97–99
  social intuition, 105
  somatic, 105, 179
  state of, 22
  symbolic, 99
  tacit, 97, 105
  transpersonal, 101–2
knowledge
  embodied, 16, 69–71, 96, 97, 100, 170
  empiricism, 92, 93
  enactive, 70
  modern, 6, 16, 89, 91–5, 96, 97, 101
  post-modern, 16, 81, 89, 92–6, 101
  rationalism, 92, 93
  social somatic, 95
  somatic, 95, 96

tacit, 97, 105, 156
Köhler, Wolfgang, 26, 27, 37, 55n11
Kuhn, Thomas, 77

L

Lakoff, George, 156
language, 11, 12, 32, 37, 41, 50, 64, 65, 74, 91, 99, 138, 143, 148, 153, 155, 156, 173, 179
learning
  behaviorism, 26
  levels of competence, 135, 161
Levenson, Hannah, 36
Lieberman, Matthew, 79, 80
life-space, 53, 175
Light of Buddhadharma Foundation International, 57
Lipton, Bruce, 77–79, 83, 140n4
literature review, 14, 19–36, 38, 45, 100, 174n12
Loder, James, 33
Lonergan, Bernard, 30
Longhurst, Leigh, 34

M

Margolis, Joseph, 10n22
Marianetti, Oberdan, 60
McGann, Marek, 100
McKee, Annie, 60
McWilliams, Spencer, 9, 9n17–20, 10
Mead, George Herbert, 10n22
meaning making, 39, 132
mechanistic approach, 6, 7
memory
  amygdala, 121, 124
  associative, 17, 159
  autobiographical, 62, 113, 117, 123, 124
  autonoetic consciousness, 116
  behaviorism, 124, 133
  coherence, 121, 134
  conscious, 113
  consolidation, 120, 121
  constructivist, 82, 120, 121
  correspondence, 121, 134
  cortical-dependent, 121
  cultural, 122
  declarative, 113
  emotions, 16, 46, 48, 61, 62, 97, 113, 119, 127, 159
  episodic, 112, 115–18
  explicit, 113
  frontal lobes, 119, 124
  Gestalt, 111, 166
  habits, 112, 165–6
  hippocampal, 121
  hippocampus, 124
  implicit, 16, 113, 114, 124-4, 134
  long-term, 111, 113, 130, 165
  meaning-making, 39, 132
  monitoring, 22, 118
  neocortex, 73, 124
  networks of associations in, 125, 134
  noetic consciousness, 116
  nonconscious, 113–14
  non-declarative, 113
  occipital lobe, 124
  optimistic bias, 118, 119
  priming, 17, 46, 48, 113, 125–34, 139
  procedural, 114, 115, 117, 122
  prospective, 117, 118
  reconsolidation, 120, 121
  retrieval, 114, 118, 130
  semantic, 116, 117, 130
  social, 17, 64, 76, 83, 109, 122, 123, 125, 127, 130–4
  subjective, 45, 54, 64, 116, 134, 157
  time travel, 16, 61, 116, 134, 157
  unconscious, 113–14, 118, 123–7, 134, 139, 166
  visional, 146
  working, 112

mental block. *See* impasse
metaphor
　generative, 138, 148
　kaleidoscope, 136
Metcalfe, Janet, 21, 23
Meyer, Susan, vii
Mezirow, Jack, 12n31, 33, 84
Milgram, Stanley, 25
Miller, William, 32, 33, 39, 111n3, 143n7
mind-body, 81, 96
mindfulness
　Buddhist, 57, 58
　Four Foundations of, 58
　Mindfulness-Based Stress Reduction program (MBSR), 58
　positive emotions and, 67–8
Minsky, Marvin, 71
mirror neurons, 80
models
　AC coaching tool: growing *vs.* closing the gap, 141
　all pivotal moments, 16, 42, 43
　coaching cycle: embodiment of mind, body and environment, 152
　coaching chain of events, 46
　cone-in-the-box, 147, 148
　control-influence-concern, 139
　Emergence of Pivotal Moments, 42
　manifestation of pivotal moments, 15, 42, 43
　pivoting: Igniting substantial change, 137
　pivoting: The power of self-organization, 48
　role of beliefs in self-organizing, 74
　role of inner knowing in self-organizing, 90
　role of memory in self-organizing, 110
　slow awakening, 42, 44
Molaison, Henry (H. M), 113
Molden, Daniel, 130n86, 132, 133n107

Moravec, Hans, 71
Moravec's paradox, 71
Mussweiler, T., 131
myth, 74, 76
　personal, 74, 76

Nelson, Peter, 101
Nescolarde-Selva, J., 75, 76
networks
　associative, 50, 123–7, 134, 136, 139, 157, 159
　small-world, 24, 25
　social, 20, 24, 25
neurolinguistic programming (NLP), 32, 42, 87
neuroplasticity, 4, 92, 138
neuroscience
　cognitive, 20, 79
　electroencephalography (EEG), 20, 22, 123
　functional magnetic resonance imaging (fMRI), 20, 22, 80, 176
　neuro-imaging, 20, 22, 64, 123
　priming research, 44
Newton, Isaac, 30, 52, 53, 175
Nielsen, J. M., 112
Nietzsche, Friedrich, 62
nonconscious, 139, 147, 161–162, 174, 177

objectivism, 5, 6, 9, 14, 15, 26, 76, 82, 94, 96, 173, 176
　approach, 5, 6, 9, 14, 173
ontology, 91, 93

Page, Linda, 78, 94, 95
Pajares, Frank, 75n5, 76, 82, 149

paradox, 71, 182–3, 183
Passmore, Jonathan, 60
patterns
  of association, 24
  self-limiting, 12
peak experiences, 163
Peat, David, 171, 172
Peirce, Charles, 10n22
Penrose, Roger, 31
perception
  figure-ground, 28, 55
  Gestalt, 27, 28, 55, 104
Pfeifer, Rolf, 70, 71
phenomenology
  duration or *duree*, 97
  lifeworld, 98
philosophy
  empiricism, 92
  justified true belief, 91
  rationalism, 92
  scientific method, 91, 92
pivotal moments
  embodied experiences, 169
  holistic, 31, 45, 170
  interactive, 170, 180
  process, 3, 7, 10, 12–14, 16, 31, 45, 155, 170, 179, 180
pivoting
  model of self-organization, 15, 16, 45–72, 77, 79, 86, 87, 96, 171, 173, 176
  pivotal moments, 2, 3, 7–16, 31, 32, 40–6, 49, 72, 103, 136, 137, 144, 155, 157, 167, 169, 170, 179–81, 184
  pivots, 1, 8, 13, 14, 19–47, 143, 151
plato, 110
Poetic Principle, 12, 40, 137
Polanyi, Michael, 97
Popper, Karl, 177, 178n24
Positive Principle, 13

pragmatism, 9, 10, 14, 49, 50, 89
Preiss, David, 36–7
present moment
  mindfulness, 57–60, 149–51
  mind wandering, 149
priming
  action, 44, 133
  anchor, 131
  construal, 132
  feedback, 17, 141, 142
  long-term semantic, 131
  process, 16, 24, 45, 48, 115, 125–28, 130–4, 139, 180
  research experiments, 44
  short-term, 130–2
  strategy, 137
  subliminal, 126
  tools (commenting, broadening), 17, 137, 141
problem-solving
  cognitive insight, 20
  routine, 22
psychology
  behaviorist, 26, 124
  cognitive, 20, 21, 100
  Gestalt, 20, 25–8, 55, 111
  social, 69, 170, 175
  transpersonal, 34, 101–2, 170
psychotherapy, 20, 28, 32–4, 36, 125, 126
Puhakka, Kaisa, 101

Q

quantum
  change, 19, 32–4, 39
  field, 174
  leap, 23
  mechanics, 92, 92n9
  physics, 4n3, 5, 31, 52, 79, 82, 86, 171, 176
  shift, 3, 32, 42, 49

Index

R

Racioppo, Vince, vii
Radvansky, Gabriel, 110, 111
Reeder, Bobette, vii
Riddle, Douglas, 60
robotics, 69, 71, 170
Rock, David, 77n17, 78, 94, 95
Rogers, Carl, 29, 39, 39n73
Rokeach, Milton, 75, 83n39, 155n36
Roper, Lyndal, 63n43, 64
Rosch, Eleanor, 57, 58, 70, 100, 150
Roth, Deborah, vii
Rothermund, Klaus, 130–2
Royce, Josiah, 146, 154n35

S

Sawyer, Keith, 21n3, 178, 178n25
Saxer, Daniela, 63n43, 64
scaling question (Solution Focused Brief Therapy), 140
Schacter, Daniel, 111, 118n39
Scharmer, Otto, 12
Schein, Edgar, 87
Schilling, Melissa, 19n1, 22n12, 23–5
science of change
    chaos theory, 171
    complexity theory, 171
    dynamic movement, 171
    holistic, 170, 171
scientific materialism, 77, 78, 85, 93
scientific paradigm, 4, 14–16, 20–36, 39, 53, 94, 173–4, 173–4, 180
seeing the thunder, 30, 31
Seelasettho, Phra Luang Por Jamnian, 58
self
    authentic, 51, 52, 173
    best self, 3
    self-identity, 42, 47
    true self, 3, 173
self-organization
    dynamic patterns of, 16, 50, 96
    elements of, 48, 50, 69
    model, 44, 46, 48, 57–60, 71, 86
    pattern-forming, 176
    phase transition, 50, 51
    pivoting: The power of self-organization, 48
    role of beliefs in self-organizing, 74
    role of inner knowing in self-organizing, 90
    role of memory in self-organizing, 110
shifts
    learning, 12, 19, 42, 49
    liminal, 42, 44
    magnitude of, 15, 41
    manifestation of, 42
    in perception, 39, 44, 45, 55–7, 173
    in perspective, 19, 39, 42, 44, 50, 129
    quantum, 3, 32, 42, 49
    substantial, 11, 14, 19, 44, 107
    timing of, 15
Shotter, John, 14
Silverman, Lloyd, 126, 139
Simmons, Annette, 31
Simultaneity Principle, 12
six degrees of separation, 25
Skinner, B. F., 26, 92
social constructionism, 6, 94, 173–4
social networking theory, 20
Sohlberg, S., 127
somatics, 31, 89, 95, 96, 102, 105, 170, 179
Sparks, William, 33
spectrum of consciousness, 34, 35
Spence, Gordon, 60
stance
    coaching, 14, 139
    growth, 140–3
    influence, 11, 13, 14, 70, 72, 141, 153
    protective, 140, 143
Stapp, Henry, 78, 85, 86

Steele, C. M., 125, 126n72
Stock, Jeffrey, 115
subconscious, 24, 25, 51, 73, 79, 178
Sullivan, Erin, 62, 63
synchronicity, 53

T

tacit knowledge, 97, 105, 156
Taylor, Kathleen, 82
Thompson, Evan, 70, 100
Thorndike, Edward, 26
thought
   patterns, 11, 55
   rational, 28, 29, 71, 105
time
   discontinuous, 175
   external, 175
   flow, 48, 53, 115, 170
   linear, 52, 120, 175–6, 175n17, 175
   Newton's absolute, 53, 175, 175n17
   perspective of, 52, 117, 175
   subjective, 116
tip-of-the-tongue, 37
Trail, Robert, 93, 94n19
transformation, 2, 6, 19, 20, 32–4, 40, 45, 50, 102, 135, 151, 173, 174, 176
transformative learning, 12, 34, 84
   habits of mind, 84
Trope, Yaacov, 132
Tulving, Endel, 111n3, 112, 116, 117, 119, 136

Turing, Alan, 71

U

unconscious, 22, 71, 73–5, 77, 85, 87, 93, 96, 97, 113–14, 118, 123–7, 134, 135, 139, 156, 159, 161, 163, 166, 177, 182
   automatic processes, 22, 73, 159
Usó Doménech, J. L., 75, 76

V

Varela, Francisco, 70, 100
Veltrop, Bill, 6

W

Wang, Qi, 123
Wasylyshyn, Karol, 35
Weinberger, Joel, 126
Welling, Hans, 28
Wentura, Dirk, 130–2
Westen, Drew, 73n1, 113n10, 113n12, 114n13, 114n15, 125, 126, 157n48, 157n49, 157n54, 161
Wilbur, Ken, 34
Wilson, Vietta, 31, 59n19

Z

Zhang, Sherry, 115

GPSR Compliance

The European Union's (EU) General Product Safety Regulation (GPSR) is a set of rules that requires consumer products to be safe and our obligations to ensure this.

If you have any concerns about our products, you can contact us on

ProductSafety@springernature.com

In case Publisher is established outside the EU, the EU authorized representative is:

Springer Nature Customer Service Center GmbH
Europaplatz 3
69115 Heidelberg, Germany

www.ingramcontent.com/pod-product-compliance
Lightning Source LLC
LaVergne TN
LVHW020329260326
834688LV00037B/942